INUIT JOURNEY

INUIT JOURNEY

BY

EDITH IGLAUER

Douglas & McIntyre
Vancouver

The contents of this book, except for the Introduction, Epilogue, and the
section titled The Outermost Place appeared in *The New Yorker* in slightly
different form.

Canadian Cataloguing in Publication Data

Iglauer, Edith
  Inuit journey

  First published in 1966 with title: The
new people : the Eskimo's journey into our time.
    ISBN 0-88894-174-9
    1. Eskimos—Canada. 2. Cooperation—
Canada. I. Title. II. Title: The new people.
E99.E7135   970.41   C79-091057-8

First paperback edition published in 1979 by
Douglas & McIntyre Ltd.
1875 Welch Street
North Vancouver, British Columbia

Map by Sheouak, West Baffin Eskimo Coöperative Ltd.
Printed and bound in Canada

CONTENTS

FOREWORD

ALTHOUGH IT was not many years ago that the first coöperatives were started in the Arctic, it seems much longer because so much has happened in their development since then.

Coöperatives not only have provided us with considerable economic strength but also hav? been the means of enabling us to manage and control many aspects of our lives which would have been much more difficult without coöperatives. Many of our business and political leaders developed in them.

Today, coöperatives are all across the Arctic in Canada, and a second generation of Arctic people now support and operate them. For the Inuit of Canada, coöperatives are a symbol of our determination to build better lives for ourselves in our land. They are our way.

Louis Tapardjuk, President
the Canadian Arctic Co-operative
Federation Limited
Yellowknife, Northwest Territories

Pauloosie Kasudluak, President
La Fédération des Coopératives
du Nouveau Québec
Montreal, Quebec

ᑕᐃᒪᐃᑲᓗᐊᕐ ᑎᓗᒍ ᐊᕋᒍᐃᑦ ᐊᒥᓯᖅᑭᑐᑯᓗᐃᑦ ᖃᖏᕐ ᓯᒪᓕᕐ ᐸᑦ ᓯᕗᓕᕐ ᖀᒥᒃ ᑯᐊᐸᑯᑦ
ᐱᕆᐊᓚᐅᕐ ᓂᖓᓂᒃ ᐃᓄᐃᑦ ᓄᓇᖓᓂ ᑭᓯᐊᓂᓕ ᐊᑯᓂᐊᓘᖅᑯᕗᓕᕐ ᐸᖅ, ᐱᔪᑎᒋ ᓗᓂᐅᒃ ᐊᒥᓯᐊᓗᐃᑦ
ᐱᕆᐊᕐ ᓯᒪᓕᕐ ᒪᑕ ᐱᕆᐊᓚᐅᕐ ᓂᖏᓂᑦ.

ᑯᐊᐸᑯᑦ ᐃᑲᔪᓯᓯᒪᑐᐃᓇᖏᒪᑕ ᐅᕆᑎᓂᒃ ᑭᓇᐅᔪᐃᑦ ᒥᖅ ᓵᓄᑦ ᑭᓯᐊᓂᑕᐅᖅ ᐅᕆᑎᓂᒃ ᓇᖅ ᒥᓂᖅ
ᐊᐅᓚᑎᑎᐹᐅᓕᕐ ᒪᑦ ᐊᒥᓯᓂᒃ ᐃᓅᓯᑎᓄᑦ ᐊᔪᕐ ᓇᕐ ᓂᐊᓚᐅᕋᓗᐊᕐ ᑐᓂᒃ ᑯᐊᐸᖅᑲᓚᐅᖏᐸᑦ.
ᐊᒥᓯᓗ ᐱᔅ ᓯᓇᑎᔭᕗᑦ ᑭᓇᐅᔭᕐ ᑖᕆᒥᐅᕐ ᑕᕗᑦ ᐊᒪᓗ ᓚᐅᒪᕈᔪᒥᔭᕗᑦ ᐱᕆᐊᕐ ᕿᐅᓯᒪᓕᕐ ᒪᑕ
ᑕᐅᖕᑦ ᑯᐊᐸᑯᑎᓂᑦ.

ᐅᕐ ᓗᒥ ᑯᐊᐸᑯᑦ ᓇᓂᑐᐃᓇᐅᓕᕐ ᒪᑕ ᐃᓄᐃᑦ ᓄᓇᖏᓂ ᑲᓇᑕᒥ ᐊᒪᓗ ᒪᓇᐅᔪᒥ ᐃᓅᓕᕐ ᑐᑦ
ᑐᖅ ᓕᑎᔭᐅᓗᑎᒃ ᐃᑐᑎᓄᑦ ᐃᓄᐃᑦ ᓄᓇᖏᓂᒥᐅᑕᑦ ᐃᑲᔪᕐ ᓯᕐ ᒪᑕ ᐊᐅᓚᑎᑉᐅᓗᑎᖅ ᓗ ᑕᑯᓂᖓ
ᑯᐊᐸᑯᓂᒃ. ᐃᓄᖅ ᓄᑦ ᑲᓇᑕᒥᐅᑕᓄᑦ ᑯᐊᐸᑯᑦ ᓇᓗᓇᕈᓃᕐ ᑎᑎᖅ ᒪᑕ ᓴᐱᓕᕐ ᑕᐃᓕᓂᑎᓂᒃ
ᐊᖅᑭᓯᐃᒐᓯᐊᕐ ᓂᕐ ᒧᓗ ᐃᓅᓯᕐ ᒥᒃ ᓇᒪᖅ ᓂᕐ ᓴᒥᒃ ᐅᕙᑎᖅ ᓄᑦ ᓄᓇᑉᑎᖅ ᓂ. ᐃᓕᖅᑯᒥᑎᒐᑉᑎᒍ ᑕᐃᒪ.

ᓗᐃᔅ ᑕᐸᕐ ᔭᒃ, ᐊᖓᔪᖅᑳᖅ
ᑲᓇᑕᒥ ᐃᓄᐃᑦ ᓄᓇᖏᓂ ᑯᐊᐸᑯᑦ
ᑲᑐᔾᔨᖅᑎᖏᑦ
ᔪᓗᓇᐃ, ᓄᓇᓯᐊᖅ

ᐸᐅᓗᓯ ᑲᓴᑦ ᓗᐊᖅ, ᐊᖓᔪᖅᑳᖅ
ᑯᐸᐃᒃ ᑕᕋᖓᓂ ᑯᐊᐸᑯᑦ
ᑲᑐᔾᔨᖅᑎᖏᑦ
ᒪᑦᑐᕆᐋᑦ, ᑯᐸᐃᒃ

To my mother and father
Bertha and Jay Iglauer

INTRODUCTION

THIS IS the story of the very beginning of Eskimo coöperatives in Canada.

One day, almost twenty years ago, I went to an exhibition of Eskimo carvings in the parish house of a fashionable church in New York City. It was the first time I had seen any Eskimo sculpture and indeed, the first time any had been shown in New York. The work was so different, so alive, that I felt I had to know more about the artists who had created those commanding human, animal, bird and sea creatures from black, gray and a mossy green stone.

Where my consuming curiosity led was to a much broader experience than I could have imagined then: the opportunity to observe and record a small series of events that were a turning point in Inuit history. The coöperatives were the Inuit's training ground for their prodigious effort to move from an isolated nomadic existence equated in recent history with semi-starvation and relief handouts to a life that has become increasingly self-sufficient; to a new pride in preserving their culture; and to the formation of native organizations to unite and represent the Inuit in their common interests.

In the winter of 1959 a small group of Eskimos who made their home around the George River in Arctic Quebec and were almost all on relief met with federal government officials in a tent while their land, rivers and bay were covered with snow and ice, and formed the George River Eskimo Coöperative. It was the first Inuit coöperative in Canada. One of the officials, Donald Snowden, whose job was to solve the puzzle of unemployment among the Canadian Eskimos, or Inuit as they now prefer to be called, gave the George River Inuit ten dollars from his own pocket to pay the required fee to register with the Quebec government. They had no money at all and before they could get a government loan to start their coöperative it had to be registered in the province in which they were living. "It was the best cash investment I ever made," Snowden said twenty years later. "That ten dollars went an awful long way."

The exhibition I attended occurred in the spring of 1960. It took me another year to find my way north, and the occasion was the second meeting of the first coöperative at the site for a new settlement to be called George River. Like a photographer who happens on the scene, I caught in the camera of my mind and recorded the earliest efforts of the Inuit to cope directly with the grave changes caused by the intrusion of the white man in their land, and the coöperative was their tool.

The novel idea of setting up a coöperative business in the Arctic wilderness that the proud but desperate George River Eskimos agreed to give a try took root and grew, until now there are fifty-two active Arctic coöperatives, forty-one of them in the Northwest Territories, eleven of them, including one that is run by Cree Indians, in northern Quebec, with assets of fourteen million dollars and annual sales of twenty-three million. They are the largest single employer of Inuit in Canada. Every year about six-and-a-half million dollars go out to coöperative members in wages, salaries, for goods produced—including the works of art cherished all over the world—and other payments. After only two decades, the Arctic coöperatives are generating more money in this annual six-and-a-half million in wages and other related payments than the total amount of loans and grants put into them by all levels of government during the past twenty years.

The idea of coöperatives was introduced to the Inuit because it seemed compatible with their traditional way of living and sharing together; a device whose use it was hoped would enable them to regain their former dignity and independence, which had suffered a disastrous erosion with the white man's presence. In this first fascinating experiment at George River, individuals involved on both sides were of unusual character. The Inuit were highly intelligent, trusting, willing to work hard; and they were steadfast. The civil servants who brought them the idea were exceptionally nonbureaucratic: pragmatic idealists determined to adjust the system to marginal natural resources and immense distances; and they and their successors, too, have been steadfast.

The health of individual coöperatives waxes and wanes with the quality of local management, which is frequently confused and susceptible to local pressures. The coöps still have severe financial troubles, difficulties with personnel whose backgrounds have not been business-oriented, and logistics problems due to geography, particularly in transporting freight. Some, like Povungnituk, Inoucdjouac (Port Harrison), Cape Dorset, Holman Island, and George River, are prospering, but many of the coöps are fragile, their chief obstacle a chronic lack of working capital. Nevertheless, the long-term result of the idea adopted by that first tiny courageous group in a tent has been a brilliant achievement, one that cannot be measured in dollars.

Twenty years ago, almost all Inuit were on some kind of welfare. Today, besides producing the lucrative prints, carvings, handicrafts, wall hangings and clothing that have graced world markets, the Inuit coöps build houses and boats; are engaged in traditional hunting and trapping; run fisheries, tourist camps, hotels, lodges, restaurants, and coffee shops; provide all kinds of municipal services such as sewage, water supply, and fuel distributorships; and have their own retail stores that sell everything from groceries and hardware to clothing, stereo equipment, washing machines, freezers and snowmobiles. They also own a DC-4 aircraft based in Winnipeg, where it is leased to a charter airline with the understanding that the Inuit coöperatives have first call on its services. It carries the green and red color stripes and name of its owner, the central agency that links all coöps in the Northwest Territories, the *Canadian Arctic Coöperative Federation Limited*, painted in English and syllabics on its white fuselage. New ventures include recording of songs; film and television production that will probably increase, since Inuit Tapirisat of Canada (the Eskimo Brotherhood) is to participate in the experimental use of a hybrid communications satellite, Anik-B, launched in December 1978; a typographical print shop at Cape Dorset that houses the Kingiat Press, which has begun publishing books by Inuit authors; and the sale of caribou antlers in the Far East for use, when powdered, as aphrodisiacs.

In the communities where coöps exist, almost everyone is involved in them. Many of the Inuit leaders who today speak for their people received early coöp training that gave them confidence to function first on settlement councils and then in broader areas outside their communities: in Inuit Tapirisat of Canada, and its regional affiliates across the North; giving testimony at the Mackenzie Pipeline Inquiry presided over by Justice Thomas Berger that ended in 1977; as elected representatives to the Council that governs the Northwest Territories; in the negotiation of the James Bay and Northern Quebec Agreement and the structures set up to implement it. Service on the boards of directors of local coöps appears to be an excellent stepping-stone for Inuit making larger decisions now about land claims. The gravest threat to the Inuit coöperatives is that there are just so many leaders in any society, and the competition for their services puts a serious drain on this limited human resource.

This book started as a series in *The New Yorker* magazine about the development of the Inuit coöps from 1961 through 1964. In 1966, the articles were published with additional material in a book called *The New People,* with the subtitle *The Eskimo's Journey Into Our Time.* In this new edition the title has been shortened to *Inuit Journey* and an epilogue has been added describing some of the changes that have occurred in the North since I was there.

The George River settlement has been renamed by the Quebec government and is Port-Nouveau-Québec on the latest maps, but when the Inuit speak of it in English they still refer to it as George River. The spelling of *Inuit,* the plural form of the word meaning "people," has lost an 'n'. *Inuk* is one person, *Inuuk* is two, and the Eskimo language is *Inuktitut.* The Inuit have standardized their spelling and writing systems after lengthy research and community surveys across the Arctic conducted by the Inuit

Language Commission, which was composed of representatives from each of the six major Eskimo dialect areas: Labrador, Arctic Quebec, Baffin Island, Keewatin, the central Arctic and the western Arctic. The Commission operated under the auspices of the Inuit Cultural Institute, an independent body established with headquarters at Eskimo Point by Inuit Tapirisat in 1973 to strengthen Inuit cultural identity.

In a world that has become increasingly cynical, a success story of the spiritual magnitude of the Inuit coöperatives deserves reëxamining for whatever we can learn that we may have forgotten. When my first article about the second meeting of the George River Coöperative appeared in print in 1961, many readers wrote me. I remember one message in particular, in pencil, on white scratch paper with blue lines. It said, "Thank you for the beautiful and profound story on the Eskimos. It reminded me of the great virtues of civilization, before whatever goes wrong goes wrong."

PART ONE
The First One

I

In Canada's eastern Arctic, there is a place called Ungava Bay. It is a huge inlet—latitude sixty degrees—projecting southward from the Hudson Strait, between Hudson Bay and the Labrador Sea. Three hundred Eskimos live along its four-hundred-and-fifty-mile shoreline, and until just a few years ago they lived very much as their ancestors had lived for several thousands of years before them. They hunted caribou and fished for seal, and when they ran out of food they picked up their tents, packed them on their dog sleds, and moved to new hunting grounds either upriver or on the coast. Not many Canadians knew of their existence, and those who did felt little concern for them; it was assumed that if they could even survive in that far-off and forbidding area, they must be getting along all right. Over the years, the white man did bring to Ungava the Hudson's Bay Company, the gun, the motorboat, the missionary, a lot of disease, and, in the brief summers when the ice melts in the bay and on the rivers that flow into it, a bit of wage employment. The Eskimos were tolerant of the white man, and even amused by him, but they continued to speak their own language, to eat raw meat and fish, and to ignore Anglo-Saxon ideas of morality and sanitation. "Eskimo" is an Indian name, meaning "eater of raw flesh." The Eskimos' own name for themselves is "Innuit"—"The People"—and it has not been for very long that they have known that any other people existed on this earth.

Yet times were changing for the Eskimos on Ungava Bay, as for all Canada's twelve thousand Eskimos. Some of the white man's products began to have a strong appeal for them—notably tea, tobacco, guns, and textiles—and in order to buy these they devoted more and more time to the trapping of animals whose furs the white man wanted to buy in exchange. Of these animals, the white fox was for a while the most valuable—at one time the Hudson's Bay Company would pay over forty dollars a skin—so the Eskimos trapped a large number of white foxes. Then, in the depression, the price of a white fox dropped to two and a half dollars, and from that day to this it has never recovered enough to keep pace with the rising price of the white man's goods. While this change was going on, the caribou, the Eskimos' chief source of food and clothing, mysteriously began to vanish, perhaps because too many caribou were being shot and too few of their newborn calves were surviving. With the threatened extinction of that staple there came the possibility that the Eskimo himself might soon become extinct.

Formerly, most Eskimos dwelt in semi-nomadic isolation, broken—if it was broken at all—only by infrequent dog-sled trips across frozen straits to Hudson's Bay Company stores in winter, by kayak voyages in the short summer, or by rare visits from white missionaries or detachments of the Royal Canadian Mounted Police. After the Second World War, the single-engine bush plane opened the Arctic to new trade and exploration, in the course of which the white man discovered that the pattern of Eskimo life had tragically changed. Caught between a growing dependence on the white man's goods and a declining ability to provide for themselves in their traditional fashion, the Eskimos were found to be slowly starving to death. At first, they were given relief handouts of the sort granted to all indigent Canadian citizens. Then, in 1953, the Canadian government, motivated both by alarm at the Eskimo's plight and by a new awareness of the economic potentialities of the Far

North, established a Department of Northern Affairs and National Resources, and since then there has been an all-out effort, led by that department, to give the Eskimos every aid that an aroused government can contrive—from free false teeth to price protection for their handicrafts—to help The People jump, literally for their lives, into the modern world.

I set out for the Arctic to observe this effort at first hand, late one afternoon at the beginning of April, just before spring, in 1961. I boarded a Canadian DC-4 commercial transport plane on its weekly scheduled flight from Montreal to a tiny settlement in the Province of Quebec named Fort Chimo, almost a thousand miles north, on the Koksoak River, not far from where it empties into Ungava Bay. I was bundled up against the cold of the Arctic winter in long red underwear, a flannel shirt, a heavy sweater, an old ski suit, two pairs of socks, gloves, ski boots, and a wool parka with a fur-trimmed hood, and I was the only woman among the sixteen passengers aboard the plane, which had half of its seats folded back to accommodate cargo and blue sacks of Her Majesty's mail. I was accompanying Donald Snowden, chief of the Industrial Division of the Department of Northern Affairs and National Resources, and one of his assistants, Paul Godt, who was head of the Coöperative Development Section of the division, on an inspection trip to the Ungava region, where since 1958 they had been carrying out the most ambitious pilot project in Canada's program to make the Eskimo once again self-sufficient.

I had first heard of Ungava only a few months earlier, when I had met Snowden in New York. At the time, he had just returned from a trip to the area, and could talk of nothing else. Snowden, like most of the other members of his department I was eventually to meet, was youthful, tough, and imaginative, and conveyed an immense impression of dedication. He was a big man with reddish hair and brown eyes, and when he got excited his eyes sparkled and he was apt to pound the table—as often as not scattering a huge pile of half-smoked cigarettes that had been accumulating in an ashtray as he had talked. "I have the most delightful job in the whole government," he told me. "I love the North, and I also love to be in on the beginning of things. Our field of operations takes in a third of Canada, more than a million square miles, and the people at the top of our department believe the government must provide the spark and are willing to experiment. We could have picked any spot in the Arctic, but it had to be an area that was badly depressed, where we suspected there were good resources not being used. In Ungava Bay, we took a close look at the human and natural resources and came up with a crash program—first, an area survey; second, if the economic possibilities seemed good enough, coöperative development; and finally, marketing of northern products in southern Canada and other places." At Ungava, he explained, the Industrial Division's two main objectives had been to find new sources of cash income for the Eskimos and to develop a form of community life for them, with the hope that if the project turned out to be feasible, it could be extended to Eskimos in other parts of Canada. By now, he said, things were going so well for the Ungava Eskimos that the Industrial Division had started to reduce its staff at the bay and was preparing to turn the new industries over to the Eskimos.

"When we began our survey along the Ungava coast east of Fort Chimo, the central community on the bay, there were one hundred and twenty-two Eskimos, twenty-eight of them able-bodied men, living a marginal existence in camps on the Koksoak, Whale, George and Korok Rivers," Snowden said. "More than one hundred miles further along, in an isolated spot in the Northwest Territories called Port Burwell, were twenty-four Eskimos, five of them able-bodied men. We found that the George River area was relatively rich in timber and fish, and that Port Burwell, where there are no trees, had great quantities of seal and some fish."

At George River, which we would visit first, the Eskimos were learning how to produce commercially its three indigenous products—timber, fish, and handicrafts—the timber, black-spruce logs, which are floated down the rivers to Ungava Bay after the late-spring thaw; the fish, a beautiful salmonlike variety that the Eskimos call *ilkalupik* and the other Canadians call Arctic char, which was now being served in restaurants as far south as Chicago and New York; and the handicrafts, crocheted articles and sealskin objects made by Eskimo women, which were beginning to sell vigorously in shops throughout Canada and the States.

On our trip, we would first stop overnight at Fort Chimo, and then go on by small plane to a new Eskimo community that was being established on the George River, a hundred miles to the northeast, whose site had been voted upon by the Eskimos camping on the Koksoak, Whale, George and Korok Rivers in 1959. From there, we would go to Port Burwell, before returning to Fort Chimo and home.

When we had parted in New York, Snowden had said, "This will probably be my last trip to Ungava. Now we know that our program works, I'll have to go on to other things. But I have a very special feeling for the place, particularly the George River, because it was the first of our projects, and I love the people there. By the way, bring a good pair of sunglasses and dress warmly. The temperature will usually be somewhere between freezing and zero."

In the plane at the Montreal airport, I looked out the window and saw our four propellers revolving. The next minute we took off, and shortly afterwards Snowden dropped into the empty seat beside me. He groped through his pockets, found a pack of cigarettes, lit one, and began talking. "Everything about this project was experimental, right out of our own heads," he began. "In the summer of 1958, the head of our Projects Section, Jon Evans, surveyed the area by foot, canoe and motorboat, with an Eskimo guide, Elijah Annanack, first on the Koksoak River and then on the George, which, by the way, was named by Moravian missionaries after King George III of England. Jon spoke no Eskimo and Elijah no English, and it's a tribute to them both that they still have the highest regard for one another. The bugs were frightful, and every page of Jon's projects notebook was black with squashed flies and mosquitoes, but he cruised up the rivers for seventy-five miles. He selected thirty-by-sixty-foot strips of land and cut down every tree with commercial possibilities in that area to record its diameter. A tree with a fifteen-inch diameter will give fifty feet of lumber, good black spruce, knotty but tight, that doesn't crack or split. It takes one hundred and fifty years to grow the biggest trees at the George River, trees that would take fifteen years to mature in a milder climate like Oregon. Then Jon talked to the people about fishing and did some test fishing on his own and found brook trout and salmon, in addition to char. We examined the neighboring Koksoak River together with tourist trade in mind, but although prospects were excellent, development would have been impossible unless some entrepreneur had magically appeared on the scene. Finally, we talked to the Eskimos about handicrafts, and the women brought things they had made to show us. They have a tremendous sense of design and amazing ingenuity in the use of local materials.

"Our conclusions were that a million and a half feet of black spruce at the George River could be used commercially— after being cut in winter and sent downriver during the spring high water," he went on. "Working with Quebec's fishery officials we decided that one hundred thousand pounds of char could be taken out of the whole area commercially each year without causing depletion and that handicrafts were potentially a big item. We also recommended commercial exploitation of the abundant blueberry crop, but we've been too busy to develop that. When I came Outside I brought fresh caught char samples along and did some of that market research myself. I left one box in Montreal with another fellow and went to Toronto, hired a taxi for the day to take me from club to restaurant to hotel dining room, showed the fish and left them with the chefs. Twelve restaurants took in our Arctic char. Now you can eat it in Edmonton, Winnipeg, Quebec City, Calgary, London (Ontario), Chicago and New York as well as Montreal and Toronto, with new markets opening all the time."

Supper appeared on a tray, but Snowden went right on talking. "Our biggest uncertainty was the attitude of the Eskimos. All they kept saying was, 'We want to stay here, this is our home,'" he continued, buttering a roll. "We started from scratch. Nothing had rubbed off on them that was incorrect, so we didn't have to undo any mistakes, but they didn't understand why we weren't sure right away that our plan would work."

He stopped briefly to eat the roll, and then cut into a piece of chicken, talking between bites. "We had our first meeting with the Eskimos from the George River area at Fort Chimo, where some of them had come to get summer work as stevedores during the short shipping season. It was in 1958, right after the survey, and we sat on the floor of the area administrator's office and explained what Jon had been doing. I remember that in addition to Elijah, who had accompanied Jon, there were Willi Imudluk, who operates an outpost on the George River for the Hudson's Bay Company, and Josepie Annanack and Stanley Annanack. You will eventually meet them. There are three Annanack families in that area. Speaking through an interpreter, we said we knew the people were thinking of moving away to avoid starvation and we discussed the idea of people in an underdeveloped area undertaking new industries to help themselves; specifically, the possibility of a commercial char fishery and how the local lumber could be used to build houses, and make boats for sale. We promised to come into the George River that winter to talk about things the people might do, but we were careful to say we could not predict whether our study would suggest a sure way for them to make a living."

Snowden had finished eating, and he leaned back, sipping his coffee. "We were all much too excited to take notes," he said, "but I do remember the tremendous intensity with which Willi Imudluk took part in the discussion, and both Jon and I thought he was an unusual man indeed. We felt that if the projects were ever to be established, his support would have to be won. He would be one of the key people. On the other hand, Stanley Annanack was suspicious of us, which we regretted but understood. After all, we weren't sure what we were doing ourselves. Everything about it was so new."

Below our plane, the Quebec landscape was an unremitting black-and-white, with no visible human habitation of any sort. After a while, the black appeared scratchy, and I guessed that the trees were becoming lower and sparser. Every once in a while, I would spot a river—a long strip of solid white. Paul Godt, a tall, thin, prematurely gray man with a gentle manner and a worried expression, had finished his supper and came to sit on the arm of Snowden's chair. I asked him to tell me a bit about himself, and speaking slowly, with an accent, he said he was born in Denmark, and had arrived in Canada ten years before as a student. At home, his family had all worked in coöperative enterprises of various kinds, so when he decided to stay on in Canada and become a citizen, he naturally pursued the family interest in coöperatives. Godt struck me as the exact opposite of his mercurial chief. The two of them began talking about the Eskimo fishermen of the George River and their catch of Arctic char. The night before, in a restaurant in Montreal, I had eaten broiled char, and it had tasted delicious— like salmon, only richer. Snowden said, "The Eskimos at the George River were feeding all those beautiful, beautiful fish to their dogs, and were fascinated to hear that people in the South would pay money to eat char. To us, by the way, the South is southern Canada, and when a person leaves the North, he goes Outside. The Eskimos thought the whole idea that people would go out of their own houses and pay for food prepared somewhere else utterly ludicrous. Arctic char retails for a dollar and a quarter a pound in the South, and from the beginning we've marketed it as a luxury item. It's a glorious emerald green when it comes out of the water, and five minutes later it turns a light silvery pink. When we first asked the Eskimos how many char they thought they could catch in a season, they had no idea, and, to complicate things further, we had no common unit of measurement. With all the unknowns involved, we knew we ran a high risk of failure. We went into the George River that following winter as we had promised, and we were meeting with the whole population—about a hundred people—in an Eskimo tent, something like twelve by fifteen feet square and eight feet high. I said, 'Could you fill this tent?' 'Oh, yes—ten times over,' they replied. Then we had to figure out how many fish we thought the tent could hold. The first year, they caught sixteen thousand pounds of char, and the next year it jumped to twenty-five thousand pounds. After the Eskimos have brought the char in from the bay in their small boats, the fish are cleaned, quick-frozen, glazed and stored in a little plant we have helped the Eskimos build at the mouth of the George River, and are shipped south by freighter."

"The George River Eskimos formed the first Eskimo coöperative in Canada in 1959," Godt said. "They bought the fishing boats, freezing machinery, and other equipment, with twelve thousand five hundred dollars borrowed from the department's Eskimo Loan Fund. That was more than two years ago, and they have already paid back twenty-five hundred. On this trip, I'm going to hold the annual meetings of the coöperatives at George River, and at Burwell, the second Eskimo coöperative to be established under our program.

"Coöperatives are a logical development in the North, since they make it possible for the Eskimos to work for themselves rather than for the white man, once they have some capital, and we've made that available to them. The one at George River is going to sell its black-spruce logs, which have been cut under the direction of one of our men, named Max Budgell, to the government for the first school to be built in the area, and the women there have been very busy producing handicrafts.

"The Port Burwell Eskimos, over a hundred miles north of the George River community, have a coöperative that not only deals in sealskins, fish, and handicrafts but runs the first Eskimo retail coöperative store in the Arctic. We keep talking to the George River people about starting a retail coöperative store, but so far they are still buying their staples at the Hudson's Bay Company outpost, run by Willi Imudluk."

"Fort Chimo sounds like a town," I said, "but I'm not really clear about what's on the George River."

"Right now, when we talk about George River, we are referring to a community hall built last year on that river twelve miles south of where it runs into Ungava Bay," Snowden told me. "Our plan calls for a permanent settlement there, to be called George River, with year-round houses for the Eskimos, who now lead a semi-nomadic existence in tents, made of canvas stretched over wooden frames. The only permanent habitation in the area now is the Hudson's Bay Company outpost."

I said it sounded to me as if there had been a remarkable change in the Eskimos' lives in the past three years or so.

Snowden agreed. "When I made my first trip to Ungava, in 1958," he said, "the housing was inadequate, the nutrition was terrible, the t.b. rate was high, and the only way the Eskimos could earn any cash was by trapping, by working for a few white tourists who went there to fish, or by stevedoring during the summer months, when supply boats put in at Fort Chimo. Many people had warned us that the Ungava Eskimos had become so used to handouts—first from the Americans, who had an air base at Chimo during the war, and later from our government in the form of relief payments—that they wouldn't take on any responsibility. The Eskimos told us they wanted to earn money, but they had a reputation as no-good slackers. Not a very promising outlook, eh? We had no precedents, but I always feel that there is a solution to every problem. When I first went to Ungava, I thought Stanley Annanack was the laziest Eskimo I had ever met. This year, he caught more fish than anybody else on the George River, and now he's planning to put up a house for himself."

I asked Snowden and Godt to tell me about some of the other Eskimos I'd be meeting. "Well, among the first will be George Koneak, our interpreter," Snowden said. "The whole Ungava thing would never have worked without him. I don't speak Eskimo, which is a very difficult language, with several dialects, and very few of the Eskimos around Ungava speak

English. You'll like George. He has a delightful sense of humor. It's so easy to fall into a misunderstanding, especially when you've been talking continuously for five or six hours. Because Eskimos think in terms totally different from ours, George not only has to translate, he must carefully rephrase everything we say. It makes him both Eskimo and non-Eskimo, which must be quite confusing. Until the end of the nineteenth century, the Canadian Eskimos had no written language that we know of, but around that time, when most of the Eskimos had become Christians, Anglican missionaries in the eastern Arctic worked out a system of representing Eskimo syllabic sounds by geometric forms—circles, different arrangements of triangles, and little hooks and crooks. You might suppose that having at least *some* kind of written language would be beneficial, but actually the effect of the syllabics has been to isolate the Eskimos. Until very recently, practically nothing had been printed in syllabics except the Bible and the prayer book, and very few outsiders could understand the syllabics. Soon, as we've told you, there will be a school at George River, and then the Eskimos there will learn English. Meanwhile, George Koneak is truly an indispensable man."

II

WE HAD BEEN travelling so peacefully over the quiet land, which was now darkening, that I was startled by our arrival at Fort Chimo. I saw Snowden and Godt slip on the parkas they had been carrying, and while I was still struggling with the zipper on mine, we disembarked onto a snow-covered landing field. Ahead was a low building where bare electric bulbs, garish in the Arctic twilight, illuminated a small group of Eskimos who stood silently watching our arrival. Directly in front of me my two travelling companions had been surrounded by a welcoming party of men in parkas. I stood a little apart, feeling very much alone, and suddenly aware that although I might still be on the North American continent, I was certainly on foreign soil. Everyone was shaking hands and talking.

"George! George Koneak!" I heard Snowden shout, wringing the hand of a handsome young Eskimo of medium height, with shining black hair; green eyes; freckles; high, flat cheekbones; and a turned-up nose. "By God, but it's good to see you!"

"We been waiting long time, Don," George Koneak replied, with a tremendous grin. "Good to see you, too, it sure is." I was introduced in rapid succession to Koneak; to Sam Dodds, the senior Northern Service officer at Fort Chimo, who was a large, genial man wearing a Scottish tam; and to Dodds' young assistant, Keith Crowe. Then I was hustled onto the front seat of a truck. Crowe slid into the driver's seat, and Snowden, Godt, Dodds, and Koneak piled into the back with the luggage. "There are no hotels in Chimo," Crowe said, speaking with a British accent. "You'll be staying tonight with my wife and me and our two little girls." We were bumping down an icy road lined with small one-story wooden houses. Crowe told me that Chimo had a population of about three hundred, mostly Eskimos, and that although its history as a settlement went back to 1830, when a Hudson's Bay Company post was opened there, it had really just been completed as a modern Arctic community, with schools, a post office, and a government health center.

After a brief stop at Sam Dodds' house—a prefabricated bungalow—where I said good night to Snowden, Godt, and Koneak, and promised to be ready for an early start for the George River the next morning, Crowe took me around the corner to a similar bungalow, where he introduced me to his wife, Edna, a beautiful Japanese-Canadian girl with long black hair. When I had peeled off my parka and boots and settled down in an overstuffed chair, she brought in a steaming pot of coffee and a platter of freshly baked jelly doughnuts. Her husband presently produced a guitar and sat down to strum it while he sang in a strange, guttural language filled with "k"s and "g"s. "That's Eskimo," he said, and translated the song he had just been singing:

> "With twenty-two ammunition
> I'm going to shoot you,
> You big owl.
> Then I'm really going to eat you up.
> You'll be cooked in jig time."

I was feeling as warm and secure as if I were in a housing development in a New York suburb, when, suddenly, an unearthly howl penetrated the house from the still, cold air outside.

"Wolves?" I asked, with what I hoped was nonchalance.

"Dogs," Edna Crowe said quietly. "You'll get used to that

sound, and anyway it usually doesn't last more than ten minutes. By the way, don't be surprised if you see small children throwing stones at the dogs. They aren't pets here. We teach our children to protect themselves as soon as they can stand up. A two-year-old was killed by dogs at Frobisher Bay, on Baffin Island, two summers ago."

I slept that night in a sleeping bag that had been stretched out on an aluminum chaise longue in the Crowes' spare room. The next morning, I awoke to see two pairs of black eyes gleaming at me through a crack in the door. They belonged to the Crowes' little girls, who, when I joined the family at the breakfast table, were busy dipping toast into their eggs. After breakfast, I left them and went next door, to a prefabricated cottage that served as the Northern Affairs office. Here I found Snowden, Godt, George Koneak, Sam Dodds and his wife, and a number of Eskimos. Mrs. Dodds told me that when she had heard I was coming along on the trip, she had arranged to supply me with a vital item of northern wearing apparel—a pair of waterproof sealskin boots, which would be ready for me when I landed at the George River. I noticed that everyone in the office was wearing knee boots of coarse blackish leather with a gray fur band at the top; they were tied with bright-colored cord, and had rounded soles, like moccasins.

George Koneak had gone into the next room, and he shouted to us to join him. We found him sitting in front of an enormous gray short-wave radio transmitter. *"Ahailaa, ahailaa!"* he called into the mouthpiece. There was a crackle, and then a rough voice answered *"Ahailaa, ahailaa!"*

"That's Willi Imudluk, at the Hudson's Bay Company outpost on the George River," Snowden explained to me. He turned to Koneak and said, "Tell him we're leaving immediately and to have the dog sleds waiting. We'll land on the river ice above the outpost."

There was some conversation in Eskimo, and then Koneak looked up from the set. "They been waiting, all of them," he said. "They setting out right now for the river." To me, he added, "They got your boots."

Snowden, Godt, Koneak, and I climbed into Crowe's truck with our luggage, and in less than five minutes we had pulled up beside a single-engine, ski-equipped plane standing in a snowy field. We got out of the truck, and I was introduced to the pilot, a thin, sandy-haired man named Al Falby. Then, after he had jumped onto a small tractor and pulled the plane around into position for takeoff, he started loading the luggage. "This is a Norseman, Canada's most famous bush airplane," he told me. "It's done more to open up the Arctic than any other machine. The snow now is wet, with no bottom, but with our skis and shock absorbers, we can take the jolt of landing under really bad snow or ice conditions."

A young and pretty Eskimo girl joined us, carrying a small bag. She had smooth, rather flat features, and was wearing a parka, a flowered calico dress, cotton stockings, and rubber boots. When I smiled at her, she smiled shyly in return.

"Mary has been in hospital here in Chimo, and we are taking her home to the George River," Snowden said. "Often, when a plane goes to these remote places, it takes Eskimos going to or from hospital. The only other way to get to the George River now is by dog sled, which means four days of hard travel. Eskimos who come to Chimo by sled for provisions usually have eaten them up by the time they get home. Chartering this plane from the private air service that runs it, by the way, costs a dollar and fifteen cents a mile, which can come to four or five hundred dollars a day, and if we don't use the plane on a given day, we are still charged for two hours' flying time—at a hundred and fifteen dollars an hour. So we must move fast."

I remarked to Snowden that I should think Mary must be cold in her flimsy cotton dress, and asked why she didn't wear something warmer. He told me that in the past the women had worn caribou leggings, but the early missionaries had taught them that it was wicked for females to go about in trousers, so now they wore dresses.

We climbed into the plane, and my companions ranged themselves on wooden benches running along both sides of the small cabin, and propped their feet on luggage. I was told to sit up front with the pilot, so I could see better. After briefly studying a map of the Ungava Bay region, Falby taxied a short way through the snow, cranked something over his head, pulled on a wheel at his knees, and we rose into the air, heading east. Looking sidewise through the Plexiglas nose of the plane, I saw that Chimo, which had seemed a sizable town the night before, consisted of a few roads lined with cottages, a little church, a scattering of other buildings, and a small waterfront on the Koksoak River, with miniature wharves. At the edges of the rough field we had just left were several tents of gray canvas, with smoke coming from stovepipes at their tops. Eskimos stood outside them, looking up at us. Except for patches of black woods on some low hills, Chimo was encircled by white snow and ice.

I looked at the instrument panel. We were cruising at a hundred miles an hour, three thousand feet above the ground, in a white haze through which the sun shone dimly. Snowden leaned forward and, raising his voice above the roar of the engine, called out the names of rivers as we passed over them—the Koksoak, the False, then the Whale. "In summer, there are white whales at its mouth!" he shouted as we crossed the last. "Before too long, we hope to catch some to process for dog food!"

To the north, the hills levelled off into a vast expanse of white, stretching unbroken to the horizon. The pilot glanced at it. "Ungava Bay," he said. "Frozen."

IN AN HOUR, the land became much hillier. As the plane began to descend, George Koneak tapped my shoulder and pointed down to two faint lines across the snow. "Dog-sled tracks!" he shouted. "We're at the George River!" The plane banked, and I saw a clump of people standing on a white, smooth-looking strip of river ice. Tiny figures of dogs sprawled nearby, with the lines from five long, narrow sleds spread out around them. We flew low over the stretch of river that was to serve as our landing strip while Falby took a good look, and then we turned, flew back, and came in for a landing. We bumped along the ice that had appeared so smooth from above, stopped, turned, and taxied over to the waiting group.

Shouts of welcome greeted us as the cabin door was opened. Our baggage was thrown out, and I crawled out after the others and jumped to the ground. Snowden and Godt were immediately surrounded by smiling men with black hair and ruddy brown skin, wearing lively-colored cloth parkas and seal-skin boots. The Eskimos came over, one by one, and shook my hand, nodding and smiling. One of them—a powerfully built young man with an air of authority, who was dressed in a spotless bright-blue parka with red-and-yellow trim—handed me a pair of sealskin boots and pointed to my feet. "This is Willi Imudluk," Snowden said. "He wants you to put the boots on right now." I sat down on my bag and tried them on while everyone stood around, smiling. They fitted perfectly. There was a deep "Aa-ah" from the men, and Willi reached for my old ski boots and popped them into a wooden box attached to the front of a sled. As he did so, Falby called down from his cockpit that he would be getting along, but would be back to fly us to Port Burwell in three days. He waved his hand and was gone, his plane climbing until it disappeared over the hills.

By that time, our luggage, including large bundles of groceries that Snowden had brought from Montreal—mostly fresh fruits, vegetables, and eggs—had been lashed to the sleds. The Eskimo men ran their hands over the sleds' cargoes, found a spot that seemed neither hard nor fragile, and motioned to Mary and me to sit down there. I saw that Mary sat sidewise, holding the lines that bound the baggage with one hand, and I did the same. Snowden and Godt had already started off on two other sleds, and Koneak was on one behind us. Everyone else had put on dark glasses to protect his eyes from the harsh glare of the bright sun on the white snow, and I slipped on mine. A husky, rather tall Eskimo, who had been introduced to me as Elijah Annanack, was standing beside our sled. I recognized the name as that of Jon Evans' companion on the area survey. Suddenly, he shouted *"Oo-it!"* at his dogs, and as, with a mighty jerk, we started to move, he ran along beside us and jumped gracefully onto the front of the sled. I soon found that my safest bet was to ride astride the luggage, as if I were on a horse, for we had climbed the bank of the river and were following a trail that was narrow and wildly irregular. The sled—or *komatik,* as the Eskimos call it—was perhaps eighteen feet long but only about sixteen inches wide; its steel-faced wooden runners were fastened to squarish wooden crosspieces, about eight inches apart, by means of leather thongs that enabled the sled to give with the stress of travelling over uneven terrain. At the front of the sled was the large covered box containing my old boots; in this the Eskimo ordinarily keeps his food and, when he is out hunting, his ammunition. The reins, or traces, were narrow, grayish straps of sealskin. Each team consisted of five or six dogs in a fan-shaped hitch, with the lead dog in the center, on the longest rein.

When I recovered from the first shock of the jolting ride and found that I was still hanging on, I began to look around me. The trail was never wider than a foot and a half, and I had to lift my feet frequently to keep them from dragging on the bumpy ground or to avoid trees and bushes—not to mention our driver, who was continually leaping to the ground to keep the sled from running off the path, or to shove it across deep fissures in the rough trail. As I looked down into these huge cracks, I began to realize what Falby had meant when he described the snow as "wet, with no bottom." Elijah had to exert enormous strength to keep the sled steady and moving forward, but he seemed tireless. As we approached a particularly steep uphill stretch, he jumped off to reduce the strain on the struggling dogs, and I decided to do the same. To my consternation, I immediately sank several feet into the snow. It was only with a great effort that I was able to pull myself back onto the sled, while Elijah and Mary waited patiently until I was settled again. From then on, whenever we reached an incline I was torn between a desire to help the dogs and the dreadful certainty that if I did, there would be a delay, not only for us but for everyone behind us, while I floundered in the snow. (Later, I found out from George Koneak that the reason the Eskimos never sank in the way I did was that they kept their knees bent as they moved, which gave them a forward and not a downward thrust.) On our right, now, were low bushes and hills, and on our left was the broad river channel, choked by massive hunks of broken ice, like pieces of a giant jigsaw puzzle. The silence was broken only by Elijah's shouts to the dogs: "Ha-rah!" when he wanted to go left, "Owok!" when he wanted to go right, and "Aa-ah!" when he wanted the dogs to stop and let the team in front pull ahead. From time to time, the team behind would surround us, and the dogs' mouths, great red jaws open, tongues dangling between enormously sharp teeth, would be an inch or two from my legs. Despite the shaggy animals' otherwise benign appearance, I was by no means tempted to reach out and pet them; instead, I would swing my legs up onto a high spot on the luggage until we had pulled away. The air was clear and warm, and I pushed back my parka hood and prepared to relax, but just at that moment the dogs began to bark, and we pulled up in front of a little white building with green trim, perched on the riverbank. We had arrived at Willi Imudluk's Hudson's Bay Company outpost. The dogs lay down in the snow, and we all hopped off the sleds.

The outpost consisted of two small, old-fashioned wooden buildings, much sturdier than the prefabricated structures at Chimo. In the larger building, before which we had pulled up, Willi lived with his family; the smaller structure, about seventy-five yards away, was the Hudson's Bay Company store. As we entered Willi's house, we passed through a vestibule in which some freshly killed and rather bloody animals and birds were lying about, and found ourselves in a square kitchen that contained a big wood-burning cookstove. Several Eskimo women in cotton dresses and sealskin boots came forward, and we all shook hands. We followed Willi into a second room, where an old lady with gray hair and very bright eyes was sitting on an iron bed smoking a cigarette, while a round-faced child played on the floor. I was told that the old lady was Willi's mother. We shook hands with her and with the child, who was Willi's four-year-old daughter; she was big for her age, and was dressed in corduroy pants, sealskin boots and a little pink jacket. There was a stove here, too, giving out so much heat that we quickly removed our parkas, and in one corner stood a large gray short-wave radio, the twin of the one in the Northern Affairs office at Chimo. Everyone except the little girl was smoking a ciga-rette, and every so often one or another of the Eskimos would produce paper and tobacco and roll a new one.

I asked who had made my sealskin boots, and Willi's young wife came forward. After I had complimented her on their workmanship, Snowden whispered to Koneak to ask the price. After some thought, Willi replied, through Koneak, that ten dollars would be about right. Now Snowden launched a dis-cussion of a recently completed logging operation, with Koneak translating back and forth, and each group waiting quietly through the translations. Soon a lively conversation began among the Eskimos, and after listening attentively Koneak turned to Snowden. "At the end of logging, everyone short of food, especially the dogs," he said. "Fifteen dog teams eat seven hundred pounds of dog food in two nights. They so short of dog food, Don, they come back after they cut twenty-five hundred logs instead of three thousand." Willi said something further, and a look of surprise crossed Koneak's face. "So they come back here and get on radio and order one thousand pounds of dog food from Hudson's Bay store in Chimo, and tell Rube, the storekeeper, to have it flown over. It costed them eight dol-lars and ten cents each, but they only get eight hundred pounds, because two Eskimos just back from hospital Outside, who were waiting at Chimo to come home here, are sent on plane."

Snowden looked first astonished and then angry as he listened. He slammed his fist on his knee, and said, "By God, that's the first time Eskimos have ever chartered a plane on their own, paying out their own money, and look what hap-pens! Whoever made the decision to throw out the dog food and return the patients was wrong, since those two people were presumably well and could have waited a day or two longer. The government should reimburse the Eskimos for that two hundred pounds." While Koneak was translating these remarks, Snowden turned to Godt and me. "Anyway, it is kind of a milestone in their economic independence, eh?" he said.

Koneak said, "They running short of dog food again, so they want to see if they can catch some seals, which will give enough meat so they don't have to order more."

When the seal hunt had been agreed on, it was time for lunch. Snowden produced some cans of sardines from the stock of groceries we had brought, and we all sat down in the kitchen on wooden benches before a table on which had been piled some big, circular loaves of what looked like raisin bread, about an inch and a half thick. "I love this bannock," Snowden said, breaking off a large chunk. "It's non-rising Eskimo bread, made in a frying pan. The more you eat of it, the more you want." I hadn't felt hungry, but I ate a whole can of sardines, along with some bannock and tea. Afterward, we all walked down to the store. It consisted of one room containing a counter and several rows of shelves neatly piled with staples: matches, baking powder, powdered milk, tea, candles, rope, cartridges, chewing tobacco, cigarette tobacco and papers, lard, thread, luncheon meat, and a few cans of Johnson's baby powder. Godt showed me some tokens, made of a special alloy, and ranging in value from five cents to a dollar, that were used as a medium of exchange by the Hudson's Bay Company. When we had finished our inspection, we went outside and settled down on the steps of the store, sunning ourselves. Meanwhile, the Eskimos were packing the several heavy components of the short-wave radio from Willi's house aboard the sleds for the twelve-mile trip in a downriver direction to the George River community hall, so that we would have a means of communication while we were there. "Our project would never have worked without these radios," Snowden said. "We have three: one at Chimo which you saw, this one, another at Port Burwell, and next summer, we'll put a fourth on the Long Liner, the department boat that tends the long fishing lines. They are sixty-watt Seaway-Marconi Radio-Telephones, and we work them on a relay system, because reception can vary from absolutely perfect to absolutely dead. If Willi had known how to work this one a year ago, his first wife might not have died. The radio had been taken apart and stored at the community hall for the winter, and although he had no idea how to operate it, when his wife became very ill he went down to the hall and tried to put the set together by himself, in the hope that he could call for help. Last summer, we taught him to run it, and now communication with Chimo and Burwell is on a regular daily schedule. All the Eskimos are very good with mechanical equipment."

On the trip to the community hall, I again rode with Elijah. The Eskimos smoked as they drove along, and those who weren't handling the reins shifted from sled to sled and gossiped quietly. When we had been driving downhill through low woods for about an hour, skirting the edge of the river, and occasionally dismounting to let the sleds move more freely across difficult spots, I heard the dogs ahead barking furiously, and we came out into a clearing, where the three sleds ahead of mine had halted before an enormous hill, which the dogs were apparently unable to climb with their heavy loads. The Eskimo drivers began rehitching the teams so that the strongest dogs could lead the way up the hill and pull the weaker ones behind them. All the passengers had dismounted, and I could see Snowden, Willi Imudluk, and some of the others well started on the climb on foot. I followed, knowing that however long the ascent took the others, it would take me twice that long. I discovered at once that not only did I sink down two or three feet at almost every step but whenever I did find a surface frozen hard enough to hold my weight, my sealskin boots, with their smooth, rounded soles, had no grip. Halfway up the incline, I had to stop, clinging by my fingers to ice on sheer rock while my feet slipped around helplessly. My clothes were stifling, and I was so exhausted that I fought back a desire to put my head down and go to sleep. I shall die here—the sooner the better, I thought, and felt only a faint surprise at my weak instinct for self-preservation. Then my feet found lodging, one on top of the other, on a quarter-inch rock projection, and since I could move nothing but my head, I raised that and looked around. Elijah, several yards away to my left, was motioning to me to cross over to where he was. I tried to move, and instantly slipped several inches. The prospect of sliding to the bottom of the slope was so appalling that I dug my fingers frantically into a piece of tundra moss and hung on. Elijah inched toward me, holding out his right hand, and I finally let go of the tundra moss with my left and shakily reached over to grasp his fingers. Slowly we moved sidewise, until I was off the glazed surface onto which I had blundered. I completed my climb alone, sinking gladly into the soft snow, since I could at least move through it, however slowly. Every few minutes, as I stopped to catch my breath, I peeled off a piece of clothing, until, on reaching the top, I was down to my new Viyella shirt, bought a thousand years ago in New York.

Elijah had gone on ahead, so I jumped onto another sled that was waiting at the top of the slope. In a moment, Paul Godt joined me, and we moved off. I folded my parka and sweater across my lap, stuffed my gloves in my pocket, and enjoyed the scenery. The sky was light and very blue, and the river had broadened, providing a wider trail for the sleds. A fresh splash of blood on the snow and some scattered feathers marked the spot where a dog ahead of us had caught a bird, and at another place we passed a battered teapot that someone had dropped.

At five o'clock, the sun went down, and the cold was suddenly piercing. I quickly put on my outer garments again, drawing my parka hood tight to keep out the icy wind. When I asked Godt how much longer our trip would take, he looked at the sky, then peered at the trees, and, having apparently spotted a few landmarks, said, "I have taken this trip only once before, but I would judge—yes, I would really say we must be about halfway from the Hudson's Bay outpost to the community hall.

Another two and a half hours will do it." It took three. After dark, the cold penetrated from every direction, and our hands and feet were so numb that we had to shift position every few minutes, and keep on the alert so as not to fall off the sled.

The trail now took us down the center of the river, winding in and out among massive icy boulders. We moved along so rapidly that we soon closed ranks with the other teams, and were travelling, five sleds together, in a long line. The only sounds were the scraping of the sled runners on the ice and the barking of the dogs. The night light was a beautiful deep blue. When I had begun to think we were going on forever, we turned a bend, and I could see the outlines of a large log building ahead, with smoke coming from a pipe on top. We had arrived at the George River community hall.

We climbed the last hundred yards, up the riverbank, on foot, passing a rectangular scaffolding I had not noticed at first in the twilight, which Godt told me was a sawmill, for which Snowden was carrying a missing part, the guide, in his knapsack.

More Eskimos were waiting to shake hands. There seemed to be dozens of them waiting—men, women, and children, all smiling—and when the last toddler had shaken my hand, a tall, quiet man with black hair turning gray introduced himself, in a reserved, courteous manner. He was Max Budgell, the Northern Affairs Department projects officer who had come in a month before to direct the logging operation here.

The Eskimos had been swiftly unloading the luggage, and now they disappeared silently on the empty sleds. We followed Max Budgell through a small vestibule and into a large room where green fish nets and dirty white animal pelts hung from the rafters. Beyond was a smaller room, with a slanted roof. We went in, and, by the light of a kerosene lamp, I could see a stove made from an old gasoline drum, a wooden table under one of two unshaded windows, and shelves lined with dishes and canned food. The only other pieces of furniture were several tree stumps—used as seats—and two tubular beach chairs. This was the kitchen, which, at night, was also to be my bedroom. After a dinner prepared by Snowden, from food we had brought with us, to which Max Budgell contributed bread he had made that day in anticipation of our arrival, we washed dishes in water made from snow heated in an open pan on the stove. Then we turned in. I slept in a government-issue sleeping bag, which I laid out on an air mattress. The men spread out their bedding on the floor of the big room, and the last sound I heard that night, and for the next couple of nights—like taps—was George Koneak blowing up his air mattress in the other room.

III

NEXT MORNING after breakfast, nine Eskimo men and several boys arrived by sled from across the river and walked quietly into the community hall. The group was led by a stocky Eskimo with high cheekbones and a black mustache on a long upper lip, who slowly settled himself into the one metal beach chair in the community hall's large room. His face was deeply lined, and I guessed that he was in his late fifties. Traditionally, Eskimos live in family or household units, with several tents near one another; in every such group there is usually one man who is recognized as the leader. In this group—whose tents were now scattered from nearby, across the George River, to points on neighboring rivers as far as a hundred miles away— it was this man, George Annanack. Snowden brought in a chair from the kitchen and sat down opposite Annanack, and Koneak perched on a box between them to interpret. The other men either sat on the floor or squatted on their heels (a position the Eskimos seem to be able to maintain for hours) or found places on boxes and crates. Koneak told us that most of the men had gone out to catch seals, fishing through holes in the ice, and that it had been agreed that there could not be a formal meeting until they had caught enough to feed the dogs.

George Annanack spoke, in a deep, soothing voice. Koneak translated: "How are they liking the char?"

Snowden replied that "they"—the people in the South—liked it very much, and that soon all of the previous year's catch would be sold.

When this information was relayed by George Koneak, there was a low *"Aa-ah"* of satisfaction from the Eskimos.

Snowden talked about a proposed salmon fishery at Chimo, and suggested that the George River coöperative might soon start a brook-trout fishery. "Do you remember our telling you about the big government and the little government?" he asked. "Well, the little government says that trout has to be filleted, with the head taken off—not left whole, like the char. You cut the backbone out too, so you just have the side of the fish, which you freeze flat in little packages." The men laughed. This was obviously a very funny idea to them.

He turned to me while George Koneak was translating. "The Eskimos have a great fondness for the Queen," he remarked, "but they understand only that the federal and provincial governments are the big one and little one, and that the name of the whole thing is Canada. We're lucky that George Koneak is a creative translator. He knows that they know things I don't think they know, and that they don't know things I think they do know. Sometimes a few words from me will require a ten-minute translation."

Several women now came into the room, the older ones bent slightly forward, the heads of the children they were carrying in their parka hoods peeping out over their shoulders. Snowden passed around photographs he had taken during the fishing season the previous summer, and the Eskimos looked at their own images with grave interest. Next, he showed them a picture of the Eskimos at Cape Dorset, on Baffin Island, who in the past two or three years had begun to receive worldwide attention for their magnificent graphic prints made either with stencils cut from sealskin or with carved stone blocks.

"George River has the first Eskimo coöperative anywhere in Canada," Paul Godt said, and when George Koneak translated this, the Eskimos nodded with pleased smiles. "The third-oldest is the one at Cape Dorset. Now, at Dorset, they have a little bakery, where an Eskimo and his wife bake bannock and the Eskimos buy it, and in the summer they have tents where people from Outside come and camp."

Snowden put in, "At Dorset, the coöperative has recently hired a white man to work for it. Many white men have hired Eskimos to work for them, but at Dorset the Eskimo people are the white man's boss." The George River Eskimos laughed heartily.

After several other matters had been discussed briefly, George Annanack suggested that we call a recess until after lunch, when the rest of the men would be back from sealing. As the group made its way out, I asked Koneak how he had happened to learn English.

"I can read it, but not write it," he said. "I was living a hundred fifty miles north of here, near government radio station at Cape Hope's Advance, and one of the radio operators, H. B. Sabean, a great man, who is now a doctor working in hospital in Halifax, taught me English. I taught him Eskimo, and he learned to write in syllabics, too. That time—1942 and 1943— I was twelve, thirteen. I saw him again when he came back to Arctic five or six years ago on government medical ship, the *C. D. Howe*, that comes every summer. I haven't seen him ever since, but we still write each other, and year before last, when he was in Arctic, I was talking to him on the radio."

Snowden explained that the *C. D. Howe* puts in at all the small settlements it can reach in the summer, to give medical examinations and treatment. "It's aircraft, though, that have done most to improve our medical service," he said. "Substantial northern communities, such as Chimo, have health stations with government nurses—Joe Ross is the one at Chimo— but for major treatment, such as that for t.b., the patients are now flown out either to a hospital at Hamilton, Ontario, or to one at Roberval, Quebec. It's a great sorrow for the people to be separated from their families, but our department's Welfare Division does a good job of keeping the families informed. Formerly, when an Eskimo went Outside to hospital, the patient's family thought he was going to die, and they might not hear a word to the contrary for two or three years. Now the family is kept informed of the patient's progress—and Eskimos nowadays nearly always come back from hospital with good clothing and good reports of their treatment."

While we were eating lunch, I remarked that I had never seen such a crowd of chain smokers as these Eskimos.

Koneak laughed. "Eskimos love tobacco," he said. "When they run out of cigarettes, they smoke butts, and when they run out of butts I have seen them slash their pockets out where the tobacco was and chew the cloth."

AFTER LUNCH, while George Koneak and Max Budgell put up the radio in the small room Snowden found a large galvanized pail and began brewing some dehydrated soup he was planning to serve the Eskimos between the afternoon and evening sessions; he put me to work stirring instant chocolate pudding in a giant red-and-white dishpan. At three, we heard the barking of dogs, and from the window I could see long, thin lines of sleds and dogs moving across the river and up the bank toward us. All told, over a hundred Eskimos were coming from their tents across the river. The dwellings belonged to about fifty Eskimos who had been living in the neighborhood all winter. Now, Budgell told me, the tents were bulging with friends and relatives who had come for the meeting. But the main group was made up of the twenty-eight men who were members of the George River coöperative, and their families.

When all the men and women had gathered in the large room of the community hall, with the older children playing outside and the younger ones playing around the grownups' feet, Max Budgell began a discussion of the recent logging operation along the river, and of the failure to cut the full quota of logs.

George Annanack, who had again seated himself in the beach chair, said, "I think I should not have held the men from working Sundays."

"Airplane pilots have to rest," Snowden replied. "Otherwise, they get careless and have accidents. It's the same with others.

Now, I want to say that we are very pleased at the way the people have worked and done things at George River."

There was a murmur of pleasure, and a deep, musical "Aa-ah" from the men.

George Annanack said he was very glad to hear Snowden say this. "When you first came, we doubted whether the co-öperative business would work," he went on, "and now it looks as if it wasn't bad at all. Also, if you people hadn't come, it wouldn't be very good living here."

"This was a new thing to us, and we didn't always know how it ought to be run," Snowden replied. "But now, because the people have worked so hard here, the government thinks this is the way it should be done in other places, too."

"We are very pleased about that," George Annanack said, "but we are worried about Max—that he will be transferred —and we wonder what the next man to come here will be like. Max is not only a good person but also he knows a lot about the work."

"Max must soon go to help other Eskimos, but we are going to send you the best man we can find," Snowden replied. I noticed that several of the women were bottle-feeding their babies, using a varied assortment of containers to which nipples had been attached. One little boy was sitting in a corner blowing his cheeks in and out, and another was playing with a balloon. Suddenly, everyone moved away from the door, and I saw an elderly blind woman being gently led into the room and seated.

"This year, we are going to try to fill the freezer with char three times, in July, August and September," Snowden said. "The man who ran the freezer last year, Leo Bereza, will be back. Just before Leo comes, he is going to get married, but he is going to leave his new wife behind, and come here to do this."

"Why should he leave her behind?" George Annanack asked.

"Here you just put your wife in the kayak or on the sled, and away you go," Snowden explained, "but he would have to pay for her trip and food, and it would cost a lot of money."

"If I were him, it would not matter the cost, I would bring her anyway," George Annanack replied.

"Leo will be the only man of ours here this summer," Snowden said. "We said that at the start we would give lots of help, but now you are well started, and we have to go someplace else, and can't send the same number of people all the time."

"The young people should hear this and remember, when the time comes to take care of themselves," Annanack said, nodding.

Snowden explained that since the government would have only one man at the freezer, the Eskimos must choose someone to work with him and learn how the machinery was operated. To Koneak, Snowden added, "They may think that it is a bad thing for us to talk about leaving, but the day will come when they will be completely on their own, and that will be a good day for them." He paused while George translated.

"*Ouga!*" George Annanack exclaimed, and several others cried out, too.

George Koneak turned to Snowden. "He says, 'No!'" Koneak translated. "He doesn't think all of your people should leave. The time will come when one of us could run the fishery, which would be good, but not now."

"We know that day is not here yet," Snowden went on, "but it is a lot closer than it was several years ago. We didn't even know then what kind of freezer was needed for char." He told the group about the plan to start a salmon coöperative among the Eskimos at Fort Chimo, and asked if anyone wanted to sign up for it. The Eskimos are expected to belong to only one coöperative at a time, and only one man, a visitor who came from the Whale River and was not a member of the George River group, indicated his desire to join the new one. He came forward and signed his first name, in syllabics, on a paper that Snowden handed him, and they shook hands. "Congratulations!" Snowden said. "You may be the first member of a new coöperative."

It was seven o'clock, and everyone was restless. The small children, after playing placidly for several hours, were now beginning to wail. Snowden announced that it was time to eat, and Paul Godt brought the pail of hot soup and some bowls into the big room. The Eskimos moved up shyly and took bowls, and when they finished the soup, the chocolate pudding was served. Then Snowden distributed chocolate bars to the children and oranges to the adults. While they were eating these, Koneak told Snowden that a woman named Lavina, who was sitting in a corner of the room, was very sick. Snowden and Koneak went over and talked with Lavina, a pale, drawn-looking girl with lovely straight features and a sad expression, and found that she had recently had a miscarriage and still had not recovered. Her mother was now with her, but her husband, who had also been ill, was in the hospital Outside. "We will try the radio at nine," Snowden said. "We'll get word to the health station at Chimo and let Joe Ross tell us what should be done."

Eskimo boys had brought us a supply of fresh clear water in large drums by sled from a nearby lake. Several young girls retired to the kitchen to wash the dishes, and the meeting resumed. The men were sitting on boxes in a tight circle, and the women, across the room, rocked their babies and watched. Now Paul Godt began handing out mimeographed sheets of paper, two to each man. One sheet was printed in English, and was headed "George River Eskimo Coöperative." The other was in Eskimo syllabics, and its heading was:

ᒍᐅᐊᐸᐸᓇᐳᐸᑲᑎᕐ ᐁᑲᕐᐊᓗᐸᐁᕐᒍᕐ

Koneak explained that the symbols meant "To the Co-op Members of the George River." The papers were copies of the coöperative's financial statement—the first thing of its kind that any of the Eskimos had ever seen. The statement reported that since its founding the coöperative had received twenty-two thousand dollars for forty thousand pounds of char. Eight thousand dollars of this had been used to pay the fishermen for the char; the men working at the freezer had been paid wages of four thousand dollars. After other expenses, there was a profit of four thousand dollars. The Eskimos struggled hard to understand unfamiliar concepts, especially those involved in the "other expenses," and Snowden and George Koneak struggled to explain such items as "advertising" and "freight." It seemed especially difficult for the Eskimos to understand why the Royal Bank of Canada had charged them eleven dollars to handle their checks. "That amounts roughly to three cents a check," Godt said. "The bank has to hire people and put up a building, and has to pay for these things." He explained that the twenty dollars spent for office supplies had bought, among other things, the loose-leaf ledgers in which the coöperative's records were kept. "Next year we can just buy new sheets of paper," he said, holding up a notebook and showing how it worked. He explained that a three-hundred-and-forty-six-dollar expense for "Storage" was for keeping fish in a freezer in the South until it was sold, and that a ninety-nine-dollar "Advertising" expense was for "a card we printed to put in restaurants to show that here was something new." A thousand dollars in commissions paid to a fish broker in Montreal for marketing the char in the South was a puzzler to the Eskimos, who couldn't understand why the broker was entitled to five cents for every dollar's worth of fish he sold. "That's because he knows how to sell it, and we don't," Godt said. Of a ten-dollar incorporation filing fee, he said, "That's to the little government in Quebec for allowing us to form a business. That has to be spent only once."

Finally, Snowden introduced the Eskimos to the concept of interest, as he explained a five-hundred-and-nineteen-dollar interest charge on the ten thousand dollars still due on their government loan. He began tentatively, "You have known us for more than three years, and we want to know if you trust us."

There was an immediate response to this, and Koneak said, "They trust you."

"All right," Snowden continued. "They may find this hard to understand, but I'll try to explain it. In the South, if I want to buy a house, I probably won't have enough money, and I'll have to borrow some. For all the money I have to borrow, I have to pay at least six cents for every dollar, probably more. Sometimes, when people in the South need money very fast, they have to pay as much as sixteen cents for the use of every dollar. So the big government has the Eskimo Loan Fund, and all Eskimos who borrow from it pay only five cents for every dollar, which is less than many white people pay to borrow money. They may wonder why anyone charges to lend money. Well, sometimes someone borrows and can't pay it back, and there still must be money enough to lend out to other people."

"So the coöperative is doing pretty good to only have to pay five cents," Paul Godt added. Then he took a deep breath and explained the distribution of the four-thousand-dollar profit. "Half went to the members, and half was used, in the name of the coöperative, to help pay off the loan on the freezing plant, so that you will own it," he said. "Elijah, for instance, got twenty-four dollars and fifty-six cents in cash. Actually, Elijah's share of the profits was twice that amount, but the other half pays back the government." He turned to George Koneak and said, "I know this is very hard for them to understand, but try to explain it."

George Koneak sighed. "It *is* very hard to understand," he said, and began the long explanation to the other Eskimos.

At nine o'clock, Snowden brought the meeting to an end, and as the Eskimos slipped away on their *komatiks,* he talked to Chimo over the radio about Lavina, the sick woman. Word came back that Joe Ross wanted her brought out on the first plane that could get into the George River area; however, at the moment weather conditions were poor at Chimo, and no planes were taking off.

After we had washed our supper dishes, Max Budgell put fresh wood in the stove, and Snowden asked Koneak to tell us a story. Our lamp was out of fuel, and the ghostly white patches of the windows gave us our only light.

Koneak leaned back in his beach chair and lit a cigarette. "I can't talk the story the way my dad did, but I'll try," he began. "A little before my dad's time, four families went out in kayaks to hunt walrus around an island called Akpatok, way out in Ungava Bay. They waited so long for walrus that the bay froze over. They couldn't use their kayaks, and the ice was too thin in places for them to walk back to the mainland, so they had to stay for winter. They got a few seals, and then they were starving. Some of the hunters were very wild, and they were all very carefully afraid of each other. Maybe someday some of the men die by a knife, or a harpoon, or a clump on the head. Two of the families were in north end of island, two were in south end. One day, a father at south end go out to hunt, and his son and cousin stay home. When father come back, he say, 'I failed again.' Cousin say quietly to son, 'Don't holler. We're going to kill him and boil him and eat him and get a few days' more life.' Cousin stab him, and he have a few holes in back, and he knew he gonna die. So he lying down all the time, and say to son, 'You may as well get water for me for the pot.' Son dying of starvation, and father and son died at same time, so cousin got two meats at same time, and ate it up, heads and all."

I shuddered, and Max Budgell poured me a cup of hot tea.

Koneak rolled another cigarette and lit it. "Just then, lady from north end came down to other tent at south end and said, 'Last night we had very nice food—a human baby.' Nobody answered. Then she said, 'On my way down, I thought I saw a fox.' After she left, man from that tent walked out to the snow-bank where she said fox was, and saw a polar-bear house. He crawled in and killed the bear, so he and his wife and son, a quite small boy, had meat, but it was eventually gone, and they were in the same position of being hungry. The boy slept very carefully right next to the mother, ever since he heard about the baby, and one day woman come down again and say, 'I wish I could eat that boy.' The boy heard that, too. Then the boy's father killed his wife and cooked her, but the boy says, 'I'm not hungry. I'm not going to touch what you eat.' And that night, after everyone sleep, the boy walked out and disappeared. That boy started from Akpatok Island and spent a whole month on the ice of Ungava Bay. At same time, my mother's father had been wandering a whole month on the ice with my wife's grandfather. These people were not hungry at all. They had found seal and whale, and one day they seen the boy's tracks. They seen his tracks for three days, and on the fourth they walked right up to that boy. He tells them what happened and that he walked out from being scared of being eaten. So he survived. These people took him along, and after a while they came to shore and walked home. The boy grew up to be a man, and that man died only fifty years ago." He paused. "That soon."

IV

AT NINE O'CLOCK the next morning, when I went outside to brush my teeth, I was surprised to see that the *komatiks* were already moving across the river ice toward me. I soon learned that the Eskimos were in a hurry to get the day's meeting under way, because they had run out of dog food once more, having had a poor catch of seals the day before, and would have to go hunting again that afternoon.

"Our main business today is an election," Paul Godt announced after the hundred or so Eskimos had gathered in the hall. "Two years ago, we elected five men as the board of directors of the coöperative. Now it is time for another election. We will not vote for all the directors each time, because then they might all be new and wouldn't know much. We will elect only one new director now."

George Annanack began to speak, slowly and emphatically. "The five people elected were supposed to guide the fishermen and tell them how to work together," Koneak translated, "but he was the only one who could talk to the people. The others didn't do anything. He is hoping it will work out better."

"The idea of having five is that if something is wrong you can talk together and go to the plant and decide what to do," Godt explained. "One man alone who does not like what is being done might not be right, and then what is decided might be wrong. This year, one new man will be elected, and next year and the year after you will vote for two men. It's complicated, but let's give it a try." He passed around small slips of white paper. "First, each man should put down the name of the man he thinks should be removed from the board. After that, we will elect a new man to the board for a three-year term, and after that the board will vote for a president."

The men looked very serious, and some took their slips of paper to the other side of the room to write on them, printing each syllabic character with great care. Godt put a hat on a box inside the circle of men, and they dropped their papers in it. Koneak read the names to Godt, who announced that a man named Johnny Baron had been eliminated from the board. Three men were then nominated to take his place, two of them being Elijah, my sled driver, and Stanley Annanack, a handsome brown-haired man with green eyes, who was George Annanack's nephew. "I would hate to have to choose between two men as good as Stanley and Elijah," Snowden remarked as more slips of paper were passed out. When the votes were counted, Stanley Annanack had been elected a director, with fifteen votes. "He got the most, so let's give him a hand," Godt said, and after Koneak had translated, everyone clapped, while Stanley grinned. Max Budgell congratulated Stanley, who turned his head aside in pleased embarrassment. Then, while everyone else sat and smoked, the five directors of the George River Eskimo Coöperative assembled, with Paul Godt, in the far corner of the room to elect their president.

I asked Snowden why the women didn't participate in the meeting. "The coöperative has no women members," he said. "There is nothing to prevent them from becoming members—although under Quebec law they could not hold office—but this is considered men's business. At the first election, we tried to suggest that the various families be represented on the board of directors and that the president need not be the same one every year, but they know exactly what they want." Now Godt announced that George Annanack had been reëlected president, getting three votes out of five. Everyone clapped, and Annanack looked pleased.

The board members resumed their places, and Snowden sat down facing George Annanack. I had never seen him look so serious. "Ever since we first came here, we have been talking about the possibility of people coming to live together in one place," he began. "We know that much of the sickness of the children and older people comes when they are living in tents and are wet, and we know that when children and older people, especially, live in houses, they don't get sick."

He stopped. Now, as George Annanack spoke, Koneak translated. "He said that before he has been moving around in so many different places," Koneak said, "but now he is not so young, and would like to get settled in one place."

"In other places, hunters and trappers live in houses in winter and go out to hunt and follow their lines in spring and summer," Snowden said.

"So that way, if people are getting together in the same place, that would be a good idea," George Annanack said.

Snowden said, Eskimo-fashion, "Aa-ah." I noticed that he was beginning to phrase his sentences the way George Koneak did, and he often nodded slowly, Eskimo-style. "Now, Willi wrote to me this winter," Snowden continued. "I had asked him, when people came to his store, to find out how many were willing to spend their own money on houses. There were three."

When this had been translated, there was an abrupt sound—"Ouga!"—from the men, and they all began to talk to Willi, who was sitting on the floor with his back against the wall, hugging his knees. Koneak listened to what they were saying to Willi, then turned to Snowden, and said, "They all think you have their names for houses already!"

Snowden was so absorbed in his subject that he did not immediately catch Koneak's words, and he went right on. "There were some who said they didn't want to move when we asked last year, and we said, 'That's fine,' because each man must make up his own mind." Then he did a sort of double take, turning to Koneak. "They've *all* decided they want to live in houses here?"

"We'll ask each one," said Koneak, and Paul Godt, carrying a pad and pencil, started around the circle with Koneak, asking each man what he wanted to do.

"Tell them it's their own decision. It's not what we want but what they want," Snowden said.

Thomas Etok, a small, wily-looking Eskimo who, Snowden told me, had been the leader of the previous year's opposition to permanent houses, put his name down for one, and Snowden and Godt looked surprised. Koneak said, "Thomas Etok say he didn't agree last year *never* to come. This winter he knew all the rest were planning to move, and that leave him all alone on the Korok River, and he say if he's left alone, he'll ruin himself. That's why he joins."

"All of them!" Snowden exclaimed. "Well, this is a surprise!"

Now Snowden again began talking very seriously to George Annanack. There was total silence, and the men watched Snowden's face intently while Koneak translated. "The government wants to make sure that never again does anybody starve to death, as people did before. To make life better, the government must work with those people who no longer live off the land. The George River people have worked very hard these last two years, but to build houses costs a lot of money. A man must get his own logs and put them through the sawmill, and he must build his own house. That is what a man must do." He was speaking now in a curious rhythm, and Koneak was rocking back and forth on his box while he translated. "But later a special man from the big government will come in who knows how to build houses, and he will help the people. He will come not just this year but for several years, because we can't build all the houses in one year. The government will pay for some of the things that go into the houses— for windows, doors, doorframes, and roofing, and for a good wood stove for every house, with an oven so the women can bake bread and roast meat, and for a toilet, which must be in a separate place, and for a sink. It should not be as hard to build the houses as it was to build this community hall, because there will not be so many logs to lift."

There was a long sigh from the Eskimos.

Snowden continued to eye the group very seriously. "I know that everyone who said he wanted a house is going to want one right away, but this year we have enough money for only six."

There was another long "Aa-ah" as this was translated.

"Three years ago we were strangers, but now we are friends, eh?" Snowden said. "The government doesn't want to decide who should build first. You must decide among yourselves."

It was agreed at once that the two families, of which Elijah's was one, who had first pitched their tents on the site of the George River settlement should have the first two houses. There was confusion about the four other houses, and a great roar of laughter went up when Koneak jokingly suggested that the matter be decided by means of a wrestling match. At last, Snowden said, "It seems to me that there is one man who is independent, because he already has a house. Willi Imudluk has no reason to want anything for himself, so I wonder if you would let him be the one who finally decides which people need houses worst of all. But before that, you should talk this over among yourselves, and we should not be nearby when you do."

Max Budgell asked to be heard. "After the community has begun, more of your people will move in from other places," he said, "and you must form a group that will be responsible for keeping the community clean, for fire protection, and for protection of the water supply." He looked stern. "A community of houses that is not run properly produces sickness worse than in tents. But I am quite sure that won't happen here. And when the community starts, the children must have a school." He stopped, and when he spoke again, he seemed to be talking to himself. "If they don't, they are lost."

Then Budgell led the men outside and staked out for them,

in the snow, the approximate dimensions of a house. When they had all watched him do this, they leaped on their sleds and set off down the river to their seal-hunting grounds.

SNOWDEN HAD INSTRUCTED the Eskimo women to bring their handicraft output to the hall after lunch, so that he and Godt could pay them for the various objects, which would then be shipped Outside for sale. At two o'clock, the hall was filled with Eskimo women in flowered head scarves, their children either riding along in their parkas or tagging behind. Each woman carried her work in a sugar or flour sack, or a corrugated box or plastic bag. Snowden and Godt sat at one side of the room while the women came forward, one by one, and handed over handsome crocheted caps and belts and marvellously fashioned sealskin birds and animals. Snowden explained to me that the previous summer the Industrial Division's handicrafts specialist, Bill Larmour, had come both here and to Burwell and encouraged the women in work that could be sold Outside, yet would maintain the high standards that gave their art its classic beauty. Larmour had also brought in yarn, materials, thread and needles, which the women had lacked.

After Snowden had examined each piece carefully and put a price on it, Godt wrote out a check for the total value of each woman's work. "We double this price for retail sale in the South, to cover the handling costs," Snowden explained to me. "We never turn down their work at the start, for then they might get discouraged. First we buy the article, and then, if necessary, we explain what's wrong."

I watched Godt write out a check for seventeen fifty for a delighted teen-age girl who had made two colored yarn belts, three hats with tassels, and five miniature animals, and another check, for fifteen seventy-five, for Jessie Snowball, an attractive deaf girl, who had also done exquisite work. Next, Jessie's mother, Dorothy, a sprightly middle-aged lady, presented her creations; when Snowden praised them, she did a little jig, which made everyone laugh. I was surprised to see the sick girl, Lavina, sitting against the wall. Snowden walked over to her and gently took her bag of handiwork. He lifted a stuffed-fur bird from a fur nest to reveal four stuffed-fur baby birds, and said admiringly, "Oh, for Pete's sake, look at this!" At this praise, Lavina smiled and put her hand over her mouth in embarrassment. She had also made a pair of children's slippers, several fur hats, and a shapeless fur pocketbook, this last being clumsily constructed, with a zipper at the top. Snowden showed me the purse and said in a low tone, "This is an example of what we don't want, and Larmour will want to see this to help her to correct her mistakes. She has tried to make something she thinks will sell in the South." Lavina, sensing that the bag was not right, leaned back against the wall with tears rolling down her cheeks, and she would not be cheered by the check, for sixteen seventy-five, that Snowden handed to her.

After the women had gone, Max Budgell remarked that Dorothy Snowball, who had several children besides Jessie, had never got married. "And now she has just adopted a little boy as insurance in her old age," he said. "Not through legal channels, but simply by means of an agreement with his parents. The women often marry late or not at all, sometimes because their parents won't let them leave home, and sometimes because they simply don't want to. The woman belongs to the man she marries, just as his dogs do, and she has definite and stern duties. She must make his boots, look after his tent, and keep his clothes in repair. Actually, I think Eskimos are much more considerate of each other and their children than we are. The harder life is, the more cheerful they become—sometimes it's unbelievable—and they possess a natural courtesy at all times. Then, the younger Eskimos have a great respect for their elders. In the old days, when parents became too infirm to travel or work, and were eating food without making any return, the young people would have to leave them behind—sometimes in a snowhouse and sometimes not—but always without food or fuel, since death would come quicker that way. Now they are able to take good care of them.

"Their habits and ways of thinking are not like ours. Illegitimacy, for instance, means little to them," Budgell continued. "A lot of the children are by white men, and that isn't frowned on, either. Anyway, there is never a homeless child. No matter how desperately poor the Eskimos are, they will always take in children. When an Eskimo girl has an illegitimate baby, she has a stock answer for the missionaries who tell her how terrible that is. 'If God didn't want me to have it, He wouldn't have sent it,' she says. Last month, when I was out logging with George Annanack and some of the younger men, we were sitting around talking one evening, and George put his arm fondly over one young man's shoulder and said, 'This chap has given me a baby!' I found out that the fellow had fathered a child born to George's daughter. George spoke of the baby with great fondness and there was certainly no suggestion of outrage, or even a wish that the young man should marry the girl, then or later. Just a normal, pleasant occurrence."

I asked whether the Eskimo women now went to the hospital to have their babies.

"Most babies are born at home," he said. "There are several midwives in each group. When a male child reaches the age of hunting—about eight—the proceeds of his first hunt go to the midwife who delivered him. If the child is a girl, the first thing she makes with her hands—a pair of mittens, usually, or perhaps boots—is given to the midwife."

Willi Imudluk came to have dinner with us, and he told Snowden and Godt that he had been thinking that the new community should have a coöperative store. Eskimos often complained to him that Hudson's Bay Company prices were too high, he said, especially since they had so little money. He added that if he were offered the management of a retail store at George River he would take the job. Even if the store did not materialize, he felt that he could make more money logging and fishing for the coöperative than he was earning at the outpost. "Some day I will live at George River, and my kids could go to school," he declared. Snowden reminded Willi that he already had a stake in the new settlement, for he was one of the four men who had built the community hall, to which

Willi replied in his soft voice, but with great firmness, "I know how heavy this building is, because I put a big flat rock under it, and it was crushed like a soda biscuit. We built this hall to last forever!"

ONLY THE MEN attended the final meeting of the George River coöperative, which started at about eight o'clock that night. It was bitter cold and already dark when they arrived, and shortly after the discussion began, the lamp faded and went out. We sat in the blackness, the only light coming from the frosted windows and the red glow of cigarettes. Occasionally, a match or a cigarette lighter would momentarily illuminate a face. The Eskimos had an announcement to make: They had picked Stanley Annanack to help at the freezer. George Annanack said, "We have picked him for three reasons: he will take very good care of the equipment; he is not afraid to talk up to anybody; and he is not a deep sleeper and can work all night."

Snowden asked if the Eskimos had decided who should have the four unallotted houses. "We have left that up to Willi," George Annanack said.

Willi began to speak slowly. "I suggest that the first of the four houses go to George Annanack," he said. "The second should go to old Sam Annanack and his wife, Stanley's parents, for when the people go to the Hudson's Bay outpost for Christmas, these two are always left behind. Stanley Annanack has six very small children, so he needs the third house, and Ned Imudluk, who lost his wife last year and also has quite a few small children, besides a very old mother-in-law, should have the fourth."

Snowden turned to Koneak. "They realize that they are all going to have houses later on, don't they?" he asked.

"They understand, Don," Koneak said. "No complaints."

Now someone found fuel and relit the lamp. Snowden, Koneak, and Willi Imudluk were lying on the floor with their heads propped against some boxes, and, as usual, George Annanack was sitting in the central spot, in the beach chair.

Snowden began to discuss the future community, explaining that the houses should not be too far from the school, and that there should be room for a seal-oil shed and for stores. "Remember that most of your supplies will come in by water, so you should be able to get to it and back easily," he went on. "And you should build on land that is well drained and gets reasonably dry in the summer. Also, the water supply has got to be protected. The dogs must be put in a compound, so that they cannot contaminate the water supply and bring illness and disease. I know people don't like to do this with their dogs, but it must be done."

I heard the low, musical voice of George Annanack. "I have been thinking of the dogs for a long time," he said. "If we put the dogs on chains, they will be suffering more than I can stand. So I think the compound is a lot better, for in there they are free to walk around and will not howl so much."

George Annanack spoke again, and Koneak turned to Snowden. "George Annanack wants to know something, Don. They are looking forward to seeing you again, and they want to know if you are coming from now on."

Snowden sat up, and slowly shook his head. There was a deep murmur.

Koneak said, "Now they know this is the last time. They are sorry to hear."

Snowden looked disturbed. "I'm going to try to get back sometime, because I like it here," he said, in a low voice. "But we have to move on to other places."

Stanley Annanack spoke. Koneak listened, and then said, "They feel very, very sorry. This new thing you people brought, what nobody had never thought before, turns out well, and they are very pleased."

Snowden seemed deeply moved, and cleared his throat several times. After a moment, he addressed Koneak. "All over the world, there are men who speak different tongues who are trying to talk to one another," he said. "You have made it possible, George, for all of us and your people to speak together. I think that's as important as anything that has been done in the whole project." He insisted that Koneak, who was embarrassed, translate this for the other Eskimos.

There were approving nods. Then came the voice of George Annanack, very deep and quiet. Koneak listened, and turned his head toward Snowden. "He says there could not be any better help than they have got from you people, because now they don't have to leave their own country. You people were to the Eskimos as their own." He paused, and then he said slowly. "We will remember you forever and ever."

Suddenly, the room was bursting with the sound of voices. Everyone was calling out, *"Nokomik! Nokomik!"* It was the Eskimo word for "Thank you."

PART TWO

The Outermost Place

I

It was time for our pilot to pick us up at the George River and fly us to Port Burwell. Early the following morning, Snowden began to look at the sky and listen for the plane, but at noon the voice of Sam Dodds was heard on the radio calling from Fort Chimo that the weather was still bad there. The plane would not be leaving.

Stanley Annanack, Willi Imudluk and several other Eskimos drifted into the community hall. Snowden produced a hard salami from his knapsack, cut off thin slices for the men to sample and watched as they tasted it. The Eskimos chewed politely until Stanley made a face. Then all started laughing and choking. Stanley held his throat and said, "I would explode if I had to eat that all day. That doesn't mean I don't like it, but just that I can feel it getting hot!"

"You aren't hurting my feelings, there are lots of foods I don't like," Snowden replied. "This is called sausage and it's made of meat that has been smoked a long time so that it will keep two years or longer. I carry it in case the plane I'm on is forced down on the ice, because sausage is rich in food value and good for a man. I know a German fellow named Erich Hofmann who is working as chef at an Eskimo rehabilitation center in the western Arctic who experiments with local products. I'll bet he could make a sausage with seal or whale meat that you would like. He's already made sausage from buffalo and reindeer meat, and seal liver."

The Eskimos laughed again when George Koneak translated this and we could hear the word "sausage" several times in their conversation as they talked among themselves. Koneak explained: "They say they too eat things that they like but the white people can't eat. They say somebody killed a caribou and smoked it once and it tasted good. It's just that we never had this stuff, saus-age, before."

"We're going to try and hire Hofmann to go all over the Arctic for us, preparing and preserving northern foods," Snowden said. He changed the subject. "What do you want most in your house?" he asked Stanley. Stanley, the father of six children, instantly responded, "A washing machine." Snowden asked a handsome young Eskimo in his late twenties named Lucas Etok the same question. Lucas turned his face away when Koneak translated the question, looking embarrassed. "Not for my house, for myself," he said in a low tone. "I never went to school. I wish I could read the white people's books."

Taking a walk that afternoon, I found I could move more rapidly over the snow, for it had a crust and I was learning to step lightly with knees forward so that I didn't sink. I stood on the hill above the community hall and looked down where the new settlement would be. The sun had a theatrical brightness, lighting the tumbled ice of the river and the low white hills, bringing a welcome splash of color to the black and white vista. Far away, an Eskimo was hunting with his gun. A hundred yards or so from me, several small pretty white-feathered birds that are northern members of the grouse family called ptarmigan were so tame that they were strolling across the patches of rock and tundra that broke through the snow. When I returned to the hall a pan full of these white birds had been presented to us by the Eskimos for our dinner. George Koneak had shot an Arctic hare that had been added to the evening menu; a lean, lanky rabbit that was hanging, already skinned but still recognizable as a rabbit, from the rafters. I had never seen a skinned animal before, and I lost my appetite for Arctic hare. However, Max Budgell plucked the ptarmigan, cutting them up and browning them in lard with turnips, onions, carrots and parsnips that we had brought along, and delectable odors began to come from :he pot where they were stewing on top of 'he stove. The ptarmigan made a fine dish, but the polite nibble I tried of hare tasted tough and stringy. We finished the last small loaf of Budgell's home-made white bread, dipping it in the stew gravy, so that evening he prepared a new batch of bread dough to bake in the morning in the oven he would put on top of the green Coleman camp stove. We watched while he cut the dough into small square loaves and I asked for his recipe. He recited all the ingredients. "When you have mixed everything in, get the dough down on the floor and punch hell out of it," he added, and proceeded to do just that. "Take all the old pieces of wood and nails out, cover it, and let it rise overnight. In the morning, beat hell out of it again."

While Budgell was starting a fire in the gasoline drum stove the next morning, he explained that the little room I was in had been tacked on to the community hall for the government's Northern Service officer. "After this short social season is over at the George River, I'll be back living in here," he said. "When the temperature hits twenty below zero, the first thing I do every morning is to take a broom and sweep off the icicles that form on the ceiling. If I don't, when the room warms up the icicles melt and give me a shower bath." The drum stove produced a surprising amount of heat, and when it was red hot it was impossible to remain in the room without removing one's coat and sweaters. As soon as the fire died out, night or day, the room became a refrigerator. At night, the cold penetrated my sleeping bag, so that I would crawl out and put on my heaviest socks and sweaters before I was warm enough to get to sleep again.

The plane did not come that day either, and in the afternoon, I asked Budgell if it would be possible to see an Eskimo tent. He picked up a stick as protection from the dogs, and

c

we set off on foot across the river and then walked up a trail into a wooded area. As we reached the top of an incline, Budgell pointed upward, and I saw, high in a tree, an Eskimo dog hanging by his back feet, quite dead. "The Eskimos will use his fur for sleeping gear and for the trimming on parka hoods," Budgell said. Walking on, we came to a clearing containing three Eskimo tents, near which was an open platform on posts six feet above the ground. This, Budgell explained, was where the Eskimos stored meat and whatever else they wanted to keep from the dogs. "They don't have much food to store, actually," he said, "but live from day to day, hunting each day for that day's food." I was curious to know if the Eskimos still ate raw meat. "They love raw caribou, and ptarmigan, and fish," he replied. "When I was logging with them last month, I didn't eat too much of it, but when the Eskimos sat down to raw caribou, they ate it to the bare bones." He laughed. "As for ptarmigan, I remember that one day I went into the cooking tent to speak to one of the Eskimo girls we had brought along to prepare meals. Her back was toward me when I came in, but she turned around when I spoke to her, and her face was covered with blood from ear to ear. I thought her throat had been cut, but she had just been enjoying a little snack of raw ptarmigan."

We were standing now before one of the tents, and Budgell knocked on its wooden door, which was about four feet high and was hinged to its wooden frame on an inward slant, which made it slam shut behind us. The structure itself was shaped something like a circus tent, with fluted rather than angled corners. Daniel Snowball, one of the older men I had seen at the community hall, ushered us in. We shook hands with him and his wife, a plain, strong-looking woman, who had been sitting in a corner plucking ptarmigan, and with his attractive daughter, who was working on a pair of sealskin boots, using an *ulu*, a small knife with a wooden handle and a sharp, rounded blade. The temperature in the tent must have been over seventy, maintained by an oil-drum stove with a thin pipe that went through the canvas roof. I noticed that the roof was speckled with little black holes, made by sparks from the stove. "It must leak like a sieve in wet weather," I said. Budgell nodded. "It does," he said. "They will probably make themselves a new tent this summer. They'll buy about sixty yards of cloth, which will cost forty or fifty dollars, and stitch it on a hand sewing machine—something most of them carry with them."

I estimated that the tent was about fourteen feet long and eight feet wide. The stove was in the center, and around the four walls were wooden bunks, or sleeping platforms, about three feet above the rough plank floor. The platforms were lined with spruce boughs, over which caribou-skin robes had been spread, and on top of these were eiderdown quilts covered with bright calico. Budgell explained that the bunks were unusually wide because the Eskimos sleep with their heads toward the tent walls and their feet toward the stove. On a shelf between two of the wooden poles that supported the tent were a radio and two books. Noticing my interest in the books, Daniel Snowball handed them to me to look at. They were Protestant prayer books, printed in syllabics. Snowball's wife, who had settled down again to tackle the pile of ptarmigan, sat near a table that held pots and pans and enamel cups. Budgell inquired about the Snowballs' food supply, and Daniel Snowball told him he had shot six ptarmigan on his first hunt that morning, and so many in the afternoon that he hadn't bothered to count them.

"My wife is a better shot than I am," he said. "She shot ten ptarmigan at one time, using a .22 rifle. Twenty-one years ago, my wife carried our daughter, who was then a baby, in the hood on her back, and was walking through the willow beds, hunting. She tripped over a willow and shot herself." His wife nodded, pointing with a smile to her thigh. "It didn't hurt. It wasn't painful," she said. "The bullet is still there."

The sunlight that filtered through the canvas, together with the heat from the stove, made me feel as if I would suffocate. It was a relief to shake hands again and then get out into the ice-cold air. As we began to walk back toward the community hall, Budgell asked, "Have you ever noticed how much the Eskimos shake hands?" I said that I certainly had. "That's an Eskimo custom," he said. "If I went to Chimo and came back again the same day, we would all shake hands when I left, and we would do it all over again when I came back."

I had noticed that the ground around the tents we had seen was filthy, and I wondered how sanitary regulations would be enforced in the new permanent community that was to be built. "I think the Eskimos will obey the regulations we suggest because they want to please us, not because they believe what we are saying," he replied. "Sometimes they think we are a little bit crazy, but they usually decide they might as well humor us. The time of the thaw is when these communities become terrible. Most of the people come down with gastroenteritis every spring. But spring housecleaning is very simple here. The Eskimos just move out—it takes them about two hours to pack for a move that may last four years—and let the rains wash through. The spring breakup starts about the first of May, and soon there are eighteen hours of sunlight every day. The snow melts and runs into the sea—not in a flood but in trickles. The ground is saturated, and water runs continually, day and night. No planes can get in or out, because they can't land on the ground, which is too soft, or on the water, which is covered with melting ice. The Eskimos move out to the coast on their sleds, which they use as long as there is any ice or snow at all. They go out on ice that would give you the shivers, it's so rotten. You expect it to break any minute, but the sleds are so long they don't exert much pressure in any one spot and act like ladders. By the end of June, except for small patches, there won't be a flake of snow on any of this land—just black rock and gray caribou moss."

I asked how he thought the Eskimos would adapt to the radical pattern of living in fixed communities. He hesitated, and then said, with great passion for such a quiet man, "Their true hope for survival is through education. As the caribou and other game dwindle, their hunting skills are dwindling, and they simply cannot live as they used to. They depend more and more on store-bought goods, and their kids, through lack of training, won't be as good hunters as their fathers were. All we can expect to do with the present flock of youngsters, because the time has been so short, is to teach them English—or possibly French, in the French-speaking areas of Canada—and the three 'R's. Because we got started later and our Arctic area is so much larger, Canada is behind Greenland and Alaska in this respect. Our population is so widely dispersed that we have to put up schools and hospitals all over the place."

We were out of the woods now, walking across the river. I had to step carefully to avoid the deep wide cracks in the ice. I wondered what Budgell would be doing, after we left. "This spring the George River coöperative will saw up the five hundred logs we have gotten and build six little boats which the Port Burwell coöperative will buy from us," he said. "We are hoping to start trading between coöperatives. Burwell, which has plenty of seals, but no trees, can exchange its seal products for our wood products. We will also repair our own boats and fishing nets. I'm not going to touch a thing myself. I didn't cut or haul at the logging upriver, before you came. I just showed the men the type of tree to cut, and counted their daily cut record. The men were paid by the log, by the coöperative. The idea is to learn by doing, the less we do for them, the better. I will go on to Burwell then to help with its char fishery. The Burwell freezer went into operation last year, and I want to make sure it keeps up the high standards with which it started.

"In a lot of ways these Eskimos resemble the Indians I worked with in Newfoundland, where I come from," Budgell continued, swinging his stick out over the ice. "These Eskimos are good in the woods and with canoes in a river, which is definitely not an Eskimo trait. All Eskimos are good in salt water, but most are afraid of rapids and the big rocks of the rivers. I am more friendly with Indians and understand them better, and they accept me as one of their own. The way Eskimos live, there is no such thing as personal privacy, and if you aren't careful you'll have people with you all the time.

They visit at all hours of the night—bringing their families too. George Koneak has been with us so much that he is able to live in both worlds, but Willi Imudluk is a very extraordinary man. He is an Eskimo who has lived entirely in an Eskimo world, and yet he can still run a Hudson's Bay Company outpost.

"No man is allowed more credit than he can pay, so Willi has to say 'no'. Yet he's popular, and I'll be damned if I see how he does it so successfully. Before the Second World War, I was representative at a Hudson's Bay Company outpost myself, in northern Labrador. My father was an old-time employee of the Bay who thought there was only one company in the world, and that places like Bethlehem Steel existed only to supply the Hudson's Bay Company with steel knives and forks."

We climbed the bank from the river. Budgell stopped at the door of the community hall to finish his story. "My father was very angry with me when the war came," he said. "My outpost was ordered closed and I made up my mind to enlist in the Canadian Army. I walked most of the twelve hundred miles to the mouth of the St. Lawrence River. It took me three months, and I travelled the whole way with a party of twenty-five Naskapi Indians. They lived at Seven Islands, where I was going, so this was just a normal trip for them. They were walking home after hunting and trapping in the North, the way we would walk home from a pub. Every night we slept on spruce boughs on the snow. My only discomfort was wet feet, because we walked in water up to our ankles and the water is so cold in spring. When I arrived at Seven Islands I was thrown in the clink until I could be identified and allowed to enlist. My father felt I had deserted the Hudson's Bay Company for another company when I joined the Canadian Army," he said with a laugh, "and he refused to speak to me."

We had another ptarmigan stew for supper that night. "My Eskimo name is *Ahigik*, which means 'The Ptarmigan,'" George Koneak suddenly revealed, while we were eating. "When I was a year old and before the spring like now, the first time I see the ptarmigan it landed on our tent. The Eskimos see something, they think it's a miracle, so they think the ptarmigan brings my name."

The night was cold and clear, and after we had washed dishes and talked about the possibility of the plane arriving to take us away the next day, Max Budgell built up the wood fire, brewed a fresh pot of black tea, and we all settled down around the stove in the little room. It was warm and cosy, and George Koneak rolled a cigarette, lit it, and began to talk about himself. At Cape Hope's Advance on the west side of Ungava Bay, where he came from, snowhouses were still being used, he said. "I can build one in two hours," he explained, "but a tent is more comfortable. A snowhouse is better when you are travelling, though, because you don't have to carry the extra load. Since I am working for the government, I live in a house in Chimo with my wife and children, but I still have six dogs. I keep, just in case I get fired, but I loan to my brother-in-law for the whole winter so they go on working. I used to like my dog teams," he remarked wistfully. "All my dogs have names, like *Tuksalik*, 'Double Eyes,' with two spots over the eyes, and *Shenunugok*, which means, 'Gray.' We make little sealskin boots for the dogs, and cut two holes for middle claws to get a grip on the ice so it don't cut their feet, but every time you stop, you have to take off the boots, or the dogs would eat them.

"At George River, the Eskimos are enlarging their teams," he said. "In 1958, only four out of fifteen families had teams. The others had died from rabies, but now every family has a team. The government brought in pups and started new teams, and when one family has enough for a good team you always give the pups to whoever wants them. If some dogs aren't working properly, you kill them, of course. There is no food to waste."

Somebody had presented me with a compass before I came north, and I showed it to Koneak and asked him if he ever used one. He shook his head. "We know the hills and valleys and slopes," he said. "Every little while we give a quick glance so we will know the landmarks and we never get lost. But when

I am going Outside in the South it is not so easy. The houses look all the same, only different in height. I was down in Quebec City last spring and I lived in hotel. When I go out, the owner gives me map and marks the hotel. I take a good look going in and out and I gradually walk down street, counting buildings, and try to keep my head. The signs, either French or English, mean nothing to me. I see a place to drink beer and I go in and hear Navy people talking English, but I didn't join. Reason—if they find out I'm Eskimo, they going to ask me all sorts of foolish things. I start out again and make a big square and come out right across from hotel. Oh boy, I'm tired, especially my feet, as if I'm carrying a hundred pounds all day. I feel hot too. I eat fresh fruit salads and banana splits, but they make you feel full and puffy and won't stay with you very long." He was afraid he had insulted us. "I don't say that's bad, but I'm hungry again right away."

"What were you doing in Quebec?" Max Budgell asked.

"I was interpreter for Eskimo who was in jail for attempted murder, for aiming a gun in a tent even though when he shot, he missed," Koneak answered. He shook his head. "He very scared Eskimo. He wouldn't eat in jail for a whole month. They asked me what he eats, and I told them, 'Leave meat for him that is frozen or raw, and see.' Frozen raw fish is especially delicious. He wouldn't touch the food, he felt the punishment, just to be there. When we come into court he sees two policemen with guns, and he shakes and thinks they are going to shoot him. 'We are in a very strange country,' I say to him. 'Try to be relaxed and follow orders.' So he says he will do that and he braved it. Finally he's freed from jail, but I hear he's back again this year. Same trouble. Same girl. He has been trying to shoot his girl friend because her parents won't let her marry him. Nobody understands why because they love each other badly. It often happens that the father says 'no,' and without parents' permission, no Eskimo girl would get married. I asked the parents of my wife, Johanna, before I said anything to her. If I said anything to her first, she'd just go inland, away from all the people which would make fun of her, and try to kill herself."

At our expressions of surprise, he wrinkled his brow, and began groping for words to make himself clear, using his hands to emphasize his points. "When an Eskimo man talks about marriage, the man's parents are always sure and the girl's parents always say no at first," he said. "A lot of foolishness and conversation can go on for two-three years before they decide. This year, my brother wants to marry a Chimo girl. She's single and had a baby by a white man who leave her like they usually do. My brother knows her a year but they are never walking together or talking alone. My father is blind and can't walk, so I talked to her parents and they agreed. Then I talked to the girl, and she said 'no.' So we dropped the marriage. She wants to marry, half and half, but I said 'drop it,' because if my brother should drag her away, like in the old days, policeman might go after him. Not so long ago, though, a man from my town married a girl he had never seen before. She rebelled until she was played out, and then he put her on his *komatik* and away they go. Two weeks later he married her at the minister and she's very happy, but I hadn't heard of anything like that happening for a long time."

Koneak poured himself a cup of fresh tea, ladling out several heaping spoonfuls of sugar into it. "It's hard to get married according to the laws of the white people, because Eskimo girl always has to act as if she is unwilling," he continued, stirring his tea. "According to Eskimo custom, as soon as a girl is old enough to work, she's ready to marry, usually from sixteen up. When the parents are agreed on the marriage, even if the young man and girl are living together a while or she has been married before, the girl behaves as if she is shocked and upset, and she cries in front of the minister. Otherwise, people would be teasing her and saying, 'Ha! You must be glad to get married, you must have been waiting a long time.' When Johanna and I married, the minister saw Johanna crying, but he knew it was the custom, and didn't stop the marriage."

Before going to bed, we went out and looked at the Northern

Lights. Wonderful ribbons of light seemed to hang, suspended, right over us, like great rippling curtains. Suddenly I heard a frightful clatter and banging, and George Koneak ran out of the hall, his green eyes gleaming, holding up a shovel and banging on it with a hammer. "I can hear them! I can hear them!" he shouted, and turning to me said, "Do you see them moving?" Before I could answer, he rushed back into the hall. When we came inside he was sitting by the stove, finishing his tea, grinning. "In Eskimo we call the Northern Lights *Uksawnee*," he said. "The Eskimos have a superstition that if you whistle and bang on something and make noise, the *Uksawnee* will reach down toward the person making noise. Eskimo children believe that if the *Uksawnee* touch you, you die. So ever since we were kids, it's a favorite game to rush out, whistle and make noise, and rush back inside again where the *Uksawnee* can't touch you. The scientists say you can't hear the *Uksawnee*, but lots of us have heard them. Did you?"

Had I heard a swishing sound?

I wasn't sure.

II

WE WERE NOT able to reach either Chimo or Burwell by radio for two days. Snowden spent most of his time trying to make a radio contact, and at seven on the third morning we were all gathered around the set as he sang the familiar refrain, "George River, Fort Chimo. George River, Fort Chimo. Do you read me? Over." There was no sound at all, not even static. "It's atmospheric," Max Budgell said. "Sometimes the whole radio network is silent and that silence can last anywhere from eight to fourteen days, usually in spring. People think their sets are broken and change all the tubes. Then again, an Eskimo with a rickety set that has a couple of wires strung between two trees for an aerial may pick up the news on a different frequency, while one of these big expensive radios can't get a sound."

He had scarcely finished speaking when an Eskimo boy ran into the hall. "We hear Burwell! We hear Burwell!" he shouted. Snowden switched the radio on again, and this time there was a welcome noise: static. When a scratchy voice called in Eskimo, Snowden moved quickly aside and George Koneak took over. "It's Noah Annatuk, at Burwell!" he exclaimed. "Noah say, 'You have blue skies two days and you didn't come! Come now! Come now!'" Koneak answered, *"Ahailaa. Ahailaa,"* to signify that he had heard Noah, and told him we were waiting to come but had not been able to reach Chimo by radio. Shortly, we heard the welcome voice of Sam Dodds calling, "Chimo to George River!" and he announced that the plane would set out from Chimo at noon, and would signal its arrival by flying low over the community hall sometime after one o'clock. Al Falby, our pilot, would land on a nearby lake and wait for us there.

In this sudden renewal of radio contact, George Koneak was able to speak with his wife, Johanna, who was standing by with two of his children in Dodds' office in Chimo. After Koneak had said hello to the children, his wife told him that her brother had just returned from a month-long caribou hunt with many caribou. "So don't worry, we have lots to eat," she told her husband. "That makes me feel much better," Koneak said. Then he relayed the message of our impending arrival at Burwell to Noah, who responded with a torrent of Eskimo words that crackled over the wires as he expressed his pleasure at this news.

Willi Imudluk stopped in to say goodbye to us, shaking hands solemnly all around before he slipped away on his sled, heading up the river to his outpost. Most of the other Eskimos whose tents were pitched on nearby rivers had left the previous day. We packed, had an early lunch of soup and cheese, and at a little after one we sighted our plane as it flew low and circled over the community hall. The men set off immediately on foot for the lake, and I climbed on the sled driven by Elijah that was carrying our baggage. Max Budgell was remaining at the hall to complete the projects. When I bade him goodbye, I boasted that I could ride with ease now on an Eskimo *komatik*. I sat down sidewise, as the Eskimos do, rather than astride as I had done before, and when the sled started off I turned, holding the lashings around the baggage with one hand while I waved at Budgell with the other. The sled lurched and I tumbled into the snow, my purse, sunglasses and gloves flying off in different directions. Elijah stopped and brushed me off, helping me to gather up my belongings. Budgell was still laughing from his perch on the riverbank when I turned again to wave, this time riding astride and with a firm grip on the lines.

The sled followed the same route we had walked over, past the dead dog hanging from the tree, and came out in the clearing of Eskimo tents. The Eskimos were outside, shaking hands with the men of our party who had preceded me. I got off the sled and, after shaking hands all around, I too set out on foot, with Paul Godt. After we had walked uphill a mile or two I began to fall behind. The lake was further away than I had thought. It was an exquisite day, but the sun was so bright that I found walking very hot. A *komatik* passed by and the Eskimo driver stopped and signalled me to climb aboard. A quarter of an hour later we came over the rim of a hill and saw the lake below. The plane had landed and baggage was being loaded into it. The sled leaped forward and we coasted down the hill so fast that I was reminded of the breath-taking toboggan rides of my childhood. We bounced across the lake ice and stopped right at the plane. The last piece of baggage went into the aircraft as I stepped off the sled. My recent host at Chimo, Keith Crowe, had rejoined us for the trip to Burwell, bringing another passenger with him, Noah Annatuk's wife, Emily, a tiny, Eskimo lady with a wrinkled face, who was returning to Burwell from the hospital. Snowden introduced her and said she did the most beautiful handicraft work on Ungava Bay and was teaching her art to the other Eskimo women. When this remark was translated to her by Koneak, she raised her hand and shyly hid her face.

We shook hands with the Eskimos remaining at the George River, climbed aboard the plane, and the aircraft door was slammed shut behind us. Falby raced the plane motor, but we didn't move. The aircraft's skis were sticking in the soft layer of snow on the lake ice, but from the lack of concern of the other passengers, I gathered this was routine. The Eskimos outside, who had backed off from the plane, now ran forward to grip the wings and rock them back and forth until they had pried us loose. On the next attempt, we took off.

As we travelled east, the hills became larger, but in every

direction there was the same white, untracked landscape. I fancied that beneath us was total wilderness, so I was really startled when after fifteen minutes we dipped over a large river as if we were coming down. Snowden shouted that we were at the Korok River and would land to refuel. I could see small figures below with sleds and dogs, and now I could even make out the double lines that the sled runners made along the trails in the snow. When we landed on the river, I was further astonished to see that the figures were George and Stanley Annanack, and the Etoks, with their large families, numbering perhaps thirty in all, whom we had last seen just two days ago. They greeted us with handshakes and broad smiles, and Lucas Etok's old father, Adam, handed us a gift of frozen char.

We waited beside the plane while four Eskimos ran to a fuel cache halfway up the riverbank and rolled two bright red gasoline drums down to the plane. Falby climbed on top of the wing, where the gas tank was located, and pumped in gasoline, and the men rolled the empty drums back up the riverbank. "That fuel cache was put here last summer for this trip," Snowden said. "When the supply boat returns this year it will pick up the empty drums and put in new ones." Our plane was stuck in the snow again when we left, and even George Annanack and Adam Etok helped rock our aircraft. It soon came free and we were in the air.

We headed northeast along the edge of Ungava Bay toward the tip of Quebec, where it borders on Labrador. Separated from the mainland by a narrow strait is a small island called *Killinek,* Eskimo for "The Outermost Place." Killinek Island is fifty-six square miles of solid rock, and on this spot, like a gatepost between the Atlantic Ocean and Hudson Strait, is the Eskimo settlement of Port Burwell. As we followed the shoreline, the Bay of Ungava—an Eskimo word meaning "Far Away" —was on our left, a mighty, motionless white sea. On our right were the fierce, black and ancient Torngat Mountains, reaching a height of five thousand feet, with deep angular lines clearly visible on the steep sides made by centuries of ice that had pounded against the cliff walls.

"Tell me about Port Burwell," I said.

Snowden, who had been looking out the window, turned around and smiled. "It's a fascinating place," he said. "Maybe because it's so remote and so beautiful. Six families, just thirty-six persons, are living practically out in the Atlantic Ocean, more than a hundred miles from any one else, on a big piece of rock that once must have been part of the northeast tip of the mainland. The settlement was named after a colonial surveyor, Mahlon Burwell, and dates back to 1884, when a meteorological station was established on the island. That was closed after two years and a Newfoundland trading post occupied the site. Around 1900, Moravian missionaries arrived, followed by the Hudson's Bay Company and the mounted police, who collected customs from vessels entering to go to Hudson Bay. For a while, there was a government air base there, but gradually all these organizations left, and by 1940 only Eskimos remained. For many years there had been about two hundred and fifty Eskimos at the settlement, but in the late 1930's and early 1940's the fox trapping was poor and they gradually went off down the Labrador coast or to the George River. The population had dwindled to twenty-four when we first went to Burwell two winters ago, and we found this stubborn group sitting on their rock without food—there was no open water that winter to hunt seals—and burning the front porches of the few remaining old frame structures for fuel. The Eskimos were about as badly off as they could be; half-starved, everyone on relief, and the average annual income was one hundred and seventy-three dollars. To buy a sack of flour at Willi Imudluk's outpost, they had to go one hundred and twenty miles by dog sled, a trip that took four or five days. They had so little money that they used up all the food they were able to buy on the trip home. Today, their average annual income is over one thousand dollars, which is prosperous by any northern standards. Theirs was the second coöperative in the Arctic, after George River, and the first to have a retail store, which has had quite an effect on their lives. Since it is so much easier to shop, they have more time to trap and hunt, which means more income.

Besides, prices at their own store are lower than those of the Hudson's Bay Company outpost on the George River, and the profits are theirs."

Paul Godt had been listening. "The store is run by an Eskimo named Henry Annatuk who doesn't know a word of English," he said. "Henry keeps perfect books in syllabics."

"What made the Burwell Eskimos prosperous in just two years?" I inquired.

"Seals, furs, handicrafts, and the attitude of the people," Snowden replied. "We always knew that potentially Burwell was one of the richest areas in the North and could again support a much larger population, but the Eskimos didn't understand how to exploit the available resources, and markets had to be found for their goods in the South. Killinek Island is close to the migration route for harp seals, and thousands of seals swim literally past the doorstep of Port Burwell twice a year, heading north in spring and south in fall. Fishery experts have estimated that five thousand seals could be taken out annually without damaging the herd.

"The first thing we did when we came in was to establish radio communications, so that if the fish freezer we proposed to construct broke down, or other disasters occurred, help could be summoned," Snowden went on. "After the coöperative was organized, with eleven members, a char fishery like the one at George River was established. The coöperative has done a thriving business in sealskins. The Burwell women have been regarded for years in the Arctic as experts in handling sealskins for the southern market, trading through the Hudson's Bay Company at the George River and at Chimo. But it was the wholehearted attitude of the people that really counted. When we came, they told us they would rather die than leave. Now they are worried about inbreeding and want more people to settle at Burwell. We are encouraging other Eskimos to move there and this winter two families, those of Thomas Thomas and Senach Anglatweena, came from the Whale River, which is between the George River and Chimo. The Snowball family from the George River has promised to try it next summer."

Keith Crowe tapped my shoulder and pointed out the window. I had grown accustomed to the magnificent sweep of Arctic views, but this was different. It had a savage simplicity: black mountains, flat white sea, and no trees to soften the bare rock and snow-topped land; overhead, cold blue sky with fleecy clouds. Truly, this was 'The Outermost Place'!

Keith Crowe tapped my shoulder again, impatiently this time, and pointed down. In the middle of this nowhere, on a sloping curve of a small island separated from the mainland by a frozen strip that seemed so narrow it hardly deserved to be called a channel, was a cluster of a dozen houses huddled together. The pilot, the only person other than myself who had never been to Port Burwell, flew back and forth twice to get a better look, and flew right into the chasm. The rock walls of the cliff on the mainland and the cliff on the island were so close on either side of the plane windows that they shut out the light, and I gasped. We landed, the plane skis sliding across the ice, and came to a stop.

III

THE ENTIRE Burwell community had come to meet us. Noah
Annatuk was the first to shake our hands. His face was seamed
with tiny lines, he had shrewd, twinkling eyes, a scraggly
mustache that drooped at the corners, and due to the absence
of teeth in the middle, a single tooth at either side of his mouth
looked like a fang and would have given him a sinister appearance, had he not smiled continuously. On the trip, listening to the men talk about him, I had learned that he had
many accomplishments. In addition to being radio operator at
Burwell, he was considered the best small-boat pilot in that area
of dangerous shoals and shifting currents, and, despite his un-
prepossessing appearance, he was also known as something of
a ladies' man. All the Eskimos looked healthy, and several of
the women and children were quite beautiful, rosy-cheeked,
with sparkling eyes. Like everyone else, the dogs had a steady
diet of seal meat, and so were far stronger and fatter than those
at the George River.

While the Eskimos loaded our baggage on the sleds, the pilot
fastened the plane to the ice, in the absence of any shelter for
it. Otherwise, it would have blown away. He tied a cover over
the aircraft's nose, and made holes in the ice through which he
somehow passed heavy ropes that he secured to the ends of
the wings. Our baggage went ahead on the first four sleds with

most of the Burwell population, and we piled on the last *komatik*. "The first winter we came, we had to walk in," Snowden observed. "The Eskimos had lost almost all their dogs."

Fifteen minutes later we arrived at a small rectangular white frame house about thirty by eighteen feet. It was the Northern Affairs Department's headquarters, a hut where Noah and his family had been living so that he could tend the radio. With our arrival, Noah had moved back temporarily into his own house directly behind, a low weathered clapboard shack from the old days that had survived the shortage of firewood, although it had lost its porch. The department hut consisted of one room, painted green and white, furnished with a beach chair, table, Coleman cooking stove, an oil heater, a wooden sleeping platform, and the large gray department radio. The room was spotlessly clean. A step from the hut was the gleaming square box of the steel fish freezer. The rest of Burwell's inhabitants lived a half mile away along the inside of the channel, in the sheltered inlet we had seen from the air.

Snowden went over to the radio and switched it on. It was dead. He noticed a small paper box on the table beside it, and while the smiling Eskimos crowded around, he opened the box. "Seal liver!" he exclaimed. "We'll have a feast!" It was after six and getting dark, and the Eskimos left to prepare their own meals, taking George Koneak with them. Koneak said he was "starving" for his favorite dish, boiled seal meat, and when he returned from dinner, he reported having consumed "four ribs, six spareribs and the shoulder blade of a seal. About two pounds of meat, I guess."

Snowden fried the seal liver, and the Arctic char we had been given at the Korok River. It was my first taste of seal liver, which was more tender and delicious than the calf's liver it resembled, and the char was even better than it had been in the Montreal hotel. Waiting for the Eskimos to return, we found dried fruits among the department's stores, and made a large fruit stew to serve as refreshment in the evening.

By eight-fifteen, the room was packed with Eskimo men, women and children. Despite their healthy appearance, they had the usual Eskimo respiratory troubles, and their coughing and sneezing was a continuous background noise during the evening. George Koneak, who frequently complained of headaches anyway, and was always "borrowing" my aspirin, asked for four and put them all in his mouth at once before he began translating.

When the meeting started, Henry Annatuk, the storekeeper, was sitting in the central spot, at the end of the sleeping platform. He was a gentle, scholarly little man with a thin mustache and timid expression. Noah leaned against the window behind him, owlish and innocent, blinking and smiling. Snowden, who sat next to the radio and intermittently switched it on, hoping for a sound, opened the meeting. "We promised Henry last year we would get people to come to Burwell to settle, and Thomas Thomas and Senach Anglatweena came from Whale River," he said. "This year we will get more good hunters, who know how to live off the land."

"We could have a hundred people here and we would get more of everything and live better," Henry said. "We need more men. I am useless."

"Tell him he got more seals than anyone," Snowden said to Koneak. Then Snowden asked Thomas Thomas, a sturdy, calm looking gray-haired Eskimo, how he liked his first winter at Burwell. "We didn't get hungry and we didn't have to go far away to the store," Thomas Thomas replied. "We would be foolish to go elsewhere."

Snowden inquired how the other Whale River man, Senach Anglatweena, liked Burwell, and a man's voice from far back in the crowd replied. Koneak said, "Senach likes it here too."

The door opened and Noah's wife, Emily, slipped into the room. She handed Snowden a pair of half-finished sealskin boots decorated with fur inlays of contrasting shades in a lovely geometric design, and indicated that she was making them for him. He ran his hand over the flawless work with awe. "These are very very beautiful," he said, and when Koneak translated this, Emily's face was radiant. She smiled, revealing that she was toothless. She left the room as quietly as she had come, and Snowden turned to Crowe and said in a low voice, "Two years ago her teeth were taken out! How could she come back from hospital now without new teeth? Anyone can see how much she needs to eat meat!" Crowe seemed worried too. "As soon as I get back to Chimo, I'll inquire about getting her false teeth," he promised.

After a discussion of fishing operations and the need for more boats and better housing, Snowden said to Koneak, "Ask just the people who were here when we first came, in 1959, if life is easier now than it was."

Several men spoke up. Koneak listened and said, "They find life much easier. The store makes it possible for the men to go hunting and they don't have to leave their families without enough food while they are gone."

The possibility of having a tannery at Burwell was broached. The current practice was to send sealskins used by the women for handicrafts Outside to be tanned, and bring them back in again to make into the stuffed animals and rugs for which the Burwell women are renowned. "Tanning used to be done right here and there is no reason not to do it again," Snowden observed. "Other people in this area could send their skins to be tanned here too."

He went on to tell them about his plans to have the German chef, Erich Hofmann, travel in the North experimenting with Arctic foods. "With all the seals here, an awful lot of seal meat could be preserved and sold throughout the area," he said. Considerable interest was indicated, and Henry remarked, "We think we could do something about the seal meat when the man comes to teach us."

All the Burwell adults had packets of white cigarette papers and tobacco, and were rolling their cigarettes and chain smoking. The air in the small room was so thick with smoke that we were all coughing now, and my eyes were burning and teary. Crowe opened the door to let in some fresh air, and we could hear the dogs howling. Snowden called an intermission while the Eskimos ate the fruit stew, returning for second helpings until it was gone, and we passed around the last of the oranges and chocolate brought from Montreal. The meeting resumed with Paul Godt discussing coöperative finances. After he had made sure the Eskimos knew what a bank was, he said, "When we get all the money left over from this year's fishing and handicrafts in the bank, we should have about six thousand dollars, but when everything is squared away, there will not be extra money this year. When you have worked so hard, you may wonder how you can own something and not have made extra money, but there are always added expenses when things are beginning, and you had to get the store started. You should make a first payment to the government on its loan with this six thousand dollars, but you can't do that. With more people coming next summer, you will need that money to buy more goods for the store."

Several men called to George Koneak, who said, "They want to pay the government back as soon as possible."

"I'm afraid I'll have to ask the government to wait for its first payment for another year," Godt replied. "Goods needed for the store will take the money."

At the end of the evening, Henry Annatuk lingered behind to tell us that he had recently killed a polar bear near the coöperative store. "I shot *my* polar bear at Cape Hope's Advance when he was coming into the dog food cache all night," George Koneak volunteered, after Henry had left. "The bear lifts the barrel of seal meat and shakes it until the lid falls off, eats, and then goes back to sleep on the ice. When he's hungry he comes back. I shot him, but he kept coming back, so the last time I shot him dead."

After breakfast the next morning, Al Falby stayed by the heater in the hut reading a western adventure story he had brought with him, and the rest of us walked along on the ice in the channel until we came around to the Eskimo houses. Having lost so much time waiting at the George River, we were in a hurry now. We had to be back in Fort Chimo by nightfall, for the plane to Montreal left there at five the next morning.

We arrived at the slope where the houses were located. They

were oddly shaped, an experiment in rigid frame low-cost housing engineered by the government, with sides on an inward slant, small windows high in the walls and sloping roofs with overhanging eaves. Our first stop was at a neat little white frame building of conventional design with a sign posted above the door reading, in English, "CO-OP STORE." I glanced in as Paul Godt and Keith Crowe entered. They were making an inventory of the stock before ordering new merchandise. The interior was just two rooms, one with shelves and a counter, the other a storeroom.

Snowden had assigned himself the job of pricing the handiwork that the women had made during the winter. It was to go on our plane for shipment to retail outlets in the South. He sent word to the Eskimo women that they should bring their finished handicrafts to him at the home of Thomas Thomas, and meanwhile he suggested that George Koneak and I go from house to house and obtain a list from each family of the special items they would want the coöperative store to order for delivery to them in the summer shipment. Koneak and I set off, armed with the huge catalogue of Eaton's Department Store, the Sears, Roebuck of Canada, from which the Eskimos would make their selections.

Snowden stopped at the first house with us, knocking on the door. We waited in a small vestibule, which Koneak said was used to keep frozen meat away from the dogs and also to store seal fat, which was used here for fuel in the stoves instead of wood. A stocky, slant-eyed young woman with a large mouth, long black hair fastened in a knot at the back, and wearing a red gingham dress opened the door. Behind her, half hidden by the long skirt of her dress, was a little boy with round pink cheeks. Her face broke into a great smile when she saw us, and Snowden said, "I want you to meet Penina. She is one of the nicest people on earth, and always just as cheerful as she is now. When I see her, I begin to understand why these people have survived."

I subsequently discovered that all the houses were almost exactly like Penina's. There was first a vestibule, reeking from the odor of the seal fat stored there, and inside a single room with a gasoline drum stove, a shelf with a radio and an Anglican prayer book in syllabics, a church calendar pinned to the wall, a cupboard or two, a trunk under the bed or doubling as a seat, and across the whole rear and sometimes another wall, sleeping platforms, usually with mattresses as well as quilts. Some houses contained hand operated Singer sewing machines and victrolas, and there was always a teapot, a frying pan of bannock and a large pot of stewing seal meat or ptarmigan on the stove. The houses were even more overheated than the Eskimo tents at the George River.

Five people were living in the spotless, green and white room of Penina's house. She motioned us to sit down on one of the two sleeping platforms that filled the rear section of the room, and told Snowden politely, with Koneak interpreting, that although she liked her new house, it would have been better had the walls been straight instead of slanted. In fact, she said, it was so damp at the edges that she would rather sleep in a tent. Koneak added, "She says she would rather have two rooms, one to receive visitors, and that she would like to put her children in school, when she sees what it has done for the white people."

After looking carefully through Eaton's catalogue and referring to notes she had made beforehand in syllabics, Penina gave me her list: one cotton dress, size twelve; one large teakettle; two pairs of children's rubber boots; two flowered head scarves; and one child's zippered snowsuit. Her husband Matthew arrived and added an eighteen-ninety-five .22 single shot rifle and a jack plane to the order.

The next house was that of Thomas Thomas. The women had not arrived yet with their handicraft and the family were sitting on the floor plucking ptarmigan. Thomas Thomas got up to welcome us and when we sat down on the beds to talk said, "This is the first house I've ever lived in. Before this, I always lived in a tent. It is cold outside, but in the house we don't feel it, and for the first time in my life, the water is not frozen overnight. My wife likes having fresh food too.

One time a polar bear came right to the corner of this house in the dark of night, a very big bear. I got my rifle but I couldn't see him well, so I missed."

"What kind of food did you have at Whale River in winter?" Snowden asked.

"We didn't get much food and the dogs died of starvation," Thomas Thomas replied. "We didn't go to the outpost often to buy because it was such a problem to feed the dogs on the long trip. We lived on relief rations and this was hard to do. When you have relief rations, if all your food is gone you can't get more until the month is over. Now when we haven't enough food, we have money to go to the store and get it. We are staying here. I don't think if I looked all over the earth, there would be a better place to live."

The women began coming in with plastic bags filled with sealskin animals, chiefly birds and polar bears, and occasionally a sealskin rug, the design appliquéd from different shades of seal fur. Snowden was soon half hidden by the bags of handicraft. He examined each item, put a price on it, and slipped a notation of the amount owed the maker in each bag, so that Godt could send the women payment checks from Ottawa.

George Koneak and I were about to leave for the next house when Thomas Thomas reminded us that he had not given his order. The family looked at the catalogue, and chose a sixty-dollar radio, a ten-dollar watch, two pairs of scissors, combs, sweaters, and four pairs of rubber boots. While we were waiting, the door burst open and Noah Annatuk entered, followed by Emily and a pretty teen-age daughter. Since he lived away from the other houses, he feared we ·might forget him. He wanted an outboard motor, a green coat, a skirt and slip for Emily, a red dress for his daughter, a mattress, and for himself, an upright piano. He asked me to find it for him in the catalogue. There was only one piano listed, for five hundred and ninety-five dollars.

Snowden glanced up and said to Koneak, "We can't order anything for the coöperative to buy that we don't think the

Eskimos can pay for. Noah knows that. Perhaps he could find something cheaper."

When Koneak translated this, Noah winked at me and we studied the musical instrument section of the catalogue. Noah paused over a saxophone and finally settled for a twenty-eight dollar accordion with piano keys. As he took his hand from the page, an ash dropped from Noah's cigarette on the floor. Frowning, he looked at his daughter and pointed regally at the ash. She quickly knelt and picked it up, carefully wiping the floor all around it.

Noah said that the men at Burwell liked to make model kayaks. Would anybody want them? Snowden looked up again, this time with delight. "Tell him the coöperative store will buy all the kayaks they want to make, because we can sell them down south."

Noah remarked that he had been talking to his relatives on the Labrador coast about coming to Burwell in the summer, and they were anxious to return. This gave Snowden an idea. "Some nights you could get on the radio after your regular schedule and tell how well things are going here," he said. "You might tell how you need more people in the fishery. You could just talk for a minute every night, not more, and mention a different thing each time, so that if the Eskimos do hear, they would know all you are doing at Burwell."

Noah was enthusiastic. "They can hear on their little radios," he said. "I will do that."

Koneak and I visited ten houses altogether. In addition to guns, clothing and household equipment, some Eskimos wanted toys for their children and victrola records, cowboy songs and square dances. Several wanted binoculars, clocks and barometers. George Koneak and I finished up before the others, so he stayed behind to help them, and I set off alone for the Northern Affairs hut to prepare lunch. I walked carefully down the slippery hill, and at the bottom I stepped on the frozen strait between the island and the mainland which would bring me to our quarters. It was strangely like walking on water, because the ice had a bluish tint and I could actually see open water at the floe edges. In fact, there appeared to be several inches of open water between the ice and the rocky shore, so I took off my glove and leaned down, putting my finger over the edge of the ice. It felt definitely wet. Although the ice beneath my feet seemed solid enough, I had an eerie feeling, each time I heard a deep hollow cracking sound below me.

I started walking again and came around a bend to where our plane was fastened to the ice. It looked small and very frail. I stopped. There was nothing beyond but snow, rocks, ice and sky. Nothing moved, anywhere. I had never experienced such a feeling of complete solitude in my life. I paused for perhaps a minute, and when I started walking again, I saw Falby running down the hill from the hut. He was calling to me and brandishing a heavy iron rod in his hand. "Are you all right?" he shouted. "Are you sure you're all right?"

"I'm just fine," I called back.

"I looked out the window and saw you stop," he said when he had joined me and we were walking back to the hut together. "The dogs have been fighting above me on the rocks all morning. Their snarling is a savage sound if you aren't used to it. When you stopped, I thought the dogs had frightened you and might even attack you. A friend of mine at Frobisher Bay had a child who was chewed to pieces by dogs."

I hadn't noticed the dogs, but now I saw and heard them, fighting over the frozen carcass of a seal not fifty feet above us. "They must have broken into one of the meat caches," Falby said, as we went into the hut. He had already eaten lunch, and soon departed to start warming up the plane motor. I opened the emergency food ration we had brought along, heated several cans of beef stew for lunch and melted ice for instant coffee. The others arrived and while we were eating, Snowden switched on the radio once again, shouting "*Magassie! Magassie! Magassie!*" the Eskimo version of Max Budgell's name, into the speaker. To everyone's astonishment, we heard Budgell reply. He had ordered a pair of sealskin boots from Burwell and he needed them, because the caribou boots he was wearing were not waterproof. Would we drop the new boots to him at the community hall at George River from our plane on our way to Chimo? Snowden said we would, and asked Budgell to relay a message to Chimo that we would arrive there about seven-thirty that evening. Any Eskimos interested in forming a salmon fishing coöperative should come to the Chimo schoolhouse at eight o'clock.

An Eskimo boy was dispatched to find Budgell's boots and we rode on the sleds down to the plane. We had added one hundred and sixty-six sealskins to our aircraft's load, and transparent plastic bags filled with stuffed bears and birds were piled around us when we sat down in the plane. When Falby tried to take off, the motor roared but the plane didn't budge, and Snowden remarked cheerfully, "The last time I was here, we had to go back and unload." As the Eskimo men began rocking the wings, a *komatik* streaked down the hill and the Eskimo boy ran up to the plane, waving Budgell's new sealskin boots. George Koneak who was sitting next to the pilot, opened his window in the nose, reached out an arm, and hauled in the boots. Falby raced the motor, and this time our aircraft rose from the ground. The last face I saw at Burwell was that of the Eskimo woman, Penina, slightly bent forward because her little boy was perched in the hood of her parka, and she was smiling her marvelous smile.

We had a strong tail wind and in an hour we were at the George River. We flew low over the community hall, and as Falby banked the plane, George Koneak opened his window and threw out the sealskin boots, one at a time. We could see Max Budgell running to get them as they fell at the edge of the embankment. He waved his arms, we waved back, and our plane began to climb again. We landed at Fort Chimo at seven-thirty, and five minutes later we were sitting at Edna Crowe's dinner table, eating baked ham, croissants, and apple pie.

I felt as if I had just come back from the moon.

IV

I HAD a leisurely cup of coffee with Edna Crowe after dinner, and when I arrived at the Chimo schoolhouse, which was new and just around the corner, Paul Godt was already telling perhaps a hundred Eskimos through a cloud of smoke about George River and Port Burwell. The schoolroom was packed. Eskimos were sitting at the desks, and standing around the sides, in the aisles and at the back. Babies and small children slept in the parka hoods on their mothers' backs, and older children leaned against their parents. George Koneak was sitting on a front desk facing the crowd, his youngest baby on his knee. He was feeding it from a bottle and jiggling it when it cried, while he interpreted. His wife, Johanna, a handsome girl with long brown hair and classic features, stood beside him, holding another child. Koneak looked weary, and no wonder. He hadn't stopped talking for seven days, except to sleep.

Paul Godt described the activities at the George River and Port Burwell, and said that recent studies indicated there were enough salmon in the waters around Fort Chimo to start a fishing coöperative there. He reminded the audience that there had once been a commercial salmon fishery in the area, but pointed out that the proposed operation would belong to the Eskimos instead of outsiders and that the money it made would be theirs. Two older men who remembered working in the old fishery spoke enthusiastically in favor of the coöperative, but others were more cautious. From the nodding of heads when he spoke, a man who said, "the people can never make up their minds until they talk about it some more," appeared to speak for the majority. I thought that this must have been the way it was with the George River and Port Burwell Eskimos when the coöperative idea was first suggested to them.

When Godt left shortly to catch the plane for Frobisher Bay, on Baffin Island, two hundred miles further north across Hudson Strait, Snowden took his place as speaker. "The people in this room know that at one time Port Burwell was a very big place and the people were well off," he said. The Eskimos indicated their interest by making the low *"Aa-ah"* sound I had heard so often at the George River. "A lot of bad things seemed to happen there all at once, and most of the people left, going down the Labrador coast and to other places," he continued. "Times are better now at Burwell and we think can be still better. Some of the people here know Thomas Thomas and Senach Anglatweena. If they hadn't liked living at Burwell, we would never talk to anyone else about going there, but today Thomas Thomas said to me, 'If I looked all over the earth, I don't think there would be a better place to live.'"

There was a murmur through the room. "With the right equipment, nets and people, you could take as many as five thousand seals in a single migration, twice as much as you could eat," Snowden went on. "But there's no good having all those seals, and all the char that's there too, and only eight or ten men. They can't do all the work. Port Burwell needs more people."

Keith Crowe said the government would pay half the expense for any Eskimo family that wanted to go to Burwell and try it for the summer. Several Eskimos said they wanted to think about it, and see what the others were doing. One old man said he wanted to wait until the salmon fishery started at Chimo, but that he had three sons and he might send one of them to Burwell now.

"Go home and think it over," Snowden said. "Last year logs were sent to Port Burwell to be burned for fuel this winter, but the people caught so many seals that they didn't need the logs. All those logs sat under the snow and the people say they may be sitting there for a long long time."

One of the Eskimos shouted that there must be a very bad smell of oil in the houses at Burwell, because seal oil got all over the sides of the stoves, while when trees were burned, they didn't smell. The other Eskimos thought this very funny, and the meeting broke up in laughter.

At dawn I said goodbye to George Koneak and boarded the big DC-4 plane that would take us south to Montreal. At the front of the passenger cabin was a stretcher and I recognized the blanketed figure on it as Lavina, the sad and lovely woman who had been so sick when we were at the George River. Sitting behind her was a tall man with glasses— Joe Ross, the nurse from Chimo, who was accompanying his patient to the large hospital at Roberval, an hour's flight from Montreal.

I walked up to the stretcher. Lavina was so quiet that I thought she was unconscious, but as I turned away she opened her eyes and smiled at me. She reached up her hand and I held it for a moment, wishing I could say something; I was speechless without George Koneak.

I took the same seat I had had going north on the plane, and Snowden sat down beside me. For the first time he looked tired, but I could see he was still keyed up and wanted to talk. He took a fresh pack of cigarettes from his pocket. "My last pack," he said. "I've been saving it for this flight." He lit a cigarette, stretched out, and said, "I've often heard that religion, taxes and politics are guaranteed to provoke an argument, but in Canada we have a fourth ingredient, our North. Every Canadian has his own solution for the problems of the North. It's marginal and highly inefficient, with its small, widely scattered population. In an undemocratic society, right now, because of the heavy expenditures required for health, education, administration, and so on, the government wouldn't give the people freedom of choice, but would probably move them south. In our society, however, which is a democratic one, once the decision has been made not to force the people out of the North, the government consciously sets itself to be inefficient. It seems to me that a nation which puts such a tremendous investment into such a small group of people is a decent place to live."

He sat up as the stewardess brought breakfast. The dawn had been gray, but now the sun was throwing a rosy light over the ham, eggs and coffee on our trays. "When you deal in concepts new to the Eskimos—and they were new to us, too—you have to keep repeating them," he continued. "You have to try and anticipate what the Eskimos will wonder about and question after we are gone, keeping to ideas, so they can work out details for themselves. I don't think we will know for two or three years how much has been accomplished at Burwell or the George River," he said, digging his fork into the eggs. "We didn't accomplish anything, really. The Eskimos did. They spoke a lot more on this visit than they ever had before, and we listened a lot more. They trust us now. That's new. We accepted their ability to run their own affairs. That's new. We had hoped they could do it, but we had no way of knowing until they proved it. It's what I call a catch-your-breath experience. What the Eskimos we were with have now is that most wonderful thing of all, the assurance that they can continue to live where home is for them and that they can do this through their own efforts.

"Say, I've got something you might want to see," he said, taking a crumpled piece of paper out of his pocket. "It's a note from old George Annanack." He handed me the small white sheet, slumped down in his chair, and promptly dozed off. It was a crudely pencilled note in Eskimo syllabics, and a translation had been scribbled at the bottom. It read:

"Even though we live a long way from each other, it's as if we live together all the time. Goodbye to you all."

PART THREE

Conclave at Frobisher

I

SMALL ESKIMO SETTLEMENTS are scattered across the frozen top of North America, separated from one another by hundreds, often thousands, of miles of the hauntingly bleak Arctic. About two thousand of Canada's Eskimo citizens live as far south as the fifty-fifth parallel, in the northern third of Quebec, where Ungava Bay is, but most inhabit the huge area known as the Northwest Territories, which begins above the sixtieth parallel and stretches for over a million square miles between Baffin Island, in the east, and the great Mackenzie River, in the west, beyond which are the Yukon and Alaska. Those who live on the islands of the vast Arctic archipelago see polar bears, whales, and seals, but no trees; in winter their view is glistening ice and snow and in summer it is soft gray tundra and black rock. Eskimo communities bear names ranging from stirring Anglo-Saxon ones like Resolute to native tongue twisters like Povungnituk. The settlements vary in size from Port Burwell's thirty-six people or the northern outpost of Grise Fiord, on Ellesmere Island, situated between seventy-five and eighty degrees north latitude, which has around a hundred, living in total darkness from November until the end of January, to the government administrative center at Frobisher Bay, on Baffin Island, which has more than sixteen hundred inhabitants.

In the two years following my first trip to the Canadian North, the Industrial Division of the Department of Northern Affairs began carefully to extend the coöperative idea beyond Ungava Bay, to other Eskimo communities that were distressed but had economic potential. By 1963, there were eighteen Eskimo coöperatives in sixteen northern settlements, all the way across the Arctic: at Aklavik and Inuvik, in the far west, near the Mackenzie River; at Coppermine, on Coronation Gulf, and at Cambridge Bay and Holman, on Victoria Island, in the central Arctic; at Povungnituk, Great Whale River, and Whale Cove, on the coast of Hudson Bay; at Resolute and Grise Fiord, in the Arctic archipelago; at Cape Dorset and Frobisher Bay, on Baffin Island; at Igloolik, on a tiny island nearby; and of course in eastern Ungava, at George River, Port Burwell, and Fort Chimo, where the Eskimos had not only established their fishery, but were also engaged in handicrafts, stone carving, logging, and were rather tentatively operating a coffee shop.

Early in February, 1963, Snowden wrote me that the First Conference of the Arctic Coöperatives was about to be held at Frobisher Bay, and he invited me to attend. "It may well mark a turning point in the economic affairs of Canadian Eskimos," he wrote. "It is the first time that the Eskimo leaders of Eskimo coöperatives have been able to get together to find out what is being done in other parts of the Arctic. It is highly unlikely that any Eskimo has ever been at a meeting involving so many Eskimo people from so many places in the Arctic. Many of the delegates may have had even less experience at formal meetings than the George River people had had when you were there. This is to be their meeting. Our role will be purely advisory and minor. I have no idea what is likely to be said at this conference."

On a Monday afternoon, in the middle of March, I joined Snowden and his party in the terminal building of the Montreal airport for the twelve-hundred-mile flight north to Frobisher Bay. With him were Paul Godt, looking, as usual, both kindly and worried; Jon Evans, a sandy-haired man of about thirty, whose job still was to survey areas where coöperatives might be set up and determine whether there were enough resources to make the ventures economically sound; Snowden's secretary, a vivacious blond young lady named Terry Chaput, who was making her first trip to the Arctic; Dr. Alexander Laidlaw, a quiet, alert man of about fifty, who was national secretary of the Coöperative Union of Canada, the coördinating agency for coöperatives in English-speaking Canada, and who was coming along as an observer; and a delegate to the conference from the coöperative at Whale Cove, on Hudson Bay—a handsome young Eskimo named Celestino Magpa, who had a crew cut and was nattily dressed in a tweed sports jacket, gray flannels, white shirt, and black tie. The other men, I was surprised to see, had on business suits, rather than the heavy pants and sweaters that are the customary northern attire. Everyone was carrying a parka, that traditional outer Arctic garment, but I knew that we could expect cold weather at Frobisher, and I asked Godt why he, Snowden, and the others weren't dressed in a style more suitable for the Arctic. "Well, in fact, Frobisher is no frontier outpost," he said. "You'll find hot and cold running water, oil heat, automobiles—even a cocktail bar."

As our plane, a DC-4, took off, I glanced at a timetable provided by its operators, Nordair Airlines, which showed that we were to stop at Fort Chimo and were due to arrive in Frobisher a little before midnight. Snowden sat beside me, and I asked him something that had been worrying me for two years. Had Emily Annatuk, at Port Burwell, ever received a new set of false teeth? "Oh, my yes," Snowden replied, smiling. "That was a really happy event, when she got her new teeth, a magnificent set, and she is in every respect her old self again." "And Lavina?" I asked, remembering how sick she had looked on the plane going home last time. "She's fine now," Snowden said, "and her husband is back from hospital too." I remarked to him that Nordair seemed to have greatly increased its scheduled flights since my previous trip. "I can't get over the speed with which things are happening in the North," he said. "We'll be having superhighways next. And when those come, I leave. But one thing we do still lack, and need badly—lateral air transportation. All our scheduled air routes in the Northwest Territories run north and south; the only east-west transportation is by expensive chartered plane. At Port Burwell, the coöperative store has to carry a year's inventory of commodities, shipped in by boat in summer, and the items that the Eskimos offer for sale—white fox, sealskins, handicrafts—cannot be moved except at great expense." He pointed to Magpa, who was sitting up ahead, and went on, "Celestino presents a perfect example of what I mean. Whale Cove, where he lives, is only eight hundred miles from Frobisher across Hudson Bay and Hudson Strait, but he must make a thirty-six-hundred-mile trip to get there. He had to go eleven hundred miles south to Winnipeg, then thirteen hundred miles east to Montreal, and now he's travelling twelve hundred miles back into the Arctic with us. Transporting the Eskimo delegates presents a real problem in logistics. If the weather is bad, the crowd from the central and western parts of the Arctic may not arrive at all."

Snowden sat back for a few minutes smoking a cigarette. Then he said, "If all goes well, we're bringing in quite a varied group. A small plane is coming from Grise Fiord, on Ellesmere Island, with an Eskimo delegate and a Royal Canadian Mounted Policeman, who was for some time the only white man there, and who has been tremendously helpful to the coöperative. He keeps the books, among other things. Another Mounted Policeman will be with the Eskimo delegate from Resolute. Two Roman Catholic priests who helped start the coöperatives in their mission areas—at Holman and at Igloolik—will accompany Eskimo delegates from those places. And you must remember George Koneak, the Eskimo interpreter at the George River. We're picking him up, along with three delegates from Ungava and two from Povungnituk and Great Whale River, when the plane puts down at Fort Chimo, which is only two and a half hours' flight from Frobisher. Our Industrial Division men in that area, Wally Hill and Don Pruden, will be with them.

Pruden, who's at the George River, is about the strongest man I've ever met—heavyset, and half as wide as this airplane. Some dogs attacked his little boy this winter, and I hear that Pruden picked up one of the dogs by its hind legs and threw it so hard that it went over and over in the air.

"Do you know why I'm having this conference?" Snowden asked. "I'm trying to find out whether there is an articulate body of opinion yet among the Eskimos in the North. Their coöperative meetings are teaching them not only how to speak but how to assume responsibility and make group decisions among themselves, and I want to know if they are now capable of expressing what is happening to them as a group. If they aren't, we're doing something wrong, but if they're really enthusiastic, we've got on the right track and we should continue. I've been at conferences in Ottawa where two or three Eskimos, frightened to death, sat in an impressive room in one of the Parliament Buildings with white people from the North representing the churches, the Mounted Police, the Hudson's Bay Company, and the government. The Eskimos were anxious and depressed about the big changes among their people, but no matter how hard they tried, they were unable to talk about their own communities and their real problems. Instead, they would fall back on something like 'I have a hole in the roof of my house and it needs repairing,' or 'I need a new boat.' I'd just hate to think that this was the way the Eskimos were going to use their right to make their own decisions—especially the decision about where they fit into modern society.

"The most encouraging thing I've seen lately is that the Eskimos are showing signs of learning how to tell us when we're wrong, and I hope we get some really loaded questions about the white man's role in the North," he continued. "I don't believe that the government is infallible, and the coöps make it possible for the Eskimos to give us hell. In this way, we are insuring that we won't have a big minority in the North that is resentful, sullen, and unheard." He turned around and called to his secretary, a few seats behind us, that he wanted to dictate a memo to her, and as he rose, he said, "This meeting is as important to me as the one we had when the people at the George River formed that first coöperative. This is a kind of act of faith with me, to show that people of different color and culture can get together. They must."

At a little after eight in the evening, we landed at Fort Chimo. I walked down the metal steps from the plane into the cool Arctic night. The sky was luminous and dark blue. The stars shone, the ground stretched far away under a white glaze, and I felt the Arctic sweep around me. I noticed that a large group of Eskimos standing on the field were staring at me—giving me an intense scrutiny of a sort I recalled from my previous trip—and I walked on over to the low, wooden airport building. Its large waiting room was jammed with people, Eskimo and white. Some of them were warming their hands at an iron stove, and others were drinking coffee that two white women served from an urn in a corner. As I blinked in the glare of the bare electric bulbs, a familiar figure stepped up to me, his hand outstretched, an enormous grin on his face. It was George Koneak. "So you come back north," he said quietly. "We glad to see you again." Behind him I saw another man whom I remembered vaguely from the George River. I had known him there only slightly. He was Josepie Annanack, a solid, broad-faced man with a black mustache, who, I learned, would be the delegate from the George River coöperative. Behind him was kindly-looking Henry Annatuk, who still was president of the Port Burwell coöperative. A moment later, I was introduced to Don Pruden, who, though he wasn't half as wide as an airplane, was broad enough, and had a formidable jaw.

When we reboarded our plane, Pruden sat down next to me. I told him I had heard about his son's ordeal, and asked how the boy was. "The lad's all right now, thank you," he said. He had a warm smile, and spoke in a soft, deep voice with a slight burr. "He's lost some of his hair from shock, and if I speak to him harshly, he sulks for a couple of days. And of course there'll be scars. I don't mind talking about it, if you'd like to hear." I said I would, and Pruden began to tell me the story. "This Sunday, the wife and I were getting up late, and the boy, who is five, and his sister, who is three, were playing outside, flying a little toy airplane in the wind. We heard the little girl scream the word 'Dogs!' and I ran out. I couldn't see the lad, but I saw the dogs—they were Josepie Annanack's—by the corner of the sawmill, a hundred yards away, tearing at something—something blue, it was, and I knew he had on a blue parka. Then I could see blood all over, and I yelled as I ran. The snow was soft and I sank in, but when I got to the dogs I grabbed one sidewise by the leg and threw it. It began to yelp, which made the other dogs stop to yelp, too. Then I got to the lad and pulled off his little rubber boot, to use it as a club. The dogs backed off, and I managed to get him into the house. I gave him to the wife, grabbed my shotgun, ran outside, and shot one of the dogs. Josepie came running, and he took my gun and shot all the others. You can never trust a team again, you know, once they've had the smell of human blood and flesh. I went back in the house, and the boy was on the floor, in shock and bleeding badly. I made a tourniquet, gave him aspirin and some other drugs, and tried to calm him." Pruden moved his hand nervously over his hair, which was short and bristly. "When the lad came out of shock, he realized that he was hurt bad, but he took it good. I sent someone right away to report it on the radio, hoping to get word to Chimo, but there was no answer, so I got some needles ready to sew the lad up if I couldn't get him out on a plane within twenty-four hours. I planned to have one of the Eskimos do the sewing while I directed him. I wouldn't trust myself to do it. Luckily, someone at a radio up the coast had heard my message, and transmitted it to Chimo that night, so at eleven-thirty the next morning a plane came to pick us up and take us to Chimo. That night, the lad and his mother were on this very same Nordair plane, and he was in hospital at Frobisher within thirty-six hours of the attack. My wife, who is the school-teacher at the George River, was gone five weeks, and we had to close down the schoolhouse." Pruden relaxed and lit a cigarette. "The children throw sticks at the dogs, but those animals are tough and they're not bothered at all. We'll have a compound built for all the community dogs by next spring."

"The dogs must have been very hungry," I said.

"Oh, no," he replied. "Dogs attack on a full stomach. When they are hungry, they are too tired to attack."

After that, we chatted in a desultory way, and Pruden told me he was born at Stony Point, on Lake Winnipeg. "My old grandfather, who was a fisherman and fur trapper, brought me up," he said. "I left home at fourteen and went to work in the mines, trapping on the side, at the same time. I tried business, but went broke, and next I went into the uranium mines, but I got silicosis, so I went back to school and then applied for a job with Northern Affairs. I'm thirty-one now, and I started with the department in 1959. I like the George River very much, and so does my wife. This is our first year there, and she began teaching in a tent as soon as we arrived. Now we have a schoolhouse, and everyone between the ages of six and sixteen has started school." He leaned over and peered out of the window. "Here's your first view of Frobisher," he said.

I glanced down. Frobisher from the air had a gala, Christmas appearance, with very white snow and brightly twinkling electric street lights. I looked at my watch. It was just midnight. We landed, and as I walked toward the Nordair building, my boots crunched noisily in the crisp snow. Once again, as I had been at Chimo, I was acutely conscious of the silent white world around me—above all, it was silent. I wondered if this was partly because, on Baffin Island, we were hundreds of miles above the timber line, and the land was so barren.

We claimed our luggage inside the building, and then, following the others, I went outside and climbed into a yellow bus. An affable-looking man with glasses who was standing in the front of the bus introduced himself. He was Alex Sprudzs, Co-öperative Officer for the Department of Northern Affairs, and he told me he was supervising arrangements for the conference. "I've kept my fingers crossed that the weather would be all right," he said. "It's eighteen below, but it's nice and clear. We're still waiting for the western crowd, though." As the bus filled up, he read off our billeting assignments. Five or six men —two or three of them Eskimos and the other whites—would share each billet, with a government official in charge of each. Paul Godt, who sat by me on the bus, said, "We have delegates from active older coöperatives staying with delegates from new ones. We hope the men will pick up as much information at night, while they sit around and talk, as they will at the meetings."

I had been assigned to quarters in one of a number of pre-fabricated rectangular structures called Butler Buildings. These are large steel shells, which are easy to ship and, since they can be used alone or strung together, are capable of being transformed into almost anything—living quarters, schools, garages, laundries, workshops. The one I was in had four apartments connected by a common hall, at the far end of which was a community laundry room with an electric washing machine. My apartment contained three good-sized bedrooms and a living room, all furnished with government-issue maple furniture, including overstuffed chairs and a couch; a storage room for rations; a modern bathroom; and a kitchen with an electric refrigerator and a modern-looking stove. All the windows in the building were frozen shut, and the temperature inside was at least eighty. This tropical heat was the greatest hazard I encountered during this particular trip to the Arctic. After two sleepless nights, I discovered the community thermostat in the outside corridor, and each evening from then on I tiptoed out with a flashlight after everyone else was in bed and pushed the setting back into the sixties, which brought the heat in my apartment down to a livable seventy. Each morning, on my way out, I flicked the control back to its previous position. That first night, though, in my desperate search for air, I picked up my sleeping bag and relocated myself on the couch in the living room, where I was astonished to see a small glow at eye level, which proved to be the light on a white Princess telephone. Whom could I call? The light beckoned all that sleepless night. My sense of isolation was so complete that it never occurred to me that I could pick up that phone and call my family in New York.

II

AT SEVEN-THIRTY the following morning, the yellow bus arrived to take us to the conference buildings. I was told that the settlement of Frobisher Bay consisted of three separate communities, and that we were staying in one known as Lower Base where most of the government employees lived, and that we would have our meetings and our meals in another, called Apex Hill, which was three miles away. The third community, of small frame houses and shacks, was the original Eskimo village of Ikaluit, just around a bend in the road from Lower Base. After fifteen minutes of bumpy riding, we were deposited at the Rehabilitation Center dining hall on Apex Hill. I had learned, as we drove over, that the Rehabilitation Center had been set up by the Department of Northern Affairs eight years earlier, principally in order to provide food and shelter for Eskimos in transit to and from hospitals, but that it had gradually assumed a much wider role in Eskimo life. Physically handicapped Eskimos or those with serious emotional problems often cannot readjust to their former, primitive way of living. The Center provided a sheltered existence for some seventy-five Eskimos, who occupied themselves with such enterprises as a bakery, a coffee shop, crafts production (mainly carving and sewing), and an Eskimo-run movie theatre. Graduates of the Center who wanted to stay put could settle down with their families and buy or build houses on Apex Hill, and as our bus had climbed the hill, I had observed a general atmosphere of activity, with the stovepipes of wooden Eskimo houses smoking briskly in the early-morning air.

The conference itself took place in the Apex Hill community hall, a five-minute walk from the dining hall. A long, low building, the community hall contained a lavatory and coatroom and a large meeting area with light-blue walls and with black curtains that could be pulled across the windows to keep out the brilliant Arctic sun. As people began filing into the hall, Snowden mounted a platform at one end and sat down, facing the rest of us, at the center of a wooden table, in front of two Canadian flags and a large map of the Arctic. He was dressed in a business suit, as he had been the day before, and all the Industrial Division men were similarly dressed. The Eskimos, two of whom joined Snowden at his table and the rest of whom were taking their places at two long tables at right angles to the dais, wore suits with white shirts and ties, or plaid jackets and sweaters, but unlike the men from the South, they all had on Arctic footwear—heavy work shoes or tasselled fur boots. Jon Evans, who had walked in with me, pointed out two priests sitting with the Eskimos—Father Fournier, from Igloolik, a severe-looking man in his thirties, with bright-blue eyes, a Roman nose, and short brown hair and beard, who was wearing the standard Arctic clerical outfit of black turtleneck sweater and black trousers tucked into Eskimo boots, and Father Tardy, from Holman, who was scholarly in appearance, with graying hair and steel-rimmed glasses, and who was wearing a formal black clerical suit and collar, but also had his trousers stuffed into Eskimo boots. Evans told me that Father Tardy was the sole representative present from Holman, because his Eskimo colleague from the coöp there had missed plane connections, and had thus turned out to be the only one of the forty-five persons expected at the conference who hadn't been able to make it. Evans also pointed out the two Mounted Policemen— both of them very young—who were sitting with their Eskimo colleagues, and I was disappointed to see that they were not in uniform. One had on a business suit, and the other, a handsome, straightbacked man with a clipped mustache, was wearing a heavy brown-and-tan striped sweater, wool slacks, and fur boots.

Behind the delegates, tables had been set up facing the dais for officials from Ottawa and for observers, and at each place was a neat brown envelope. One of the envelopes bore my name, and inside it were a lined pad; a pen and a pencil; several printed pamphlets about coöperatives; the latest issue of the Northern Affairs Department magazine *north*; a list of the Eskimo coöperatives, in the order of their incorporation, with the names of the delegates they were sending to the conference; the agenda for the five days of the conference; and a program, which had a green cover ornamented by an impressionistic black stencil of two Eskimos shaking hands. The program was printed both in English and in syllabics.

Leafing through it, I found greetings from the Minister of Northern Affairs; a message from the Commissioner of the Northwest Territories; a statement by Snowden of the meeting's purpose ("What you decide here will be of great importance to Eskimo people far into the future . . ."); a suggestion by Godt that the Eskimos "look ahead to the day when the coöperatives in the North form their own big coöperative to undertake . . . things which individual coöperatives cannot do"; a message of welcome from R. J. Orange, the Regional Administrator at Frobisher; and a description of the coöperatives by Alex Sprudzs. I read that the membership of the coöperatives now totalled five hundred (representing, with their families, more than twenty-five hundred Eskimos), and that their products were currently selling at an annual rate of about half a million dollars.

While we waited for the scheduled nine A.M. opening of the conference, I first chatted with my right-hand neighbor, Dr. Laidlaw. Then a slight, wiry fellow with a lean face and a wry expression slipped into the seat on my left and introduced himself as Jack Veitch, Coöperative Development Officer for the western Arctic. He told me that he and his colleagues in the western group had not arrived at Frobisher until three-thirty that morning.

At this point, Snowden began to speak over the public-address system. "It is ten minutes to nine, and I would like to start, even though we are ahead of time," he said, by way of opening the meeting. First he introduced the Eskimos at the table with him—a tall, distinguished-looking, immaculately dressed man of about thirty, known simply as Simonie, who was the head of the Frobisher Bay housing coöperative and a leader in the community, and the interpreter, a local resident. The latter began translating Snowden's remarks into Eskimo very haltingly, and seemed to be having a great deal of difficulty. I looked around for George Koneak. He was sitting on the edge of his seat at the side of the room, his mouth open and his hands tightly clasped, listening intently. Simonie made a one-minute welcoming speech first in Eskimo, then in English, which was followed by a few words from the eastern Arctic Coöperative Development Officer, Richard Nellis. The interpreter was now in deep trouble, scratching his head and pausing for long intervals while he gazed helplessly at the ceiling. Snowden leaned over and spoke softly to him for several minutes, and then said to the assemblage, "This conference brings to Frobisher Bay many people like me, who don't speak Eskimo. This is a new experiment for all of us, and we must have patience with one another. We have talked it over and decided that it is better to start with an interpreter I am used to." He called to Koneak, who quickly came forward, stepped onto the platform, and stood beside the table. Koneak said a few words in Eskimo and smiled, and everyone seemed to relax.

Snowden went on, "Four years ago almost to this very day, the first coöperative was started in the Arctic. None of us thought at that time that we would be sitting down with so many people from coöperatives right across the Arctic. . . . If we tried to write down what coöperatives are, we would have as many different answers as there are people in this room, and it's because we have different ideas that we are here today. For the first part of our meeting, delegates will talk about what they are doing. We are going to hear a lot of things that will get our thinking straight on what coöperatives are and what they can do for us. So far, most of us think in terms of the money that coöperatives can make for the members, and there's nothing wrong with that. Coöps are the best way I know to make money in the Arctic." He was speaking rapidly, and Koneak was interpreting tensely, in short sentences.

Suddenly Koneak stopped talking in Eskimo. "Excuse my language," he said to us in English, "but I use as much power as I have to bring it out in one piece."

Snowden said, "At the start of this week, it may be for you—as it is for me—something that makes me very nervous, because I have never done this before. But it will get easier as we get to know one another better." He introduced the delegates, who stood up self-consciously as their names were called. There was one woman delegate, a dour-looking Eskimo named Mrs. Bessie Irish, who was wearing a red cotton dress and blue sweater, and had straight black hair hanging to her waist.

"She's from my territory—from Aklavik," Veitch whispered. "Bessie is unique. Hers is the only coöperative composed solely of women. They make and sell fur garments." He shook his head sadly. "Bessie won't be able to talk," he said. "She'll clam up when her turn comes."

As an alert, high-spirited Eskimo from Fort Chimo, Noah Angnutok, was introduced, I noticed that Wally Hill, the Industrial Division's man at Chimo, was sitting next to him with a small child on his lap. Behind me, I was aware that Don Pruden, who had risen from his place, was pacing nervously to and fro, and I asked him in a whisper who the child was. He explained that Hill's wife was in the hospital having a baby, so Hill had had to bring their smallest child with him.

"What's wrong with you?" I asked Pruden. "You seem nervous!"

He looked anguished. "I *am* nervous," he said. "Josepie Annanack is going to speak first, because the George River was the first coöperative, and Josepie is just about the shyest man in the world. He'll never be able to do it!"

Snowden was winding up his introductions with the two Mounted Policemen. "If I may make a personal remark, I want to say how delighted we are to have the coöperation of the R.C.M.P.," he said. "Thanks for being here." He then mentioned the half-dozen others present, among whom, in addition to Dr. Laidlaw and myself, was an anthropologist, Dr. Frank Vallee, from the government's Northern Research Center. Finally, he outlined the rules of procedure: "Simonie and I will be co-chairmen of the meetings. Anyone who wants to talk must stand up, and the chairman will ask him to talk. If lots stand, the others must sit down. Now we'll have our first report."

Snowden called the name of Josepie Annanack. Annanack came up onto the platform, and Snowden made room for him to sit next to Koneak, who was now seated at the end of the table, the original interpreter having withdrawn to the audience. Annanack lit a cigarette, and his hands were shaking so violently that he quickly thrust them under the table. Snowden moved his chair nearer to Annanack, to bring himself, Annanack, and Koneak into a little half circle, and said, very gently, "I would prefer to make this first report a discussion among three people, just the way we talked at the George River." He was speaking carefully, and there wasn't another sound in the room as Koneak translated. Hill's little boy had fallen asleep in his father's arms. Almost all the Eskimos had begun taking notes in syllabics, and I was struck by the seriousness and dignity of the proceedings. Snowden went on, speaking to Koneak, "Say to Josepie that you and he and I have talked many times. I want him to tell me about the coöp at the George River and forget about the other people here." Snowden was now leaning over so that his large frame practically blocked Annanack's view of the assemblage. Koneak interpreted, and everyone waited breathlessly for Annanack to speak. Pruden, back in his seat, put his head in his hands. Annanack slowly brought his arms up onto the table, crossed them, and leaned on them. Then he took a deep breath, and began to speak. His voice had an unusual mellowness, which I recalled from my previous trip as being characteristic of the George River men. As soon as he started talking, Snowden sat back. After every few sentences, Annanack would stop and nod to Koneak, who would translate into English.

Annanack said, "When the people of the government came to the George River with this new idea, we could hardly understand, and didn't realize how good it was. Before, we were mostly short of food. There was not enough game and we hardly got anything. We had to go ninety miles by dog team to Fort Chimo for government relief. We thought we should go to another place so we could live better. When the white people brought in this new idea, we decided to wait and try. Now we make money at home and feel much better." He halted, looked around, and said, "I'm not the best man for speaking. It doesn't come into my head all at once, and I have to stop for thinking."

Snowden nodded. "I wonder if Josepie would tell us what his coöp does," he said. "The others don't know and would be interested."

Annanack explained that in the winter the members cut logs and in the summer they fished, and he told about a new chemical called Biostat, which they used to keep the fish from getting soft while they lay on ice in the boats bringing them to the freezer that the coöp had set up. He said that the coöp was also making small boats, and had sold some to the Port Burwell coöperative. Snowden remarked, "This is one thing we'll see more and more—the coöps will be selling to one another."

Henry Annatuk, president of the Port Burwell coöp, stood up. Snowden recognized him, and Annatŭk said, "We have no wood at Burwell, so we would like more boats and also a price that is a little bit less."

Several other Eskimos rose, to ask Annanack about Biostat and about the boats. Then there were queries about pricing and marketing, which Josepie could not answer. Snowden answered for him, and then said to Koneak, "It is important that we should all understand what happens in a coöp. I'm not sure whether the Eskimos do things because the white man thinks they should be done, or because they want them themselves. I myself want to know this."

There ensued a long conversation in Eskimo between Koneak and Annanack. The latter moved restlessly in his chair, and asked Koneak several questions. Koneak suddenly began to talk in Eskimo with considerable emotion, clenching his fists. I knew that until Eskimos completely trust a white man, they usually tell him what they think he wants to hear, and I wondered whether the small drama we were witnessing represented Annanack's struggle between his desire to answer Snowden truthfully and his natural distrust of a roomful of strangers, half of them white. Finally, Annanack began to talk in a low voice, holding his hands tightly gripped before him. He said, "The coöperative idea came from the white people. We could take the idea, and it works well. We never tried to produce before, because we had nothing to produce with, so we would not refuse to do this, as long as we thought we could do it. Now we have a chance to build with something, among our own people."

Annanack looked uncertainly at Snowden, who said, "That was a difficult question, and Josepie has answered well. The whole idea for a coöp did come from the South, but it is now something that belongs to the George River. Do they feel that it is something they *must* do or something they *want* to do?"

When Koneak translated this, the Eskimos laughed, and Simonie said a few words that made them laugh again. Annanack, relaxed and calm, lit another cigarette, and said, "As we were working along at the beginning, we never thought of this, but everyone realizes now that the people can do something, and that's why every year it's getting better. We do not always make a good job, we are a little bit short of equipment or it breaks down, but we like very much to proceed as much as possible."

Snowden announced that it was time for lunch, and, with a nod toward Annanack, said, "As the first delegate to report, he has had the most difficult job that anyone will have this week, and he has done it so well. It will be easier for everyone else, now that we have seen how it can be done."

Everyone applauded loudly.

Walking over to the dining hall, I asked Snowden if I had only imagined that there had been a struggle between Koneak and Annanack over the answer to his question. "I'm not sure, but I think George was trying hard to explain my question to Josepie," Snowden said. "I asked that question because the Eskimos have never been at a formal meeting before, and right from the start I wanted no confusion in anybody's mind about the purpose of this one. I wanted everybody in the room, Eskimo and non-Eskimo, to understand that I wished the Eskimos to say what they really wanted to say, and not be dominated by us. Since Josepie was the delegate I knew best, and the first speaker, I wanted this idea established, through him, for the entire meeting. As for my asking whether the coöperative idea was something they wanted or something they felt they must do, if the Eskimos had felt they were not making their own decisions, I would have considered our whole technique wrong, and would have changed it."

At lunch, it was agreed that the conference was off to a fine start. On one side of me sat a young Eskimo who spoke perfect English. He told me he was Paul Oolateetak, and that he was from Resolute, where he had learned his English working at the Royal Canadian Air Force base. I asked what his coöperative did. "We sell polar-bear skins," he said. "We had twenty this year, but I only shot one bear myself."

WHEN THE afternoon session began, Henry Annatuk, from Burwell, was seated on the platform ready to start talking, but before he could begin, Snowden announced, "I want to do as little work as I can. I wonder if Simonie would take over as chairman?" He said this so casually that it wasn't until Simonie had started to conduct the meeting in Eskimo that it became clear what had happened. The conference had become an Eskimo affair. Now it was the white people who had to wait for the interpreter to tell them what was going on.

Brushing the hair back from his eyes, Annatuk spoke in a low tone, and with a quizzical, half-amused expression on his face. Burwell's story was similar to the George River's, he said. The Eskimos had been destitute and about to leave when "the people from Ottawa" came along with the coöperative idea and showed them how to harvest their rich resources. He told how in four years, the Eskimos had built up a flourishing fishing, handicrafts, and fur business, and, because they were a hundred and twenty miles from the nearest Hudson's Bay outpost, how they had established the first Eskimo-run coöperative retail store in the Arctic. Seals were very abundant in their area, and they had such a plentiful supply of seal meat, for feeding both human beings and their dogs (reputed to be the fattest in the North), that he said the Industrial Division had sent a food expert into Burwell with a portable cannery to experiment with the canning of the meat for sale to other settlements.

Of all the delegates to the conference, the next speaker was the one I was most eager to hear. His name was Oshaweetuk, and he was a noted carver from Cape Dorset, the west Baffin Island community where the magnificent walrus-ivory carvings and prints made from stone blocks or sealskin stencils, already well known in the American and European art world, originated. In 1959, Oshaweetuk had walked into the office of James Houston, the government administrator at Dorset, and himself an artist, and, noticing a package of Player's cigarettes on the table, had remarked, of the familiar picture of the bearded sailor on the wrapper, "It must be terrible to have to paint this little sailor on every package every time." Houston had replied, "But that isn't the way it's done," and the next moment he had introduced Oshaweetuk to the art of printing. Taking from his desk a walrus tusk on which Oshaweetuk had incised likenesses of familiar Arctic figures, and some ink and tissue paper, Houston had, by good luck, succeeded in printing a fine impression of the various objects—caribou, a man in a kayak, a goose, a walrus—that were cut into the tusk. Upon seeing the print, Oshaweetuk had said, "But we could do that!" He and his companions did, making printing blocks and stencils from more easily worked materials, and the Dorset community went into the Eskimo-art business. Soon afterward, they formed the third, and the most prosperous, of the Arctic coöperatives.

Oshaweetuk, a slight, neat, highly intelligent-looking man, walked to the platform, took his seat with dignity, and began to talk. "Before the coöperative started, the people suffered," he said. "They didn't have much ammunition and they didn't have lumber for kayaks. Now they have lumber, but they also have money to buy outboard motors, so they don't use kayaks much." Describing how Houston had provided the Eskimos with the technical knowledge that enabled them to produce the prints, he said, "A lot of people didn't know how to carve and were learning from each other—both the ladies and men, even myself. At first the price was not very high, but as we get better the price is going higher. We also learn which carvings make the better price, but now the prints are higher priced than the carvings. We can afford canoes to travel on the sea, and, working for the coöp, we can buy ammunition. That way, we get a better life." He lit a cigarette, and said, "In the beginning, we tried to make the prints fancy, but they were not as good as the prints made from an idea. Now the prints are not even pretty to look at, but they are higher-priced than the pretty prints. The way to make prints, you draw an idea on paper and carve a copy of it on soft stone and use it like a stamp. If the stone is nice and smooth, and the carving is well done, you can make lots and lots of prints. But the ladies' prints are always higher-priced than the men's prints." Everybody laughed, and someone asked him why. He smiled. "Because the ladies are not thinking only about animals, like the men always think, but of something from their own ideas." He paused, then said quietly, "The help we got from Jim Houston we still have, and it is still growing. Before he came along, we could hardly go hunting and could not afford even a half gallon of coal oil. Now everybody can get more of anything, because Jim Houston helped us. We are still thankful to that man, and can never forget him."

Simonie asked if there were any questions, and Father Tardy rose. Speaking with a heavy French accent, he asked, "What kind of 'elp Mr. 'ouston give to you? Did he teach you 'ow to draw?"

"At the beginning, people didn't know how to start," Oshaweetuk said. "Houston showed them how."

A small man named Pauloosie Seuak, from Povungnituk, who was sitting up front, near the platform, bobbed up and asked, in a staccato tone of voice, "Who is the boss at Cape Dorset—the white man or the Eskimo?"

Instantly, Oshaweetuk said, "The white man."

Snowden turned quickly to Simonie. "Could I clarify that?" he asked Simonie. "Would it be all right?"

Simonie nodded, and Snowden said, "At Cape Dorset, the leader is a white man, in the sense that two white people from the South work for the coöperative, one as manager of the coöperative and one as manager of the retail store, but the coöp, not the government, pays their salaries. If I am Prime Minister of Canada, and I don't like one of these two men, I cannot have him fired. Only the members of the Dorset coöp can fire him. People really control their own affairs when they can hire and fire their people, so although the two men seem to be leaders in some ways, they are actually the paid employees at Cape Dorset."

Pauloosie Seuak's turn as speaker came next, and he described the stone-carving industry at Povungnituk, a settlement that has become almost as famous for its art as Cape Dorset. "The carvings have to be a certain size to sell, not larger than is measured by the hand, from the middle finger to the middle of the thumb, standing on a base," he said, holding up his hand and demonstrating. "The small sell easier than the big."

In a few minutes, there was a coffee break, during which Seuak took Snowden aside and, with snapping eyes and in rapid-fire Eskimo, hastily translated by Koneak, described the events surrounding his presence at the conference.

"Did you know that I was chosen by the people, by the Eskimos, but the white men had chosen someone else?" he asked.

Snowden scowled and said, "No, no, we wanted the Eskimos to choose the man they wanted to come."

Seuak rushed on to tell how he and the mission priest at Povungnituk, who had helped found the coöperative, had taken a trip to Quebec City to promote the Povungnituk carvings. There the priest had been injured in an automobile accident. "So I returned home alone, and when I get back, I learn that the priest and the government man picked someone to come here already before, without asking the people," he said. "But I was told by the people, 'We want you to go along instead of the other fellow to represent Povungnituk.'"

Snowden told Seuak that this had been the right procedure, and that he was glad things had turned out that way.

THAT EVENING, I accompanied several Frobisher residents to the town's only night club. Often known as Gallagher's, from the name of its proprietor, it was a series of shacks pushed together and covered with red shingles. Its official name was the East Coast Lodge and Tavern, and it was divided into two sections known as the Rustic Room Grill and the Captain's Corner, but the most popular name for the whole place was the one the Eskimos used—the Easty-Coasty. The interior, which had low ceilings, shaded lights, and bamboolike tropical decorations, looked more like a stage setting for "Rain" than a cocktail lounge on a snow-covered, treeless island. A glass of beer cost fifty cents, and a steak cost six dollars. Several quietly drunk Eskimos were sitting at a table on one side of us, and several quietly drunk white people were sitting at a table on the other side, and nobody got out of hand. "They run a pretty fair show here," a man who worked in Frobisher said to me. "We hear that whiskey is ruining the Eskimos here, and I wouldn't deny that some have been affected, but a three-week waiting period has been imposed on orders at the government liquor store, and that has checked a lot of impulse buying."

I asked if the Eskimo and the white populations mixed much.

"The schools are integrated—they're three-quarters Eskimo and one-quarter white—and there is some mingling on that account, but generally the whites just do not mix with the Eskimos," he said. "They aren't interested. We have some basic prejudices to break through here, especially among people who only come north to make money. Not all our government agencies have helped, either. In 1959, for instance, when a man from another department went into the office of the Northern Canada Power Commission to suggest that the Commission should hire Eskimos, he was summarily told to leave. But last fall the Commission finally took on four Eskimo lads, to train them as power-plant operators. We are working all the time to break down barriers. The Department of Transport, for example, still operates a bar that doesn't welcome Eskimos. But give us time. All that will change."

III

DURING THE next three days' meetings, Snowden sat at the back of the room listening to the individual reports, while Simonie served as chairman. The spokesmen for the coöperatives described a wide assortment of their activities: fishing for trout, cod, and Arctic char, which was being sold as a luxury item by now not only in southern Canada, but in the United States, France, and England; arts and handicrafts production; fur trapping; boatbuilding; and the operation of tourist camps. Four coöperatives now ran retail stores, and two had credit unions—called in Eskimo *qikartissivik*, which means "the place where the money is stopped."

When Paul Oolateetak, of Resolute, spoke, he said that his coöperative had appointed Constable Bell, the Mounted Policeman, to be its treasurer. "He was to look after the money, because no one else was too good at adding," he explained.

A man from Chimo stood up. "Is the coöp paying the treasurer?" he asked.

Oolateetak said, "No. He is paid by the Mounted Police and it is part of his duties."

Constable Bell promptly popped up and said, "But it's a good idea!" This brought a roar of laughter.

Then the young policeman told how, at the Canadian Air Force base in Resolute, he had set up a table in the mess hall to sell the Eskimos' carvings to the servicemen. "A group of carvings is gone in half an hour," he said. "Almost every Eskimo family has at least one member working at the airbase, so the income from carvings is extra spending money, and the Eskimos use it wisely—on stoves, beds, and other furniture. Everybody is now one hundred per cent behind our coöperative, although at first there were several who sold their carvings under the counter. That pulled prices down, so we had a meeting and explained this, and since then the Eskimos have found that prices have been twenty to thirty per cent better."

Akpalleeapik, the delegate from Grise Fiord, on Ellesmere Island, which is about seven hundred miles north of the Arctic Circle and about a thousand miles south of the Pole, was introduced as representing the northernmost coöperative in the world. (I later learned that he had never seen a tree.) Akpalleeapik, who was a famous hunter, had a small mustache and a round haircut, and he was nervously chewing gum as he sat down on the platform to talk. He said he had formerly lived on north Baffin Island, and explained, "The reason I ended up at Grise Fiord, the government was moving people from the east coast of Hudson Bay to Grise Fiord, because they did not have too good a life in their old place. I was asked to teach them how to live in darkness, which I already knew from north Baffin. Where we live, darkness comes from November through January, and then it gets brighter and brighter and will eventually be brighter than where other places are." The Grise Fiord coöperative's activities were similar to those at Resolute, which is two hundred and fifty miles away to the southwest and is the nearest settlement. He went on, "Since very few people knew bookkeeping, we had to turn to someone who did know—Constable Currie—and since we have turned to the R.C.M.P. for help, we feel we have done well."

Henry Annatuk asked if there were fish at Grise Fiord, and Akpalleeapik replied, "If you want to live there by fishing, you might as well give up the idea of living, because you are going to starve pretty fast. Sealskins are our main source of income, and we also hunt polar bears and trap white fox, and are getting quite a lot from carvings."

During the coffee break that day, Dr. Vallee, the anthropologist, remarked to Snowden that the tensions were breaking down and people were beginning to make jokes. Snowden was pleased. "There was an undercurrent of suspicion among the Eskimos that the whole show at Resolute and Grise Fiord was being run by the Mounted Police, but it's obvious to everybody now that the Eskimos understand just what they are doing," he said.

As we returned to our seats, I noticed that Akpalleeapik was nowhere to be seen. Koneak reported that Akpalleeapik was ill, and had waited only to give his report before being taken to the hospital. "Probably the flu," Paul Godt said to me. "That's what usually happens when someone from an isolated community comes into contact with a lot of other people."

It was the turn of Noah Angnutok, from Chimo, to talk, and there was one message that he was determined to deliver. He said, "The members of my coöp want me to say, if there are men from Ottawa at the conference at Frobisher, that the people of Chimo wish to have a store. If I can't get an answer right away, I would like an answer sooner or later for my people back home. We have a Hudson's Bay store in Chimo, but everyone looks for something that costs less than in the Hudson's Bay store. My people are happy, never sad, but they will be very happy to get this."

Angnutok then spoke of the current activities of the Chimo coöperative, but before he sat down, he looked straight at Snowden, in the back of the room, and said, "Chimo would like to know. We haven't got an answer on a store. Will we get an answer here?"

Snowden got up—reluctantly, it appeared. "I was rather hoping you would forget, but not really," he said. "We will discuss this later in the week."

I asked someone afterward why Snowden had been so uncharacteristically evasive. "This is the gray area that government people must stay away from, and they do," my informant said. "It is a hellish problem, because the fact is that where there is already a Hudson's Bay Company store, as there is at Chimo, the government officials are not allowed to help set up retail stores in competition." I assumed that he meant they were prevented from doing so for political reasons. "Dr. Laidlaw is here as a private citizen, representing a powerful union of southern coöperatives, and he looks interested," he said. "Perhaps he'll come up with something."

When the report from the coöperative at Holman was called for, it was the scholarly-looking Father Tardy who rose to give it, since his Eskimo colleague had missed his plane. He was extremely nervous, and obviously something was bothering him. Speaking in halting English, he began by telling us that in 1960 there had been five cases of tuberculosis among the Eskimos in Holman, and that he was certain that a prime factor in this had been the inadequacy of the living quarters—unsanitary shacks built of old boxes, canvas, and paper. "Something had to be done to alleviate, so I thought of developing local industry," he said. He started the Eskimos making tapestries of sealskin, with appliqué designs in different shades of fur, and then decided that a second industry was needed. In 1962, he saw his first Cape Dorset print. Since the artistic talent of the Holman Eskimos had already been demonstrated in the tapestries, he decided that they should try making prints, and he found an article in *Beaver,* the Hudson's Bay Company's magazine, that described the Cape Dorset process of making stencils and printing. "We try to make, using poor paper and ink, but the first time, not good," he said. "At last, we find a nice paper that worked, so we make our first print collection. We hanged the prints, everybody came and looked, and we arrived at conclusion we liked and they are really our own. The Eskimos choose the fifteen best and we send to Canadian Eskimo Art Committee in South. None are accepted, and letter comes back that says prints are not really Eskimo and that somebody tell Eskimo 'ow they should do it." In an agitated voice, he said, "I wish to defend our prints against this comment and get your impression of them."

Slides of the prints were shown. They depicted Eskimo figures and polar bears against a background of mountains in perspective. Puzzled by the rejection, I later sought an explanation from some of the government men. I was told that the Canadian Eskimo Art Committee—a group of five experts, one of them James Houston, and the rest from Canadian museums and art publications, who met at irregular intervals to give the Eskimos guidance on such matters as the quality, printing, and pricing of their art works—had said that the prints from Holman showed real promise, and were not bad for a first attempt. But because no other Eskimo drawing had ever had background or perspective, the committee felt that the prints revealed a degree of white influence not evident in the work from Dorset and Povungnituk. The committee had urged the Holman Eskimos to try again.

I subsequently saw photographs of some of the sealskin tapestries made under Father Tardy's supervision. Intricately worked into the fur design were figures depicting the Last Supper and the fourteen Stations of the Cross; the figures wore Grecian-style robes, and grapes and tropical leaves had been painstakingly appliquéd around the borders. It was obvious that Father Tardy had become confused about the delicate line separating the imposition of ideas from the teaching of techniques. This distinction, however, seemed to be quite clear to the Eskimos, who, during a coffee break after Father Tardy had spoken, spiritedly discussed the matter, through Koneak, with the government officials. I heard one of the officials say, "I remember Jim Houston telling me that he would never think of telling an Eskimo what to draw, any more than he, as an artist, would ever think of drawing the way the Eskimos do. He also believed that the Eskimo *should* reject anything imposed on him, because his thinking is so different from ours. The whole philosophy of art is involved here." He added, "But it would be wrong for any white man to speak of this to Father Tardy. It will have to come from an Eskimo."

When we returned to the hall, Simonie reopened the discussion of the Holman prints, and sought Oshaweetuk's opinion.

The Dorset artist rose slowly and faced Father Tardy. "First off, I would like to ask how did the people start to develop the prints?" he said. "When I have heard that, I will talk about them for a little while."

"They have never been teachered, just by themselves," Father Tardy said. "They tell each other what to do—it is purely Eskimo. Our first appreciation was by the Eskimos themselves. Everybody said, 'This is our country, something belonging to us.'" He raised his voice. "The Dorset man said before, 'The best art is what comes from a man's mind.' Each Eskimo community has its own way of expressing itself. I could do it the way the committee wants and our prints would be sold, but they would not be pure Eskimo!"

"Thank you for all the information," Oshaweetuk said, in a soft voice. "These prints, we like them very much, but we don't know how much money you would get if you sent them south to the same place we send our prints. Even those that come entirely from the Eskimo, we don't know how much."

"If you like them, we don't see why they shouldn't sell at a good price," Father Tardy said eagerly. "I want you to see that there is no white influence in these prints." There was an electric quality in the quiet room. "I would refute all the arguments," he continued. "They have been judged already by the Eskimos."

Oshaweetuk said, "We never had a chance to meet before, but I hope you can understand what I try to say. People at Dorset did not get information on what to draw from elsewhere. But are those drawings from Holman not followed from pictures that came from other parts of our country? Those drawings, they must be by people who have seen Cape Dorset prints before. Or was this information passed in a letter?"

"Maybe one of them saw a print made by Cape Dorset from the magazine, but he didn't know what it was, because he didn't know 'ow to read," Father Tardy replied.

Oshaweetuk asked, "Do you supervise for the coöperative at Holman?"

Father Tardy said, "Yes, I 'elp the people with paperwork and bookkeeping. I find I 'ave to give a model for 'andiwork, but no one does for prints. In our coöp, I'm just the secretary, and in the rugs I 'elp the women with the drawing. But in the prints the drawing are supervised by the man who did not get here."

At this point, Simonie gently suggested that perhaps it was time to move on to the problems of another delegate, and he proposed that Father Tardy and Oshaweetuk continue their discussion in private.

There was something very touching about Father Tardy's appeal, and I sought him out at lunch a day or so later. While we ate, he told me that he belonged to the Oblate Order of Mary Immaculate, that he had come from a little town on the French Riviera, and that during the Second World War he had been in the French ski corps. "There, I saw so much death it was a relief when I received my call and went into the Church," he said. "Five days after I was assigned to my present post, I was in the Arctic. Believe me, it was a tremendous shock to go so suddenly from the Riviera to the Arctic."

I asked him how he liked the Arctic, and he smiled.

"The Eskimos are a primitive but interesting people," he said. "I like living at 'olman. I use my big room as a chapel, and besides I have a bedroom and small kitchen, but I am too lazy to cook. In the middle of day, I 'ave small lunch of fish; in evening, caribou. I don't take time—mostly eat meat and fish." He laughed, and touched his receding hairline. "Maybe diet makes me lose 'air. There are about one 'undred and ten Eskimos at 'olman, and twenty-four are Catholics, but the main thing is not straight missionary work. We look to improve whole community by charity and advice and by the medical, which is always the same. I get instructions by radio from doctor or nurse, and slowly get knowledge. If serious, I ask for plane."

We ate in silence for a time, and then he said, "The thing

I enjoy most in Arctic is we 'ave time to think. My faith goes deeper and deeper. If I 'ad any doubts, I could not stay, not one day more."

THE DELEGATE from Great Whale River, on the east coast of Hudson Bay, was a tough little dark-skinned Eskimo with very fine features, named Pauloosie Napartuk. Looking at the wall and smoking furiously as he talked, he said, "This winter, when we learned that delegates from all over are meeting in one place, we are very glad. I want to say thank you very much. I did not pay my fare, not even one penny, and I don't know much about coöperatives." I looked on one of the information sheets that we had been given and saw that Napartuk's coöperative, although it had been incorporated two years before, listed only one activity—carving.

Napartuk said, "I make notes here. Each delegate as he reports, I have down on my sheet of paper, but I won't blame my people if they can hardly understand, because they are hardly organized. No one has come to tell us more about the coöperative since two winters and one summer, and we are tired of waiting. Someone should have come sooner, and specially. The people haven't done much carving this year. We have people who can carve, and people who can make things, and fishermen, and also we can build canoes. We don't understand what we should proceed on, but no doubt we are going to be feeling like really getting started after we have been talked to."

Snowden asked to speak. "We know that we can't start a coöperative on a sound basis just by sending one of our men into a community for two weeks, no matter how good he is," he said, "but we now have only two coöperative officers for the whole North—Dick Nellis for the east and Jack Veitch for the west. It is too big a country for two men to handle. We also have only two officers in Ottawa, Paul Godt and Alex Sprudzs, and as there are more and more coöps, more and more work keeps them away from the Arctic. We know the problem Pauloosie has. Others have the same problem, and we are very,

very sorry. We don't know how long it will be, but we will send someone as soon as we can."

Simonie's deep voice interrupted. "Are there any whales at Great Whale River?" he asked.

Napartuk replied, "The whales are getting scarce, because more ships come in and make more noise and the whales don't come back as often as before, but our place is still called Great Whale River, just as in the old stories." He turned back to Snowden. "So no one has come to us since the first time, and this program was catching us before we fell down," he said. "Before the coöp, it was just as if we were sleeping. The people from Ottawa came and woke us up. After I get back, I will tell my people we must try and do something for ourselves."

When it came time for Mrs. Bessie Irish, from Aklavik, to give her report, Veitch's worries about her not being able to talk proved unjustified. She sat down at the table on the dais, lit a cigarette, and began to speak, in a low, pleasant voice, and Veitch whispered to me, "Good—she's relaxed. She's under control." A few minutes later, Veitch said in an awed voice, "My goodness, if she tries to tell her whole story, they'll have to shut her off. She'll never stop!" She described how she had trained twenty women to make fur mittens, slippers, parkas, and other articles. The parkas made of muskrat sold for a hundred and seventy dollars, those made of sealskin for approximately two hundred. Despite Veitch's fears, Bessie eventually did stop talking, closing on a splendid note. She suddenly tossed her head, waved an arm in the air, exclaimed "Old Aklavik will never die!" and was silent.

Noah Angnutok stood up. "Are only ladies working, or are there men, too?" he asked.

Bessie puffed on her cigarette, and smiled. "Well, you know as well as I do that among our people the men catch the animals, the women sew the fur, and the men never go near it again," she said.

Everyone laughed except Angnutok. "Is there no man who helps the ladies in the coöp?" he asked.

Bessie gave him a contemptuous look. "There is no man who helps in the coöp, and no men who are interested in sewing," she answered.

"In Aklavik, do you have a coöp store?" Angnutok asked.

"Not yet," she said.

"Do you have trees?" he asked.

"More trees than *you* could shake a stick at," she answered, and picked up her papers and cigarettes and left the platform.

AFTER THE rigorous daytime schedule, the delegates and government men usually spent the evening sitting in their quarters and talking, or else visiting around, but occasionally some went to the Easty-Coasty. On a couple of evenings, there were square dances at the community hall, in which the Eskimos participated enthusiastically. Snowden's superior, R. A. J. Phillips, the Associate Director of the Department of Northern Affairs, looked in on the conference on his way back to Ottawa from a trip to the western Arctic, and while he was there he took me to my first curling match. We arrived on foot at a long, narrow building in the Lower Base area, in front of which half a dozen cars were parked, all with their motors running to keep them from freezing in the twenty-below-zero cold. Inside the building was the curling rink, with two ice-covered alleys, each eighteen feet wide and a hundred and twenty feet long. On each team were four players, who, by turns, sent the curling stones—smooth, rounded stones that had curved metal handles—gliding down the ice to a circular target area, while two teammates, brandishing oddly elongated brooms, tried to control the stones' movement by brushing the ice before or behind them. There are times when almost everything that goes on in the Arctic seems dreamlike and unreal, and you wonder what you are doing so far from home. I felt this way at the curling rink, and also later when I visited a house that belonged to the owner of Frobisher's only three taxicabs. The house, built on an A-frame, had a two-story living room that overlooked the enormous expanse of Frobisher Bay, and the view from its picture window at night was wonderfully clear. I could see the peaks of the frozen whitecaps in that immense body of water, which was solid ice now for fifty or sixty miles. Inside the house, we sat back in deep chairs and listened to an electric phonograph, which shifted from Bach to jazz. Occasionally, I got up to take a better look at the incredible view.

The next morning, I was taken to see the new Eskimo Housing Coöperative of Frobisher, whose president was Simonie, and whose members—many of them government employees—using capital borrowed from the Eskimo Loan Fund and their own labor, were building themselves modern residences. When Simonie had given his report, he had mentioned the difficulties in building the houses, which were near Apex Hill. The prefabricated parts had come by ship, and there were many missing. Blueprints and parts hadn't always matched, and the electric wiring had just arrived by plane, with us. Despite these handicaps, fourteen houses had been constructed, each consisting of three bedrooms, a bathroom with a chemical toilet, a combined kitchen and living room with an oil heater, a storage room, and a porch, and each costing its Eskimo owner thirty-five hundred dollars. Simonie's house, though not quite finished, was on display. The interior was cheerfully painted and papered, and had a pine-panelled divider between the living room and the kitchen, and spotlights in each room. The oil heater had not yet been turned on, but even so the house, with its flowered wallpaper and soft colors, had an atmosphere of warmth and cosiness.

Later, Mr. Orange, the regional administrator, took me on a tour of Frobisher. It had originally been a small Eskimo settlement, and its modern history had begun during the Second World War, when the United States Air Force established a base there. In 1955, the Department of Northern Affairs started developing the present community as an administrative center for the entire eastern Arctic. Orange, a lean, blond man in his late thirties, was responsible for overseeing five hundred thousand square miles; he had a staff of a hundred and twenty-five people at Frobisher, and fifty more in twelve outlying settlements on Baffin Island, on the nearby Melville Peninsula, and in the high Arctic, and he spent half his time travelling by single-engine Otter plane through his outsize district.

As we started off on our tour, in a government station wagon, Orange told me he had lived in town for two years, with his wife and their three children. "I am enthralled with the Arctic," he said. "It's bleak, it's barren, harsh, and cold, but, boy, it's beautiful!" We stopped first at the various units of the Rehabilitation Center, on Apex Hill: the sewing cottage, where parkas and fur boots were being made; the crafts storeroom, in which row upon row of Eskimo stone carvings stood awaiting shipment to the South; the carving workshop, where a sad-faced, almost toothless Eskimo was polishing a black soapstone bird he had just made. This man, Orange said, had once been the best lumberman in his community, and one of its leaders, but after a series of illnesses he was unable to readjust to his old life.

Leaving Apex Hill, we drove past the Hudson's Bay store and toward the Lower Base. The road climbed and we passed a steel skeleton, which Orange told me was the beginning of a new, twenty-eight-bed hospital, to replace the present thirteen-bed one. "We're on Astro Hill now," he went on. "If we go ahead with our present plans, we'll be building a six- or seven-story town building here pretty soon. The Lower Base is really a temporary town, and we expect the permanent town to be here." He turned down a curving road that took us to the Eskimo village of Ikaluit. I noticed some wood-and-tarpaper shacks, but there were also many solid frame houses. "This is the traditional camping ground for more than nine hundred Eskimos, and many still move out of their houses into tents here in summer," Orange said. We passed a stray dog—the only Eskimo dog I saw in Frobisher—and a man on foot dragging a dog harness, and then I caught sight of two vehicles, driven by Eskimos, that were entirely new to me. They had skis on the front end and tractor treads at the rear. One, a bright-yellow machine with an exposed leather seat behind a plastic windshield, was about the size of a motor bike. "That's a Skidoo," Orange said. "It costs about six hundred dollars.

has a gasoline motor, and is used by some Eskimos instead of a dog sled, although the Skidoos are not quite as reliable." The other machine, which was bright red, looked more like a small tractor. Orange said that this was an Autoboggan, which cost somewhat more and could pull heavier loads.

Going on to the Lower Base, we passed a large quonset hut that contained a branch of the Bank of Montreal, and then more prefabricated buildings, housing a barbershop, the Frobisher laundry, a second Hudson's Bay Company store, a crafts shop, and the post office, and then we zoomed down the open road, past the civilian air terminal and the adjoining airfield, to the former United States base, which had been part of the U. S. Strategic Air Command until only a few months before. Orange stopped outside a huge, square building. "One hundred and thirty-five Americans, whom we almost never saw, worked, played, and lived here," he said. "This building has the only gymnasium within five hundred miles—a beauty, too—and the best bar in Frobisher. It cost six and a half million dollars and its various interior levels have a total floor space of one square mile." He drove around to the airfield. "A row of airplanes was always poised on this strip, ready to go up on five minutes' notice, if it had ever been the real thing," he went on. The production of large new aerial tankers that could refuel bombers in midair had made the S.A.C. setup obsolete, he said, and the entire twenty-million-dollar installation had reverted to the Canadian government, which planned to use part of it for government offices, and as a school and residence for pupils from all over Baffin Island. Just before he turned the car to take me back to the meeting on Apex Hill, he gazed for a moment at two big black birds sitting on a post. "Ravens," he said. "We love them, because they are the only living things in the sky at this time of year."

WHEN ORANGE brought me back to the community hall, the last of the eighteen coöp delegates had finished delivering his report, and Jon Evans was describing the efforts of the Industrial Division to find additional sources of income for the Eskimos. They listened closely and took notes as he outlined a new government plan that would allow them to borrow from the Eskimo Loan Fund to buy boats, and then told them about a fish that scientists had found in Ungava Bay—a "big fish, very flat, called halibut, which lives at the bottom of the sea." He added that shrimp were also believed to exist in Ungava and Hudson Bays. Finally, he told of the canning experiments being made with seal and whale meat, and announced that canned seal meat from Burwell would be served that night at supper. (The Eskimos complained that the canned meat, which I found smoky and oily, had too much seasoning, and ate very little of it—but the competition was stiff; the menu also included roast beef, a luxury item for any Eskimo.)

Snowden was now back on the platform, sitting beside Simonie, and at the close of Evans' speech he opened the meeting to general questions.

Celestino Magpa rose, and, speaking in English, said, "When summer comes, Skidoos could be shipped to us by boat. How much could be taken off our taxes for the purchase of Skidoos? Would we get a tax concession, like the farmers do on their machinery in the South?"

Snowden looked amazed at this sophisticated question, and I glanced over at Paul Godt to see his reaction. He, too, looked amazed, and I heard him mutter, "Say! Isn't that fascinating!"

Snowden looked hard at his hands for a moment, and then said, "Celestino is raising a whole new idea, and one that is very, very interesting. In the South, the government gives lower taxes to special kinds of business. The farmers get a tax rebate for a farm machine because it is a harvesting agent, and Magpa considers the Skidoo a harvesting agent. He is suggesting that Eskimos, who fish in the sea and hunt on the land, are doing a certain kind of farming in the North, so they want a certain kind of lowered tax, like the farmers in the South. Have I interpreted you correctly?"

"Correct," said Magpa.

"It's a wonderful question," Snowden said. "Canadians in the South have been trying to settle that kind of question for a hundred years, and we could spend a year discussing it. As a beginning, this is what we will do. The Industrial Division will undertake a study of the types of equipment and vehicles used in hunting and trapping, and see if any tax aid can be given. I think none can be."

IV

By Saturday morning, it was evident that the conference couldn't possibly end that day, as it was scheduled to do, but must continue on Monday. Then it would have to end, because almost everyone was scheduled to leave on the Tuesday-morning plane for Montreal, even though a number of the delegates were suffering from flu. Coughing and sneezing could be heard throughout the hall. There were several empty seats on Saturday, and, for the first time, Hill's little boy, who had a bad cold, was not with him.

The meeting was thrown open to general discussion, and Noah Angnutok repeated his demand for a coöperative store in Chimo. This time, Dr. Laidlaw rose to reply. "I hope that during the summer we will be able to send a man from the Coöperative Union of Canada to help you organize your stores where you wish to have them," he said. "This man will be an experienced person, but he will have to have an interpreter. We must convince the people that they can run their own business."

Napartuk rose and said excitedly, "Now I have information to take back, and I am proud! Dr. Laidlaw says the big coöps want to help the small coöps in the Arctic. Perhaps we can't go fast enough at Great Whale River, but we don't want to stop. We need help! Somebody put it down on a piece of paper, so nobody forgets us!"

Both the Eskimo delegates and the government representatives at the conference had repeatedly mentioned the need for a central marketing outlet in the Canadian South for Eskimo carvings, prints, and handicrafts. The Department of Northern Affairs was handling the marketing of Arctic handicrafts, but other art works, except for the much-sought-after prints, which were selected, priced, and distributed through the Eskimo Art Committee, were marketed individually. A committee of four Eskimos—Oshaweetuk, of Dorset; Angnutok, of Chimo; and the delegates from Povungnituk and Coppermine—met with Godt and Dr. Laidlaw on Sunday afternoon to discuss the formation of a marketing agency that would be financed by the Eskimo coöperatives, and the first business on Monday morning was a report on their meeting. They not only recommended that such an agency be established but felt that it should have eastern and western warehouses and sales offices, and that shipping costs should be pooled, so that Grise Fiord Eskimos would pay no more to export their goods than Eskimos closer to the South.

Snowden suggested a vote on the project, saying, "Now the delegates must decide, as a group, whether to recommend to their coöps that the central agency is a good idea and should be established. Everyone knows that the delegates here cannot make a final decision for their coöperatives. If the delegates recommend an agency, then my people will prepare a paper in Ottawa telling every coöperative how such an agency can be set up and what it will cost. After all the coöperatives have had a chance to study this paper, then *they* must take a vote."

Napartuk stood up, and said, "Before we go home to a lot of questions, we want to know: Is this going to be a better life?"

"My answer is yes, but that is only *my* answer," Snowden replied. "I say yes because more and more is being produced by the coöperatives all the time, and they will be able to pay for a central agency. I also believe that responsibility should be taken out of the government's hands and put in those of the coöps, where it belongs. This doesn't mean that the government is losing interest, though. We are always available for advice." He said to Koneak, "Do they understand what they are voting for? They must vote for what they believe, not what we think."

Angnutok said, "Suppose when I get back to Chimo, my people don't like that vote I made here at all. What should I do? Let them crawl all over me?"

"You are not making a final vote here," Snowden explained. "When your people have studied our paper, they will decide yes, we like the central agency, or no, we don't."

"So we could raise our hands here, even though we don't know what our people are going to do," Angnutok said. "They decide later at home."

Snowden said, "I will ask who says yes and who says no, and you can't vote both ways." Turning to Father Fournier, from Igloolik, he added, "Father, I am going to take one vote from each coöperative, so I will take the vote of the Eskimo, Kolaut, from Igloolik."

The vote recommending that a central marketing agency be established was unanimous.

The meeting recessed for lunch, and I walked up to Snowden, who was smiling. "We had two major objectives here," he said. "The first was education in the broadest sense. I knew that if the people in Grise Fiord became aware that the people in Chimo were thinking the same way about pricing, or about hiring white men to work for their coöps, or about establishing retail stores, they would get a sense of unity and, all together, would have a voice. The second objective was to determine whether it would be possible for the Eskimos eventually to have a marketing agency of their own. We thought it would seem like a farfetched idea to them, and the most we hoped to do was to familiarize them with the thought." He pulled his parka over his head, and as we started toward the dining hall, he said, "Of course, we had a third objective—to find out how effective our own work had been. When we got on the plane at Montreal, we were terribly afraid that the conference would be a farce. A lot might be said, but if the Eskimos weren't discussing, arguing, and constantly questioning what was being said, it would be a failure. I began to feel that it would be a success when our plane stopped at Fort Chimo on the way up. A number of the delegates had had to wait there for about a week before flying up here, and our men at Chimo told us they did nothing but sit and talk among themselves about their coöps—about what they were doing and how they were doing it."

When we returned to the hall from lunch that last day, all the delegates and all the government representatives —except for Jon Evans, who was in bed with a high fever—were present, though many of them were still half sick and coughing. Even Wally Hill's child was back, looking pale and sleeping heavily in his father's arms. Snowden opened the session by asking the delegates to help compile a list of the things that white men were doing for the coöperatives and that the Eskimos, with proper training, could do for themselves. The government planned to provide such training, Snowden said, but first it had to know what was needed. It was finally decided that priorities should be given to courses in bookkeeping, motors and motorized equipment, electricity, English, and store management.

During the coffee break, I encountered George Koneak, who had been so busy that we had scarcely exchanged a word in days. I asked how he liked Frobisher Bay.

"I find it very interesting, because I have never been here for longer than an hour before, but I wouldn't want to live here," he said.

"Why not?" I asked.

He shook his head. "Too many people," he said. "It costs too much to live here. There are too many little places to go in the evening to spend money, and I am the type of man who would spend it."

Koneak was suddenly called to the back of the room to interpret, for Orange and Snowden were conferring there with Henry Annatuk, of Port Burwell. Orange was telling Snowden that an unknown disease, believed to be hepatitis, had killed most of the dogs at Cumberland Sound, on Baffin Island, about two hundred miles north of Frobisher. Only two hundred dogs had survived out of a dog population of a thousand, and there were five hundred Eskimos in that area, in desperate need of replacements. "The Eskimos' camps are anywhere from twenty to a hundred miles from the settlement of Pangnirtung," Orange said. "We had to set up an airlift to bring people from the camps to the settlement to get their supplies." Snowden thought that the Burwell Eskimos might want to sell some of their fat dogs to the government, which could fly them into Pangnirtung within a few days. Annatuk agreed to this proposal, and the deal was closed. Burwell would sell forty dogs, at ten dollars each, and Orange hurried off to arrange for their transportation.

When the session resumed after the coffee break, Henry Annatuk had an unexpected question: What kind of opposition could the coöperatives expect from the Hudson's Bay Company in the near future? Snowden fielded this one deftly to Dr. Laidlaw, who rose and said, "You should not spend time finding fault with the Hudson's Bay Company. Work hard instead to build your own business. You can expect prices in the Hudson's Bay stores to come down when you establish your coöperative stores. But one thing to remember is that, unlike the Hudson's Bay Company retail store, each coöperative store must stand on its own feet. It cannot depend on other coöperatives to maintain it. The Hudson's Bay Company can operate one store without a profit when it is competing with a coöp, and make it up someplace else, because the Hudson's Bay Company is very big. Last year, its operating profit was ten million dollars."

"Was that money from Eskimo land?" Napartuk wanted to know. "The Hudson's Bay Company is surely a strong and powerful mountain!"

"If it is a mountain, it was people who built the mountain," Dr. Laidlaw replied. "If the coöperatives are going to have strength, they must join with bigger coöperatives in Canada." He had a suggestion. He invited the Eskimos to send one of their number to a conference of his organization, the Coöperative Union of Canada, which was meeting in the South the next month.

There was a buzz of excitement when George Koneak translated the invitation, but no action could be taken immediately, for it was now dinnertime. However, we hurried through our meal and reassembled in the hall, though almost everyone still had his packing to do. Snowden opened the final session by announcing, "In exactly thirty minutes, this conference is going to end." He went on to say that the delegates must now pick the man who was to go to the meeting in the South, and that this man must be able to speak English, so the choice should be limited to the six Eskimo delegates who were bilingual. A written vote was quickly taken among the Eskimos, and Simonie was chosen.

When Simonie heard the news, he stood up, looking very proud. "So you're the people to choose me," he said. "I can go. Probably I will feel shaky, but I will try and do the best I can for you." He went on, "My head was half asleep at our first meeting, so I didn't say much. I don't want to hold you longer, but I'm very glad we had a chance to get together, and everybody is satisfied about this conference. Wherever you people are going, and many go a long distance, God bless you all!" There was huge applause as he sat down.

Donald Snowden looked at his watch, and I looked at mine. It was eight o'clock. We had been meeting continuously from eight-thirty in the morning until six-thirty at night, except for mealtimes and on Sunday, for seven days, and I was tired. Snowden looked exhausted. He said slowly to the group, "This conference has done many things for all of us. It has made friends of people who didn't know one another before. But the most important thing I've seen this week has been that the people of the North are beginning to control their own affairs. There's a long way to go, but I can't think how a better start could have been made, and the coöps were represented by as good men as there are in the North, or anywhere."

The Eskimos had stopped taking notes and were looking at Snowden. Suddenly embarrassed, he picked up a pencil and began making scratch marks on a sheet of paper before him. "We have seen what a week's meeting in the North, the first of its kind ever held, can do," he said. "In my work, I attend many meetings in many places, but I can't think of any as satisfying as this has been. I have never been at a meeting where people worked so hard. Thank you all for coming, and I hope we meet again soon."

Then Snowden stood up abruptly and said, "The First Conference of the Arctic Coöperatives is adjourned." George Koneak repeated his words in the Eskimo language, and the Eskimos quietly began gathering up their papers.

PART FOUR

A Change of Taste

I

FROM TIME to time, I inquired about the progress of the Eskimo
food canning experiments being conducted by the Industrial
Division. Early in 1964, I was told that the products were
about to be tried out in Eskimo communities and I was invited
to accompany officials of the Division into one of the testing
areas. Meanwhile, I had picked up quite a bit of information
about Eskimo eating habits.

The Eskimos, following the semi-nomadic way of life that
existed until almost now, would set off each day from their
tents or snowhouses to hunt or fish for that day's food. If a
man came back with more game or fish than his family needed,
the family at once shared it all with neighbors. In winter, as
a slight hedge against future hunger, some food was cached
under stones in the Eskimo camp, along trails, or near trap
lines, but storing enough to feed a family and its dogs over a
long period of scarcity was impossible. A single Eskimo or a
single dog would regularly consume about three pounds of food
a day, and a single family might include a dozen or so people
with seventeen or more dogs. Moreover, when food was plentiful, the Eskimos, with memories of past hunger, would gorge
themselves with no thought for the next day, until there was
nothing left. Recently, the Eskimos have depended more and
more on some items from the white man's store—tea, especially,

and flour to make bannock, which is filling but not nutritious. Other foods bought at Hudson's Bay Company stores would sometimes be consumed on the slow dog-sled journey from the store back to camp. Quite often, in late winter and early spring, there was no meat, no fish, and, finally, no bannock. Then the Eskimos suffered, sometimes starving to death before help could reach them. In recent years, Eskimos moving from lonely camps into permanent settlements have not solved the problem of malnutrition, for they have been doing less hunting, and their hunting skills have declined. Canada's Arctic administrators reluctantly believed that because of the Eskimos' preference for their own foods, their improvident eating habits, and their stoic acceptance of hunger, the only way to guarantee them an adequate year-round diet would be by giving them regular ration handouts of southern staples, the white man's food. In 1961, when I visited the Arctic for the first time, I heard this view challenged by Snowden, but that challenge seemed to me nothing more than a highly imaginative idea: to help the Eskimos drastically change their way of feeding themselves by giving them an economic stake in changing their habits. At the time, I thought the concept staggering—and implausible.

When I accompanied Snowden and Godt to the George River in 1961, our coöperative meeting was interrupted twice, for half a day each time, while the Eskimo men took their dog sleds down to the bay and hunted seals to feed themselves, their families, and their dogs. It was not simply a matter of the Eskimos' running low on food; they were out of it completely. Even their bannock supply had vanished, for their famished dogs had got into the flour bags. Finally, when we dug into some supplies we had on hand and prepared a meal for the Eskimos, it was the only meal they had that day.

The next morning, while Snowden, Godt, and I were waiting for the Eskimos to return from one of their hunting trips, we sat on boxes and tree stumps in the community hall, and talked about the shift that Canada's Eskimos were making from temporary camps to settlements complete with health stations and schools. It was then that Snowden said suddenly, "Eskimo food habits have been changing in the new settlements—for the worse. As the Eskimos get more and more cash in wages—for example, from government work, logging, and construction—they don't hunt and fish on their own so much, and must supplement their diet with purchased food. When they can't catch their own food, which is rich in the protein and fat they need in this cold climate, they eat bannock or our canned foods—which they don't always like the taste of, and which are too high priced and by no means always available, since they must be shipped from the South. I've been thinking for quite a while that what we need in the North is Eskimo canneries for Eskimo foods—walrus, seal, whale, fish, and the rest. An Eskimo-run fishery where there are plenty of whales, or where there is a regular seal-migration route, could bring in more fresh food than could be immediately consumed locally by humans and dogs. This could be canned on the spot and sent all over the Arctic, and Eskimos could buy it in stores. If they decided they didn't want to buy it, we could sell it in the South. A dollop of properly prepared beluga-whale meat on a cracker might make a fine hors d'oeuvre. Either way, the canneries would provide jobs and money for the Eskimos, but what I would hope is that they would like the canned food well enough to buy it themselves."

I said that Arctic canneries sounded like one of the craziest notions I had ever heard of. Snowden kept right on talking, introducing the subject of Erich Hofmann. "He has made a serious study of cooking methods all over the world," Snowden said. "He was once in the French Foreign Legion in Indo-China, where he served as chef for a general. He sleeps only a few hours a night, and in his spare time he experiments with canning and pickling everything that grows. No living thing is safe from him. He has a positively wild interest in preserving food. The Industrial Division is going to hire him, and I believe that within five years he's going to make it possible for the people of the North not only to feed themselves but to make a profit doing it." Snowden mentioned his intention of canning Arctic foods to a few of the George River Eskimos before we left there, and again when we were meeting with the people at Port Burwell.

Erich Hofmann went to work for the Industrial Division the following spring, and a sample of the seal meat he canned at Burwell in 1962 was served one night at dinner at the Frobisher Bay conference in March of 1963. Now, a year later, after two seasons of experimenting he had canned sufficient Arctic food, of different varieties, to make possible a large-scale survey to see whether the Eskimos liked the new products well enough to justify the establishment of regular Eskimo canneries. There had been some small-scale preliminary testing of canned Arctic meats for both men and dogs, but now sample cans of eighteen kinds of whale and seal products were being distributed in eleven widely separated settlements—in northern Quebec, in the District of Keewatin, and on Baffin Island. The Eskimos were being asked to sample the food and write their opinions of it anonymously on the backs of the can labels. I was told that if I wanted to learn something about the results, I could accompany Snowden and his party when they went north in March to pick up the labels and talk to the Eskimos.

Probably the most interesting results would come from the District of Keewatin, because the Keewatin communities contained both coastal Eskimos, whose traditional diet was sea animals and freshly caught land game, and inland Eskimos, who were believed to have taboos against eating food from the ocean. The Keewatin, two hundred and twenty-eight thousand square miles of land so bleak and empty that much of it is called the Barren Grounds, lies in the Northwest Territories directly north of Manitoba Province and is known for some of the coldest, windiest weather in the Western Hemisphere. Its only inland settlement is on the shores of a thousand-square-mile body of water called Baker Lake, and is the focal community for the Caribou Eskimos—so called because of their spiritual affinity with and physical dependence on the caribou. I was scheduled to fly by regular airline first to Ottawa and then to Churchill, a Hudson Bay port at the north end of Manitoba. From there, our party would take a chartered plane three hundred miles north and almost two hundred miles inland to Baker Lake Settlement. From Baker Lake, heading first east and then south, we would hop along the coast of Hudson Bay to four more Eskimo settlements: Chesterfield Inlet, Rankin Inlet, Whale Cove, and Eskimo Point.

IN OTTAWA, I had a chance to talk with Erich Hofmann, who was momentarily resting between Arctic canning excursions. I found Hofmann, a tense, slender, blond man with cold blue eyes, in a cubicle at Industrial Division headquarters. His desk was piled with canned goods, and the floor was entirely covered with equipment for a small portable cannery, with which, he told me, he had been able since 1962 to preserve about a hundred and fifty thousand pounds of experimental Arctic food. As he talked about food, in a heavy German accent, a fanatical light came into his eyes. "My portable cannery cost less than two thousand dollars and it can be set up in a day, yet it can preserve almost fifteen hundred pounds of food daily," he said. "I use propane gas to heat steam retorts. Improvisation is my watchword. Sometimes I have to melt ice for water and then boil it—a dreadful process. Mostly, my troubles are with weather. Bad weather slows down hunting and fishing, and heavy winds blow my tents over. The foods we are testing are seal and whale that I canned in various ways several months ago at Whale Cove, on Hudson Bay. Thirty-eight thousand pounds of seal had been stored there for me in a government freezer, and the Eskimos went out and caught me some beluga whales. Their wives worked late into the night preparing the whale meat for processing."

Hofmann sighed. "The people at Whale Cove are good workers, but when I asked them to help me, I learned that a miserable old man had put a taboo on the cans, so that nobody would touch them. These are primitive people, and a taboo is quickly imposed. I found out too late who the man was. I went away to the Tha-Anne River and canned some whale meat there for a while. Then I came back to Whale

Cove and made a friend of that man. I was then able to employ the people I needed for my canning operation."

I asked him to tell me about some of his other efforts at canning northern food, and he said, "I did my first experiments for the Industrial Division in Wood Buffalo National Park, in the Mackenzie District of the Northwest Territories. I canned buffalo pemmican, buffalo brisket, corned buffalo brisket, buffalo soups, and two kinds of buffalo sausage. Then I went farther north, to Inuvik, in the western Arctic, and canned salt herring, pickled herring, muskrat pepperonis, pickled smoked muskrat, and whale meat loaf. I intend to keep right on going. You have to know the Eskimos before you find out what they really want. They like caribou, and I make it so nice, like beefsteak. But there is not much caribou, and by law it cannot be sold through commercial channels. In the central Arctic, the people at Eskimo Point, some of whom still live in snowhouses, like spiced foods. At Whale Cove, I found primarily raw-meat eaters—a different people altogether. They have plenty of fresh meat all year round, which was why we picked the place for our canning. In the east, at Port Burwell, where the Eskimos catch many seals, they want the complete flavor of fresh seal in the cans. No spices. In the west, I added cloves to take away tastes and odors strange to the people. In my travels, I also put up lake trout, cod, whitefish, and Arctic char in cans. Char is like salmon, but not so juicy, and it sticks to the sides of the cans, so I had to add brine. As for seal, I have canned seal meat with onion sauce, also seal flippers and seal heart sweet and sour, and I make a very fine seal-liver pâté. I have to keep experimenting. I am also canning food for the Eskimos' dogs, and I've just found out that I did not put enough whale oil in the food for the dogs in the Mackenzie Delta. The Eskimos said the dogs sat down and made funny faces. In the Keewatin, the dogs thought there was enough oil."

As I rose to leave, Hofmann said, "The general opinion is that we have a market for our stuff. During your trip, you will see. I think we will have plenty of market in the North, and, besides, lots of people are asking for our products in the South, so we can send our surplus there. You will see."

FROM OTTAWA, our party of four flew twelve hundred miles north to Churchill, where we spent the night in a small wooden hotel. The temperature was twenty below zero, but I found the air crisp and invigorating. At nine-thirty the next morning, I waited in bright sunshine to board a large red single-engined, ski-equipped plane, the Canadian model called an Otter, which would carry our group around Keewatin. After the pilot and co-pilot had loaded the plane with valises, sleeping bags, and supplies, we climbed aboard and settled ourselves in metal seats on each side of a narrow aisle piled with equipment that we were to deliver at various points. Sitting in front of me was the other female member of our group, Sheila Stiven, a Scottish-born young woman who was the Industrial Division's crafts supervisor, and who had come along to discuss crafts activities with the Eskimos and with her field staff while we checked the results of the food tests. Across the aisle from me was Snowden, and in front of him was Gordon Gibson, who had recently been appointed Executive Assistant to the Minister of Northern Affairs and National Resources, Arthur Laing. Gibson, a pleasant, studious young Canadian in horn-rimmed glasses, was a graduate of Harvard Business School, and he was on his first Arctic inspection tour. All of us, including the pilots, were dressed in parkas, heavy pants, boots, and mittens.

The plane trembled with the effort to build power, everything loose inside it rattled and vibrated, and I caught my breath when we rose and I got a full view of the majestic Arctic landscape. Soon, peering out through my small window, I could see dark leads of open water in the ice of Hudson Bay and the small shadows of snowdrifts on the white ground below; the scene became a white-on-white abstract painting of limitless proportions. It was intensely cold in the plane at first. The cabin gradually grew warmer, but there was never enough heat for me to remove my parka. Just as I was wondering if our engine wasn't making a more than usually deafening noise, Snowden said, "The Otter sounds different from any other plane to me—like a great big washing machine. It's a wonderful plane, and I have a sense of security in an Otter that I don't get in any of the smaller aircraft they use up here." He pulled off his mitts and lit a cigarette. "One of these days, single-engined aircraft based in Arctic settlements will pay their own way by flying trappers to their trap lines and back and flying seal hunters out to the floe edge. Every year, the sled dog is of less importance in the North," he went on. "More and more, the Eskimos are following their trap lines not with dogs but with Skidoos and Autoboggans, and these little machines can be transported by plane right to the trap lines."

Snowden opened his dispatch case and pulled out some papers. "Each of the types of food we're trying out has been tested in a government laboratory and given a high rating for cleanliness and nutritional value," he said. "All of Hofmann's recipes will be given to Eskimo canning plants if production seems justified. Incidentally, the first time Eskimos ever bought food that they had formerly been used to catching themselves was in 1959, when we set up our fishery for Arctic char at Frobisher Bay. Now we've sent out a letter to the various Eskimo councils explaining that whales and seals, which can be caught easily in summer, have been put in cans for eating during the winter, when animals are hard to catch and the people are hungry for meat. We ask the people to tell us the truth about whether they like the meat in the cans and whether they like it well enough to buy it at the same price as the white man's food. We've had preliminary reports from Povungnituk and from Great Whale River. At Povungnituk, Eskimo fishermen took some of the canned food out in their boat, and when they were stranded by a storm, they ate it. Their opinion of it has been reported as 'most favorable.' Several white people at Povungnituk tasted it and were also enthusiastic. The Hudson's Bay Company storekeeper said that if the Eskimos liked it, he would accept it for retailing at a price lower than competitive southern canned goods. At Great Whale

River, the members of the Eskimo council met, tasted the food, and announced that they would like to can their own whale and seal meat and sell it through their coöperative store. They had definite preferences. They liked best whale meat cooked in gravy without salt or spices, and liked least the seal tripe cooked in gravy with rice, tomatoes, and onions. They advised that more fat be left on the whale *muktuk,* which is the outer layer of whale skin—an Eskimo delicacy. The council members also suggested that seals caught in summer and fall would be better for canning than spring seals, and that females would be better than males, and they told us that the younger the seals were, the better they tasted. They liked the Eskimo syllabic printing we put on our can labels. This is the first time they've been able to tell from the label what's inside a can."

Halfway between Churchill and Baker Lake, our pilot received an emergency radio call from a settlement we had just passed over, asking that we go back and pick up a family of four who had been passengers on a DC-3 that had developed engine trouble and had been forced to land. Our plane circled back on its course and, an hour later, came down bumpily on a small landing strip at the edge of Hudson Bay. An Otter, I now learned, has a normal passenger capacity of nine or more, and our baggage had to be pushed into the center aisle to free some unused seats behind us. A little girl, a woman carrying a baby, and a middle-aged man scrambled on board. The man, it turned out, was the school principal at Baker Lake. His wife told me, as she opened a handbag, took out a bottle, and gave it to the baby, that they had had to leave their luggage, containing most of their clothing, on the crippled plane, and had no idea when they would see it again. Our plane began to taxi for a takeoff but was brought up short when its skis scraped on something that felt to me like rock. The pilot later told me it was drift snow that had been blown and pulled by the wind until it was actually as hard as rock, and could easily have knocked the undercarriage off the plane. Now he turned the plane in circles, rolling and twisting it, in an effort to get it airborne. The skis shrieked, and we were shivering, because the co-pilot had opened his window to see better. A buslike vehicle that Snowden told me was a Snowmobile, which had tractor treads at the rear and skis in front, like the Skidoos and Autoboggans I had already seen in the Arctic, came slowly out from the settlement, and a Royal Canadian Mounted Policeman and several Eskimos got out. They began to rock our plane by hand to free it, and suddenly it bounced hard three times along the ground and we rose into the air.

THREE HOURS LATER, we arrived at Baker Lake, settling down on a landing strip marked off by red kerosene cans on the frozen ripples of the lake's surface. We were met by the administrator of the settlement, Barry Gunn, in a Snowmobile. After driving skillfully up the gently sloping shore of the lake and winding among snowdrifts and houses, he deposited Miss Stiven and me at a small prefabricated cottage. This turned out to have a gleaming modern kitchen and bath with every convenience but one—running water. Gunn explained that a vital valve was missing from the water system of the building, and that we had therefore been supplied with an enormous container of lake water, which we were to boil on the stove for cooking and washing. After we had done our unpacking, which consisted mainly of unrolling our sleeping bags onto the beds, we walked over to visit Gunn and his family, whose house was nearby. He was a short Scotsman with blond, wispy hair, a soft burr, and a mild look of surprise, who came to the Arctic some years ago as a schoolteacher and married an Eskimo girl. They had five children, and as Miss Stiven and I came in, Mrs. Gunn was giving the three older ones their supper. Gunn, Snowden, and Gibson were deep in a discussion of community problems, so I glanced over Gunn's small library, which seemed to be one of the best collections of books about the North I had seen. Half listening to the conversation, I soon realized that Gunn obviously had one of the most difficult areas in the Arctic to administer. Of a total of nearly five hundred Caribou Eskimos, three hundred and fifty lived in the settlement of Baker Lake itself, and the others were scattered in primitive camps along the surrounding lakes and rivers in a region so desolate and devoid of resources that, in the years before 1958, when the government assumed responsibility for their welfare, many of them died of starvation. Being on relief had further demoralized people already listless from years of inadequate diet. However, the Industrial Division had recently discovered that these primitive people possessed considerable artistic talent, and it was now encouraging them to do some remarkable stone sculpture—the sale of which, it was hoped, would improve their economic lot. Snowden was particularly interested in the Baker Lake Eskimos' reception of the canned products, because, as the most primitive of the inland Eskimos, they were believed to have strong taboos against eating food from the sea—or, as they called it, animals without legs. I had heard that the Caribou Eskimos were among the strangest people on earth, resisting change, stubbornly pursuing their wild way of life. Gunn said that he had not yet had a chance to conduct full-scale tests among them but that he was not optimistic, and he promised to send Snowden the full results later.

After a while, Gunn excused himself to take care of some administrative duties. Snowden and Miss Stiven were conferring with the crafts officer for the Baker Lake region, Gabriel Gély, a cadaverous Frenchman with a long red beard, so Gibson and I decided to take a walk around the community. The Baker Lake Eskimos were very different from any I had previously seen. Most Eskimos laugh readily, but these people were silent and rarely so much as smiled. Many looked prematurely old, and some, whom I guessed to be in their sixties, were, I later learned from Gunn, twenty years younger. Quite a few still wore the fringed caribou-skin parkas peculiar to this area, but far more wore ragged, threadbare parkas of clay-colored cloth, which heightened the tragic cast of their dark, sad faces. When Gunn took us all to call on the Roman Catholic missionary, Father Joseph Choque, in his study in a small red shingle church beside the lake, the priest leaned against the geranium-lined sill of a window that overlooked the water, and said, in a soft French accent, "Here, each family has lost someone—often its leader—from starvation. The stone carvings are a help, for some of the Eskimos now finally have money for food. But if they had more spirit, they would all have more courage to work and go hunting, and leaders would show themselves. Now every family thinks only of itself."

II

WE LEFT the following morning, taking Gély with us, and for two hours our plane followed a long, narrow estuary that connected Baker Lake with Hudson Bay. At the entrance to the ice-filled bay, we swung down to land at the small settlement of Chesterfield Inlet. As we descended, I could see a cluster of cream-colored frame buildings, which, I was told, included a Roman Catholic mission and a school for Eskimo students from Chesterfield and other parts of the Arctic. The buildings looked old-fashioned and comforting, rising two or three stories on a bleak and rocky point. When we got out of the plane, a vigorous middle-aged priest in a black parka strode toward us. After greeting Snowden, who introduced him to us as Father Ducharme, he asked us all to lunch at the mission. We were expected, for Father Choque, at Baker Lake, had told Father Ducharme over the shortwave radio the previous night that we would be spending the afternoon at Chesterfield Inlet. All through the Arctic, there is constant radio communication between settlements, especially at night when the priests and teachers set aside special hours to talk with one another. I sometimes stood outside in the profound quiet of the evening and felt that I could almost hear the chattering of innumerable radio voices over the invisible waves around me. The radios were most responsible for the tight-knit, small-town quality that united the widely scattered communities of each northern area into an entity.

Father Ducharme led the way to the mission, his steel-rimmed glasses steaming in the cold, his black habit beneath his black parka flapping about his booted ankles. On the ground floor of the two-story mission hospital, we entered a dining room, where the first thing that caught my eye was a bowl of white hyacinths standing on a sideboard below a crucifix that hung on a white wall trimmed in blue. We were joined by our pilots, and by a young lay teacher named George Demeule, and we all took our places at a long table, covered with printed oilcloth, which held platters of steaming food, presided over by the school principal, a nun named Sister Arcand. She was almost six feet tall and wore a sweeping tan robe, over which were the usual black-and-white garments of a nun; a heavy silver crucifix hung from her waist, and her head was encased in a short black headdress with a stiff white inset, which encircled a round and beaming face.

After a sumptuous meal of chicken soup, meatballs, several vegetables, plums, and homemade cake, Snowden turned to Sister Arcand and said, "Well, Sister, I am pleased to see you looking so healthy, since I hear you ate some of our canned whale *muktuk*."

There was a shout of laughter from Sister Arcand. "I was the only one who did—the other sisters didn't dare to," she said. "I was sick for three days. I couldn't look at food—not even coffee. Oh! Oh! I was so disturbed! They said it was my imagination. They asked me, 'Sister, haven't you ever been hungry?' Gracious! I would have to be *really* hungry! That smell of oil lingered all through the school!"

Snowden was grinning. "Sister, I'll bet you eat *muktuk* secretly every night," he said. Shaking her head, she laughed again, and removed her glasses to wipe her eyes. "What about the Eskimos? Have they tried it?" he asked.

"Oh, yes," she said. "We distributed all the cans to the adults in the community six weeks ago. The labels have been returned with their comments, and we have them here for you. We let the children have a taste, too."

Demeule spoke up. "It was like a party with the children. I had two grades in for coffee and cookies, and they passed up the cookies in favor of the *muktuk*. I was surprised at how much they consumed. About half of the children have been sent here from Igloolik, which is five hundred miles away, near Baffin Island, and they have seal and whale at home. I helped distribute the canned goods to the local adults, too. When they came here for our weekly movie, I made an announcement. I said, 'If you wish to go to the kitchen, Sister Arcand will give you some cans of new food.'"

"And did they go?" Snowden asked eagerly.

"Yes, yes, they all came," Sister Arcand said. "We had just enough cans to go around."

"Could I meet with the Eskimos?" Snowden asked. "Do you think they would talk?"

"Oh, yes, they like meetings," the teacher said. "It will only take a few minutes to round most of them up."

It was decided that the meeting would be held in the schoolhouse, a single-story, four-room building facing the bay, and we put on our parkas and hurried over there. We sat down at small desks in the primary classroom, and Snowden began looking over the can labels that Sister Arcand had saved for him. Soon we were joined by about sixty of the settlement's one hundred and forty Eskimos—old men, a few young ones who were not out hunting that day, and women of all ages, carrying babies in their colored parka hoods. Several boys in blue jeans and blue shirts came in, too. They were students at the school, and, with one of them acting as interpreter, Snowden explained to the Eskimos why we had come.

"It is very important to find out whether people in the North like these foods or not," he said. "Tell us what you *really* think of them." He began holding up the various products, which were all in twenty-ounce cans of the sort commonly seen in our own grocery stores. The various kinds of whale meat bore red-and-white labels on which was a drawing of an

Eskimo sitting in a kayak holding a harpoon aloft. Seal-meat foods had green-and-white labels, with a drawing of a standing Eskimo holding a seal on the end of a line. At the top of each can were two uncapitalized words—"ilkalu brand"—and below was the message in English:

PRODUCT OF CANADA
A fish delicacy produced by Canadian Eskimos under supervision of the Department of Northern Affairs and National Resources.

The contents of each can were described in Eskimo syllabics at the top of the label and in English at the bottom. Besides whale *muktuk*—smoked or plain in oil—and *muktuk* sausage, there were, among others, smoked whale meat, whale meat in gravy, whale meat in gravy with onions and tomatoes, whale meatballs, whale heart, smoked seal meat, seal meatballs, seal pemmican, seal flippers, and seal tripe in gravy.

Snowden held up a can of smoked seal meat and said, "Some of you didn't like it. Why?"

A young man said, "It's just meat. I can eat it, but I don't like it."

"That's the way I feel about it, too," Snowden replied.

Another man said, "I didn't like it, because I'd never eaten smoked meat before."

Snowden called out to the schoolboys, who were sitting in the back of the room, "You boys—you've tried some, eh?"

"'I like the smoked meat," one replied, in English. "But I like the seal meat with no gravy better. Just the meat. Only it tastes a little different from fresh meat."

An elderly Eskimo raised his hand. "The whale meat without salt tasted like earth," he said.

One of the women raised her hand, smiling self-consciously. "I like whale meatballs with onions," she said. "I like them warm."

A man added, "I like this one, too," and another said, "Yes, I can eat it."

Finally, Snowden held up a can of *muktuk* sausage, and it

was greeted with enthusiasm. "If you could buy this in the Hudson's Bay Company store, would you?" he asked.

"Yes! Yes!" several voices called out.

"Why does everybody like this?" Snowden asked.

"The taste," a woman said.

"How do you like to have it?" Snowden asked.

"Heated," said a young woman.

"Cold," said an elderly man.

Snowden asked the Eskimos whether they would buy *muktuk* sausage in preference to a Canadian commercial luncheon meat called Klik, and they all said they would.

When the Eskimos had departed, Snowden sat down with the interpreter, who went carefully through the comments on the backs of the returned can labels. Some of the labels bore comments in syllabics such as "I don't like this meat" or "Not for food," but many more bore the notation "ᘜᘪᗄ"—syllabics for "This tastes good." When Snowden totted up the results, he found that the three kinds of *muktuk* and the seal meatballs were the best liked, and the whale meatballs the least popular.

Since few Arctic airfields are equipped for night operations, we were anxious to leave Chesterfield Inlet before dark, but first Sister Arcand wanted to take us on a quick tour of the student quarters. It was a three-story building, in which we saw a boys' and a girls' dormitory, with neat rows of beds, and with young Eskimos standing at the doorways and smiling shyly when we walked in. We also peered into the dining room, which was furnished with long wooden tables and benches, and into a spotless kitchen, where a brown-haired young nun was busy at the stove. On the way out, Sister Arcand marched us into a large walk-in icebox—a suitable acclimatization for the biting outdoor air and for the frigid interior of our waiting plane.

As we buckled our seat belts, Gabriel Gély, who was sitting behind me, leaned forward and remarked on how readily the Chesterfield Inlet Eskimos had responded to Snowden's questioning. "At Baker Lake, I don't believe one Eskimo would stand up and talk like that," he said.

THE FLIGHT took us only forty-five minutes, but the sun had set and it had begun to get dark by the time we arrived at Rankin Inlet. This settlement was established in 1957 as the site of the North Rankin Nickel Mines, Ltd., which functioned only until 1962, when the quality ore ran out. The mine operators, instead of importing unskilled labor from the South, had recruited Eskimos from all over the Keewatin. Some of the Eskimos returned to their original settlements after the mine shut down, but more than three hundred remained at Rankin, and many of these had to go on relief. The Industrial Division had been considering the idea of establishing tourist camps or small industries to revive the economy, and Snowden wanted Gély to see some pottery that the Eskimos had produced at the instigation of a new crafts officer.

From inside a black Snowmobile that met our plane, I peered out at rows of small lighted houses, some with brightly illuminated vestibules made of translucent ice blocks. We pulled up in front of a very long wooden building, which looked lower than it actually was because snow had drifted almost to the tops of its windows. Directly beyond it was the large complex of the closed mine, its tall, narrow shaft building rising bold and black against the deep-blue sky. We got out and entered the long wooden structure, which had formerly been the mine bunkhouse and was now being used by the Department of Northern Affairs for a health station, a crafts workshop, and transient accommodations. Passing a neat white dispensary room, where an Eskimo woman was sitting on the edge of a high hospital bed, we walked down a long corridor with small bedrooms on both sides. Farther along, we came to a large central area that contained kitchen equipment, a handsome old pool table, and some wooden dining tables. Here we were served dinner by a buxom, red-haired woman with glasses, who introduced herself as Mrs. Frances Wipfler, and who told me that she and her husband had migrated to Canada from Munich several years earlier. After the meal, the men were assigned sleeping quarters in the bunkhouse, and Miss Stiven and I were shown to a nearby cottage, similar to the one we had used at Baker Lake, except that here the water system was working only too well. When I turned on the cold tap, the water gushed forth boiling hot, and in the course of our stay, which lasted two days, we learned that in order to get the water cool enough to brush our teeth, we had to leave the tap running all the time. Because the ground is partly frozen even in summer, Rankin has what is known as a "utilidor" water system, with pipes running from building to building above-ground inside foot-square wooden ducts. Directly inside each duct is a large metal pipe, and inside that are three smaller ones, carrying cold water, hot water, and steam; the steam and hot-water pipes keep the cold water from freezing—and, in fact, when the cold water in a house is used infrequently, as it was in ours, they give it a thorough heating.

After breakfast the next morning, we tramped through the snowy streets to the house of the Industrial Division's local projects officer, Ron Milligan. As it happened, Milligan was away, but his wife was waiting to give Snowden information on the food tests. It was Sunday, and a beautiful sunny morning, and we passed numerous Eskimo families on their way to church. The radiance of the day seemed to be augmented by the ringing of the church bells, and the red, green, and blue parkas of the Eskimos, with their children running along behind them, added to the loveliness of the scene. Outside the Eskimo houses, dog sleds and Skidoos sat side by side. Mrs. Milligan served us some coffee and Scotch shortbread, and while we were eating she told Snowden, in an accent that she identified as straight out of Aberdeen, that her husband had held a food-sampling session for Rankin's white residents one recent evening and they had liked the food so well that they had suggested that it be sold, finely chopped, in small cans for hors d'oeuvres in the South. She told us that the sampling by Eskimos had been done under the supervision of an Eskimo named John Ayarak, and that a home-economics teacher in Rankin had conducted further tests with Eskimo women.

That afternoon, following lunch at the big bunkhouse, Snowden sent Louis Voisey, a local white trapper whom he had hired as interpreter for the occasion, to fetch Ayarak, who was the maintenance man in the mine's boiler house—the source of Rankin's electricity.

Ayarak turned out to have a precise and practical mind; he responded with a quick nod when Snowden thanked him for distributing the food samples.

"How did you give out the food?" Snowden asked him.

"I gave it to the ones who would do what they were asked to do," Ayarak replied, through Voisey. "I went to eighteen houses. Some of the people looked worried when I came in, because they thought they would have to pay for the cans. I told them that these were being given out just for them to try but that later they would have to buy from the store. I said that this meat was from last summer, made in Whale Cove, and that if they had shot a seal and tried to save it that long it would have gone bad, but this way it could keep for a long time. I said that it was the first time Eskimo food had been canned for Eskimos, and that if they liked it, more would be made up. I said it was better to have this than canned food from the South, because the money earned would come back to them. Eskimos who can't hunt could work in the plant. The ones who are hunting would bring their catch to sell, and the others could buy after it's put into cans. That's what I told them."

"You did it just right," Snowden said. He asked Ayarak which people had received the samples.

Ayarak pulled a small notebook from his pocket and consulted a list of names neatly printed in syllabics. "Two I chose work for the government, one works for your crafts officer, one is a carpenter, two are on relief, one is fairly old and is sick, and so is not trapping, and the rest are trappers," he said. "I gave it to the ones who have lived on the coast and liked seal meat, to see if they liked it in the can also. Then maybe the inland people would hear how it was, and want to try. Some inland people, after they saw the label, wouldn't even look at the whale-meat can."

"If they hadn't known from the syllabics what was in the cans, they might have tried it, eh?" Snowden asked.

Ayarak nodded. "Yes, they might have eaten it," he said. "But all think it's a good idea to know what's in the can. I hear from Eskimos that when they buy a can and don't know what's inside and then don't like it, they are throwing money away."

"I want your help," Snowden said. "We made this label. What else should be on it?"

"It's O.K. without even a picture, as long as you have what it is and where it is made," Ayarak said. "That was the first time I'd ever seen syllabics on a can, and I told the Eskimos that it was the first time I'd ever seen it."

Snowden asked Ayarak how he himself liked the food.

Ayarak took off his cap and shyly patted his black hair, which was neatly parted. "There are seven in my family," he said, smiling, "and the small kids said it wasn't very good, but they don't know what's good or bad. The grownups and the ones at school age liked it. The first can we tried was plain *muktuk,* and we liked it, but some said if it had a little bit of fat, just a little bit, it would be very good."

"How about *muktuk* sausage?" Snowden inquired.

"*That*'s the one we liked," Ayarak said. "The thing nobody wants to see ever again was the insides of the seal or whale—the tripe. Eskimos never eat the guts, and they know it's guts and don't want to touch it."

Snowden asked Ayarak whether he would buy the food in the Hudson's Bay Company store if he could, and Ayarak replied that he would. He added that he thought Eskimos out hunting would like to take it with them, and went on, "Now they have no better food than biscuits or flour. This would keep them warmer."

A discussion of trapping followed, in which Voisey joined. Voisey was a husky man, a member of a family that, according to Snowden, was renowned up and down the coast of Hudson Bay for its trapping skill. Increasingly, both Eskimos and white men now hunt with Skidoos rather than dog teams,

Voisey said, and they travel in pairs instead of alone, as they used to do. "We used to take a couple of days to go forty or fifty miles, and on a Skidoo we can do that in one day," Voisey explained. "Skidoos are cheaper to maintain than dogs, too. It costs about a thousand dollars a year to feed a dog team if you have to buy the food, and I figure that gas, oil, and repairs for a Skidoo cost about six hundred. The disadvantage is that if you get stranded somewhere and have to walk in from your trap lines, you can't eat your Skidoo."

Ayarak said that there were twenty-seven Skidoos in Rankin, and perhaps only a dozen dog teams. "I have no dog team but have a share in a Skidoo," he explained. "If the Eskimos here had enough money, all would have Skidoos."

Snowden began sorting out the can labels that Ayarak had collected, and as Voisey translated the Eskimo syllabics written on the backs, Snowden kept a written tabulation of the comments. There were again many comments of "ᒪᒪᑐ"—"This tastes good"—and one Eskimo wrote that the *muktuk* "would keep us warm in winter." Several didn't like the flavor of the smoked meats, and the seal tripe was almost universally disapproved, drawing such comments as "No good," "Not clean," "Waste of time to make it," "Fix it up," and "Smells rancid." When Snowden counted up the opinions, he found that the different kinds of *muktuk* were again the most popular, with the seal meatballs, the canned seal meat, and the whale meat with gravy or with onions and tomatoes close runners-up.

Soon after Voisey and Ayarak had left, Frances Wipfler beckoned me from the kitchen, and we talked while she fixed the vegetables for supper. "I'm against that Eskimo food—all that fish stuff and whale," she said. "It smells. I can't stand the smell. Maybe you'd like it, but I don't think so. The night I opened the cans for the white people here to taste, I opened about fifty cans, until I had no more pots. I was tired like a horse. I had my whole oven full of stuff. The *muktuk* looked nice, like mushrooms, but so spongy." She locked her arms across her chest and sniffed. "The smell of seal or whale makes me sick. Like when Louis Voisey was here today, I smelled his sealskin boots as if the room was full of them. I thought I might have to leave. I am almost six years here, and I never get used to that smell."

Before our departure the next day, Snowden made two calls. The first was at a small cottage where Miss Nelson, the home-economics teacher mentioned by Mrs. Milligan, held classes for Eskimo children and housewives. Miss Nelson was a plump, alert young woman in high-heeled shoes, a trim gray flannel skirt, and a flowered blouse, and she wore pearl earrings and a matching pearl necklace. She settled herself firmly at her desk to tell us about the food testing she had carried out, and we sat at tables in front of her. In addition to the traditional black-board, the room contained sewing machines, washing machines, a small cookstove, an ironing board and iron, and tables covered with hand-weaving equipment that Miss Nelson had been using that morning to instruct some Eskimo children, who were now out at recess. "Frankly, I was rather disappointed in the way the whole food thing was handled," she said briskly. "I don't use an interpreter, so I put the cans out and let eight women who were here look at them. We heated up the contents and tasted all the way around. I hadn't a clue as to how the things should be served, so it was a bit of a shemozzle. I had never seen whale meat in that form, so I didn't know what to do with it. Serving instructions should be printed in syllabics on the cans."

"That's an excellent idea," Snowden said.

"What the Eskimos do with the foods and what we may think is the best way to use them may be entirely different," Miss Nelson continued. "I would have preferred to go into the homes individually and devise ways of preparing the food. It has possibilities, though; it really has."

The children were returning from recess, so we left. On the steps, Snowden turned and watched them racing into the class-room. "I like to think that the Eskimos would really be far better off if the food is a success," he said.

We went on to our next stop, the Hudson's Bay Company store, which was housed in a large, white building whose interior looked like that of an American supermarket, except that the stock was more varied, ranging from food, through shoes, to refrigerators. Snowden found the storekeeper, a youngish man named Casey Jones, and explained his plans for marketing the Eskimo foods. Jones had heard about the tests, and he was interested when Snowden produced a notebook in which he had made tabulations of Eskimo preferences and told him that he hoped there soon would be a small permanent plant canning foods to be sold all over the eastern Arctic.

"Have you any idea about prices?" Jones asked.

"A twenty-ounce can might retail for up to seventy-five cents," Snowden said.

"We sell a lot of canned goods, and I hear that some of your products are pretty good," Jones said. "As far as I'm concerned, I'd like to stock them, and I don't see why they shouldn't be a big success."

"I'm not too worried about it," Snowden said casually. "If it interests the country, it will stay here."

Talking to Jones, Snowden had been the detached government officer, but now I noticed that he was humming as we left the store and started back to the bunkhouse. We collected our luggage, said goodbye to Gély, who was going back to Baker Lake after observing the new pottery project, and were driven to the landing strip. Our red plane, which had seemed such a frail and chilly shelter at first, had by now become familiar and almost cosy. After twenty-five minutes in the air, we arrived at Whale Cove.

III

So FAR, as we had travelled around the Keewatin, I had been amazed at how unlike each other the Eskimo communities were, despite the lack of variety in terrain and resources. There was the desperate sadness of Baker Lake; the old-fashioned sunniness of the Chesterfield Inlet mission; and, at Rankin Inlet, the transitional, uncertain quality of an abandoned mine town. At Whale Cove, I knew, I would see something still different. The settlement, comprising some two hundred Eskimos, had been founded by the Department of Northern Affairs in 1959, after a number of Eskimos had died in scattered Keewatin camps from the hardships of a terrible winter. Eskimos who wanted to continue to trap and hunt were encouraged to settle at Whale Cove, which had been selected because it had a good harbor and good supplies of seal, whale, fish, and game nearby. Here, inland Eskimos were introduced to coastal living and to concepts of communal organization and hygiene. At the beginning, the whole population had been on relief, but by 1962 the number was down to a handful, and the Eskimos of Whale Cove had the first and only coöperative retail store in the Keewatin District.

Our plane landed far out on the harbor ice. We had started walking toward the settlement when a machine resembling a large yellow dragon rumbled toward us. It was one of the largest vehicles I had ever seen, and I learned that it was known as a Muskeg Tractor. Miss Stiven and I climbed up beside the Eskimo driver—a handsome, round-faced young man with a crew cut, who looked vaguely familiar to me—and the four men hopped into a massive open wagon that was hooked on behind. Halfway to the shore, though, our conveyance stalled, so we got out and began walking again. It was thirty below zero, the coldest it had been on the trip so far. My nose grew so numb that I felt I must wiggle it hard to keep it from freezing.

That evening at the cottage of the local administrator, where Miss Stiven and I were spending the night, from the broad front window I watched Eskimo children playing on the swings of a school playground across the way. Though it was after ten, it was not very dark, but the temperature had fallen even lower. The children's laughter rippled musically in the sub-zero air as they swung higher and higher. Beyond, at the foot of a gently sloping hill studded with the small houses of the settlement, the land curved around a sheltered cove. In the clear night air of the Arctic, electric lights sparkle, and at the edges of this tiny community it was easy to see where the lights stopped and the dark blue of the uninhabited, empty land began.

In the morning, after breakfast, we went down to the coöperative store, which occupied part of a large steel warehouse by the water. The place seemed crude by comparison with the luxurious Hudson's Bay Company store at Rankin Inlet, since it consisted simply of a partitioned-off section of the warehouse, in which counters and shelves held food, clothing, tobacco, ammunition, Skidoo parts, and larger items such as outboard motors. A white man standing behind a cash register introduced himself as Bernard Fredland, head of the Intercontinental Mission at Whale Cove, and told us he had been a missionary in the North for the past fifteen years. He said that, since he spoke Eskimo, he was acting as storekeeper for the coöperative until a young Eskimo who had been selected for the job could complete a training course in the South. Three Eskimos were in the store, one of them being the attractive young man who had driven the tractor out to meet our plane the previous day. Now I recognized him as Celestino Magpa, whom I had met the year before at Frobisher Bay where he had asked the fascinating question about whether Eskimos could get a tax rebate on the purchase of Skidoos, just as farmers in the South received tax allowances on the purchase of harvesting machinery.

Magpa shook my hand, smiling. "I knew it was you, but I wait to see if you remember me," he said, in English.

I said I hadn't forgotten his question at the conference, and had often wondered where he got the idea.

From beneath the counter he produced the catalogue from Eaton's—and said, "I was thinking about that question for two years. The Eskimo doesn't use the Skidoo just for fun but for hunting and trapping. I noticed that Eaton's had two machinery prices—one for farmers, one for other persons. I asked someone to explain, and I thought of that question."

Magpa acted as interpreter for the two other Eskimos, whom he introduced as directors of the coöperative. (There were four directors in addition to Magpa, but two were away hunting.) Snowden discussed the operation of the store, the food-testing program, and the projected canning operation. He said that the Department of Northern Affairs was considering the construction of a small permanent cannery at Whale Cove, and observed that since canning is a summer industry, the building might serve as a crafts center in winter. Magpa interpreted in a sharp, firm voice, and periodically fired questions at Snowden, referring to a notebook he carried. His questions were those of an efficient businessman in a hurry to get things done: Would Erich Hofmann be coming to can, and, if so, when, he wanted to know, in order that the seals could be hunted at the proper time and the meat would be ready for Hofmann. Would other settlements want canned dog food, and, if so, how much? Magpa himself had some doubts about the current method of preparing meat for dogs. "A lot of guys told me that the dogs don't like ground meat, and get thinner and thinner," he informed Snowden.

Snowden and Magpa next began examining labels from cans

of food that had been tested among the Eskimo families of Whale Cove, and it was apparent that their preferences were going to parallel those of the other Keewatin communities. Everybody liked the *muktuks*, and hardly anybody liked the whale meatballs or the tripe.

Snowden asked, "What would the coöperative's directors think about selling some of our remaining stock of *muktuk* sausage in the store here?"

His suggestion was instantly approved, and it was decided to put the food on sale the following morning.

"How about a little sausage for us all right now?" Snowden suggested.

A can was brought in from the stockroom, and since no one seemed to be able to lay hands on a can opener, Magpa picked up a large, shiny, new hatchet from a shelf and cut the top open. This was my first opportunity to taste any of the Eskimo canned foods, other than the canned seal meat at the Frobisher conference, which I had not liked, and I took a deep breath and bit blindly into a piece of the gelatinous-looking, cream-colored sausage, which was passed to me on the point of a hunting knife. It turned out to have a crisp, chewy texture and the mild flavor of lightly spiced mushroom, along with another taste, which I had never encountered before. The second time around, I was as eager for my share as the others.

When the can was empty, Snowden turned it slowly around in his hands and asked whether the Eskimos who had migrated to Whale Cove from inland communities liked seal and whale meat.

Magpa consulted with the directors. "The people from inland like the *muktuk* very much," he said. "I myself tried it out on one young man who told me he didn't like seal or whale meat. So I say, 'O.K., come home for supper.' My wife cooks, and he doesn't know it is whale, and likes."

I was curious to know what other sorts of canned foods the Eskimos were already familiar with, and Fredland told me that in the store orange juice and apple juice sold very well, and so did sardines, corned beef, and luncheon meats. Cans of peaches, pears, and apricots that came in by ship during the summer were always gone before Christmas, and then the Eskimos would buy dried fruits.

Presently, Fredland and Snowden went into the storeroom to check the stocks of Eskimo food, and I asked Magpa to tell me a little bit about himself.

He cracked his knuckles once or twice, eyeing me guardedly, with his head cocked to one side. Then he smiled, and said, "I was born at Arctic Bay, on Baffin Island, in 1937. Someone adopted me when I was a little baby. All my family are still alive, but I never saw. I was taken south to Igloolik by dog team, and when I was ten, I went to the school at Chesterfield Inlet." He paused to light a cigarette, and continued, "Then I was working at the mission, starting when I was fifteen, for four years—fixing pipes, driving, anything. The mine started in Rankin Inlet, and I worked for three years three hundred and fifty feet underground. I liked that best."

I asked why.

He scratched his head, and finally said, "When we work on the surface, it is stormy and blowing in winter, and in summer it is too warm to work. Underground, it is always the same. After the mine closed, the Department of Northern Affairs asked for a powerhouse operator at Rankin, and after one year there I became powerhouse operator at Whale Cove. I am also interpreter for the department and the first president of the Whale Cove coöperative, which I organized. I didn't go hunting the whole year, but I read anything—something different every day."

He cracked his knuckles again, and suddenly asked, "Would you come to visit my house and my family?" I said I would, whereupon he declared, "Then we will go now."

We left the store, and when we had walked perhaps a hundred yards, he stopped. "Want to see my boat?" he asked.

When I nodded, he opened the door of a large shed, in which the Muskeg Tractor and several other vehicles belonging to the department were stored. At the far end, sitting on wooden horses, was a beautiful little white motorboat with red trim.

"I bought the boat for seven hundred and ninety-five dollars from Casey Jones, at Rankin Inlet," Magpa said. "He had it two years. I use it to take my wife and five children out for rides. I also have a Skidoo. All the Eskimos with enough money would buy Skidoos. One of the Eskimos with me at the store today, Thutungi, had a good dog team before he got a Skidoo, but then he forgot all about his dogs and gave them away." Magpa added that his Skidoo had cost seven hundred and sixty-five dollars, and I realized that I was in the presence of the Keewatin's foremost Eskimo expert on capitalism.

"How do you manage to do all this?" I asked.

Magpa stared at me, seeming puzzled for the first time. "So. I've been working all my life," he said quietly. "I work eight hours, five and a half days a week. When I deduct taxes, I sometimes have three hundred or more dollars a month left."

Magpa's house was a two-room wooden cottage, the two rooms being a small bedroom and a big kitchen. A large German shepherd dog, which, he explained, was just a household pet—an almost unheard-of luxury among Eskimos—padded toward us as we entered. Magpa's wife, a plain, good-humored woman with a broad face, stood by the kitchen sink, smiling. Magpa and I sat down at the kitchen table and talked for a few minutes, and he told me that he planned to buy a three-bedroom house soon, for thirty-five hundred dollars. By now it was almost time for me to join my party for lunch, and I said goodbye.

That evening, the Eskimos of Whale Cove—there must have been almost a hundred present—came to the coöperative store to hear about the canned-food program. Magpa sat on a counter to interpret for Snowden, who was standing behind it with Gibson and Miss Stiven.

Snowden began by asking how many people in the room had helped make the food products used in the tests, and hands were raised all over the room. Walking over to a large wall map of Canada, he showed the people where the canned samples had been sent and told them what the various communities had thought about them. Then Snowden outlined plans for a permanent cannery at Whale Cove, and the Eskimos listened with close attention.

A man with a drooping mustache said loudly that he had "liked so much the canning work" of the previous summer, and a man behind him repeated his words. After translating these two remarks, Magpa added one of his own. "A lot of us wondered how it would be, the canning, when it first started, but it seems to work out very well now," he said.

After some discussion of food preferences, Snowden called on Gibson, who said that the Minister of Northern Affairs had asked him to tell the Eskimos how very happy the department was at the way things were going at Whale Cove.

When Gibson had finished speaking, Snowden suddenly shouted, "Whose store is this?"

Magpa translated, and the Eskimos laughed, and shouted back *"Uvaguk!"* ("Ours!")

"Do you like the idea of having your own store?" Snowden asked.

The Eskimos cried *"Ayii!"* ("Yes!"), and everyone was still smiling as the meeting broke up, and they all went out the door and up the hill to their houses.

The next morning, before our party left for Eskimo Point, which was to be our last stop, Snowden, Gibson, and I went to the coöperative store to see how well the new food was actually selling. Soon a woman came in and bought four cans of *muktuk.* She was followed by two men, who bought powdered milk, biscuits, and three more cans of *muktuk.* Two women accompanied by a little boy moved up to the counter to order a large supply of staples; at the end of the order I heard the word *"muktuk,"* and several cans were added. This group was followed by a woman in a caribou-fringed parka. She collected an order of rolled oats, flour, biscuits, powdered milk, tobacco, cigarette papers, and several cans of soup, and then she hesitated. After a minute, she asked for four cans of *muktuk* in oil, two cans of seal meat cooked in gravy, and two cans of *muktuk* sausage.

"We're in business," Snowden said softly. "When you get a woman from the inland country to buy whale and seal meat, things are really changing."

Within a few minutes, we were bound for our plane in the big tractor with Magpa. In the wagon behind it were four mammoth bales of white-fox furs; the Whale Cove coöperative was sending the furs, which were valued at more than ten thousand dollars, to the Hudson's Bay Company's fur auction in Montreal. When the bales had been loaded onto the plane, we took off.

WITHIN AN HOUR we landed at Eskimo Point, a relatively old settlement, with a population of almost two hundred inland and coastal Eskimos. The food tests there had been conducted by the Anglican minister, an athletic-looking young man named John Marlowe, who greeted us at the door of his house wearing a gray sweater over his black habit and clerical collar. The results seemed to be similar to those we had been given elsewhere. While the Reverend Mr. Marlowe was talking, I glanced out his living-room window, from which I could see dog teams and Autoboggans intermingled on the adjacent road. Beyond, far out on the ice of Hudson Bay, was the low, round dome of an Eskimo snowhouse—the first I had ever seen. Mr. Marlowe was now telling Snowden about the abundance of life in nearby waters. "At the end of June," he said, "you can see the Arctic char coming down the Maguse River, fifteen and twenty together, their silvery fins sparkling in the water."

"I am convinced that the feeding of the Arctic population must be based on the wealth of food in these northern waters," Snowden said. "If the Keewatin can feed its people, why, surely, the whole Arctic can be made self-sufficient."

LESS THAN twenty-four hours later, we were flying toward Churchill. Snowden reached into his knapsack, pulled out a can of fruit juice, and opened it. While he was drinking it, he said, "Well, the experts told us that it was highly unlikely that Eskimos would ever pay cash for natural food caught by other Eskimos, and we've seen them doing it. The experts also told us that inland Eskimos would never eat coastal food, and now we know that the inland people who have tried our food have liked it. Some of us think that the Arctic could yield enough food, year in and year out, to feed and make fat and healthy far more people than live in the North today, especially as we find ways to use every scrap of raw material. After all, the Japanese harvest large quantities of plankton from the sea, and the Russians, we're told, have evolved deep-sea-fishing techniques so efficient that nothing at all is wasted. I simply don't know how much food the Arctic can produce, and neither does anyone else, but I believe that within five years foods that are totally strange to us, and not very damn familiar to the Eskimos, either—after all, they'd never heard of whale meatballs before— will be on the shelves of all the stores in the North. And I'll bet they'll sell so well that there won't be enough to go around, which means that more and more Arctic people will be employed in food processing."

When we landed at Churchill, Gibson and I transferred to a plane for the South. Miss Stiven went off to inventory Churchill's crafts warehouse, and Snowden remained behind to finish up his work. A few weeks later, on his return to Ottawa, he sent me word that the coöperative store at Whale Cove was selling four times as much Eskimo food as tinned meat from southern Canada, and that in a month the Eskimos had bought four hundred cans—half the supply on hand. He also reported that Barry Gunn had obtained a surprisingly favorable response to canned seal and whale meat from the inland Eskimos at Baker Lake.

The next news I had of Snowden was that he had left the Department of Northern Affairs, feeling that his groundwork had been done, and had gone off to head the Extension Service of the Memorial University of Newfoundland, bringing its educational opportunities to the people in that underdeveloped area. Jon Evans, who succeeded him as chief of the Industrial

Division to the Department of Northern Affairs, informed me
that a total of forty-five hundred can labels bearing Eskimos' comments on the food had been received in Ottawa, and that
Erich Hofmann had produced thirty thousand more cans of
Eskimo food at Whale Cove for ultimate sale in Hudson's Bay
Company and Eskimo coöperative stores. Hofmann had also
stirred up a thousand or so more cans of his imaginative samples, which this time included corned and roasted seal meat,
whale-meat goulash, sweet-and-sour whale meat, whale-meat
paste, walrus meat in Spanish sauce, sealburger in tomato
sauce, pickled whale flippers, and walrus flippers vinaigrette.

A few days after I had heard from Evans, I was standing
in the kitchen of my New York apartment and wondering
what to have for dinner. I opened a can of seal meatballs—
part of an array of Eskimo foods that I had brought back all
the way from Whale Cove wrapped in my sleeping bag, at
an excess-baggage charge of six dollars and eighty cents. I
heated the seal meatballs in a saucepan and took a taste. I
decided I didn't care for them. So I opened a can of *muktuk*
sausage, made from that outer layer of whale skin that the
Eskimos consider so delicious, and ate a piece on the end of
a fork. It still tasted fine to me—just fine.

PART FIVE

No Past History

I

It was my special dream some day to go back to George River. I wanted to see what had happened to the one hundred and thirty-five Eskimos who had made the momentous decision I had witnessed in the lonely log cabin in 1961 to abandon the nomadic life of their ancestors, form a new community, build permanent houses and send their children to school.

George River, the pilot project which the Canadian government hoped would provide the answer to the dilemma of how the Eskimos could remain in their home country and be independent, was unique in my experience; it had no past, no old buildings, and was to be inhabited by individuals with no pre-conceived ideas about community life. I had last seen it from the air as we were flying away, and the site on the bank of the frozen George River was revealed to me then as a very large slope, bounded on three sides by high black rock hills. The sun had shone over a hill to the east, casting an iridescent light across the snow and across George Annanack's small fishing boat, frozen fast in the river at a lop-sided angle. The flimsy sawmill, and the log cabin, which had seemed so large when we were meeting inside, had appeared small and lost in the great emptiness all around them.

At the Frobisher Bay conference, Don Pruden, the Industrial Division's projects officer now permanently stationed at

George River, had urged me to return and see how it had changed. I knew this big, friendly man well enough to have respect for his keenness of mind and depth of human perception, and since he spoke Eskimo, I would not need an interpreter. Furthermore, his wife, Gwen, was the schoolteacher at George River.

I had always assumed that I would carefully plan my return, but as it turned out, my visit was totally unplanned and unpremeditated. In the summer of 1964, I flew north with some Canadian officials to visit a remote lake on Baffin Island. When we arrived there, ice floes prevented our plane from landing, and so we headed south again, the mission unaccomplished. On my way home, when the plane stopped at Fort Chimo, I decided on an impulse to get off and charter a plane to take me to George River. I arranged with the pilot not only to fly me there but to pick me up again two days later, in time to catch the next scheduled southbound plane at Chimo for home. The area administrator, Lucille Beauchamp, radioed George River about my impending arrival, and I changed into my summer Arctic outfit of blue jeans, rubber boots and parka. I packed a few extra clothes in my knapsack, and carrying that and my sleeping bag, I set out in a dilapidated bus driven by Mrs. Beauchamp for the lake from which the plane would take off. Fort Chimo, a settlement that I had seen before only in winter, looked in summer like a small, sad western cow town without cows—dusty, with a few low trees, and several dirt streets lined with single-story prefabricated houses. As we chugged along, I saw a white frame Hudson's Bay Company general store, a coffee shop in an old quonset hut, two small churches, and, down by the waterfront, Eskimo tents, several warehouses and docks. At the end of a crazily bumpy road that chewed its way for a mile through scrub trees and rocks, we came to my plane, a shiny red-and-white Cessna, resembling a small, elegant car on pontoons, which was anchored in a lovely little lake. There were seats for three passengers, one beside the pilot, and two behind him, and as usually happens in the Arctic, where chartered-plane costs had risen to a hundred and twenty dollars an hour, the charter expenses were being shared by two other people, who had been waiting for a third party to come along. One was an Eskimo boy named Joshua Annanack, whose father, Josepie Annanack, I had met when he attended the Frobisher conference as George River's representative. Joshua, who was returning home from a stay at Chimo, was in one of the two back seats, and I climbed in beside him, where we sat with our shoulders braced against several sleeping bags, which are required equipment on all small Arctic aircraft in case of a forced landing. The other passenger, sitting in front with the pilot, was Fred Lueder, the Industrial Division's Area Coöperative Officer who was going on to Port Burwell.

As our plane taxied down the lake and rose lightly into the air, Lueder, a blond, jovial man, said to the pilot, "Try not to crash, will you?" Then he lit a cigar, turned halfway around and commenced shouting local news to me over the roar of the engine. "Nothing much going on this week at George River but fishing," he said. "How long has it been since you were there? Three years? You will find everything changed. The coöperative has done well right from the beginning, and it has added a retail store. I go there next week, when the big cargo boat makes its annual delivery—three hundred and sixty-seven tons of supplies this time. What was at the settlement when you were there?"

"Just the community hall, the sawmill, and an old fishing boat," I said.

"The sawmill is still there, and the coöp is going to build more fishing boats," Lueder said. "When we built a warehouse this year, we had to keep the sawmill going continuously. The logs come a hundred and twenty miles down the George River, and half of them were lost because the boat that was supposed to pull them from the current and ashore broke down and they went out to sea. Even so, eleven houses were built, making a total now of twenty-four. Until Christmas, everybody was busy building, but then caribou showed up not far away in especially large numbers. Then most of the Eskimos went hunting about a hundred and fifty miles south along the river. In the spring, six families went to the Labrador coast on an experimental, organized seal hunt. Supplies were brought to them by aircraft. The Eskimos caught about a hundred and ninety seals, and the coöp sold the seal skins for twenty-eight dollars each." He paused to relight his cigar. "Do you remember Willi Imudluk?" he asked.

I was silent for a moment, recalling my previous arrival at George River. I remembered how like toys the Eskimos' sleds and dog teams had looked from the air before our plane had landed on river ice above Willi Imudluk's Hudson's Bay Company outpost, and how when we had landed, I had been surrounded by smiling men with ruddy brown skin and black hair, all shaking my hand.

"Last time, Willi was the first person I met when I got off the plane," I said. "My Eskimo sealskin boots, which I still have, were made by his wife, Selima."

"Willi has moved to George River," Lueder said. "The coöp decided to establish a retail store, and, after a close vote, Willi was elected store manager. The Hudson's Bay outpost was closed as there would not have been enough business for both stores in that area. My job was to help price the goods and train the manager, but Willi had already had nine years of experience. He does all his accounting in syllabics and keeps very good books. On his own, Willi is also starting a tourist camp up the river. He bought the Hudson's Bay Company buildings, and is moving them to a beautiful island in the George twenty-five miles from the settlement. If he can make a go of it, it will be the first Eskimo-owned-and-run tourist operation in the North."

I leaned my head against the windowpane and closed my eyes. It was only three years since Willi had said to us at dinner after the final coöp meeting that some day he would live at George River and send his children to school.

I opened my eyes. We were travelling at a hundred and ten miles an hour at an altitude of about two thousand feet, and I could see the shadow of our plane clearly below, moving over scrubby green and yellow vegetation, gray rocks, and rusty brown water holes. The Arctic in summer was a new world to me—low and rolling and soft-colored, with wonderful hills, shading from lavender to mauve to deep purple, easy on the eyes, with none of the glare that made sunglasses indispensable in winter. The water in the wide rivers, placid from above, was a clear, rich blue, but Ungava Bay, to our left, was a dark greenish hue, with little white eddies and of so great a size that no land was visible beyond. We approached a broad, winding river with sloping banks. "The George River," Lueder said. We began to descend. As the plane banked, all the sleeping bags and other gear behind Joshua and me fell on us; by the time we had disengaged ourselves, the plane had landed in the river and was taxiing bumpily across the water. We were moving into a large cove, around a bend from the mainstream of the George River. We passed an anchored Eskimo fishing craft, called a Peterhead boat, with a cabin and a mast that rose high above the water, and we stopped. Coming toward us was a big canoe with an outboard motor, and standing up in the canoe were five or six Eskimo men, their parka hoods down and their faces vaguely recognizable to me even at a distance. In the center of the boat, sitting erect with her arms folded across her chest, was an attractive brown-haired young woman who was peering anxiously in my direction.

The canoe came alongside the plane; the pilot opened his door and climbed out on a pontoon. Joshua and I handed him our baggage, which he swiftly passed into the canoe. I moved slowly across the slippery surface of the pontoon and stepped into the canoe, watching my feet carefully. When I looked up, it was into the smiling, intelligent, familiar face of Willi Imudluk.

II

WILLI SHOOK my hand with an enthusiasm that surprised me.
I remembered him as remote and austere in comparison with
most of the other Eskimos. Otherwise, he looked just as I
remembered him—close-cropped black hair, deep-set eyes, long
nose, and pointed chin. Before I could sit down I shook each
of the hands that were thrust shyly toward me. I recognized
a young man named Mark Annanack, who motioned to a
cleared place in the canoe and said, in English, "Sit here."
The white woman who had sat quietly while the Eskimos
were greeting me, now smiled and said, "I'm Gwen Pruden.
We didn't know until this afternoon that you were coming,
and Don left yesterday with Brian, our seven-year-old, to camp
out on the Ungava coast. I expect Mark could interpret for
you, but I imagine you really want to see Don. You could
go to his camp, which is three hours from here by canoe, or
else the pilot can drop Don a message telling him you are
here, and he will come back."

I had certainly counted on Pruden's being at George River.
"I'm afraid I've only two days here," I said.

"Well, then, we must get Don back, because if you went
to the camp and the weather changed, you might be stuck
there a week or two," Mrs. Pruden replied. Anticipating the
problem, she had placed a message to her husband in a sealed

tin can, which she now gave the pilot, who agreed to drop it at Pruden's camp. "If Don waves his arms, that means he is coming home, and you can radio me," Mrs. Pruden told the pilot. I protested at the trouble I was causing, and she laughed. "When Don's away, I'm in charge, and something's always happening," she said.

The plane departed, and our canoe headed for shore. For years, I had carried in my mind my first view of George River: after hours of travelling down a narrow trail in an ice-choked river, we had turned a bend and seen, first, a wispy curl of smoke in the half dark of the Arctic evening, and then the tiny cabin in the middle of a snowy wilderness. The view I now beheld bore no relation to that memory. I saw a small dock and a cluster of little pale green buildings nestled into the side of a brown hill. My eyes searched for something familiar and found the frail wooden frame of the sawmill roof, but added to it was an extension larger than the original structure. Finally, looking up to the top of the bank as we approached the shore, I saw the old log-cabin community hall that I re-membered. On the wall facing the water was a big sign with the word CO-OP painted in large red letters on a white back-ground. Towering behind the hall, which did not seem big enough to have possibly held one hundred and thirty-five peo-ple, was a new square frame structure. Beyond were the gently terraced lines of green, boxlike houses. I turned uncertainly toward the Eskimos, who were watching me, and who in-stantly understood my confusion. Willi spoke to Mark, who said to me, "The hall where meeting was held when you come before is now coöp store. Behind, we build a warehouse for store supplies."

The canoe's motor was turned off, and we glided toward the shore. Everyone jumped out and waded through the shal-low water to the beach. Now I could hear the steady shriek and whirr of the sawmill. Four men who were lifting heavy logs and feeding them into the saw paused long enough to wave at us when Mrs. Pruden and I started climbing the slope from the river. We had to stop frequently while I shook hands with

Eskimos, but Mrs. Pruden hurried me along, past the store and a schoolhouse, past green houses from which Eskimo women and children were emerging, across a small gully and up another incline to where four frame buildings stood in a row by themselves. These were governmental structures: first the Prudens' house, overlooking the entire community; next, a house for a new school principal, who had not yet arrived; then, Pruden's office; and at the end of the line, a building to accommodate visiting nurses and other transients. Mrs. Pruden ran up the steps of her husband's office, and I followed into a bare room furnished with a desk, two chairs, and a familiar looking gray radio—the one that had been brought by dog sled three years ago with us from Willi Imudluk's outpost and reassembled at the community hall for use during our meetings. It was still the only regular means of communication between George River and the outside world, including Fort Chimo and Port Burwell. Mrs. Pruden swiftly turned it on, and I heard the voice of the plane pilot calling George River. He told us he had dropped the message to Pruden, who had waved his arms to indicate he was coming home.

When we came down the steps from the office and started back to the Prudens' house, a small group of Eskimo men standing at the top of the incline moved hesitantly in my direction. In addition to Willi Imudluk and Mark Annanack, I recognized Mark's older brother, Stanley, whom I remembered as having the largest teeth and greenest eyes I had ever seen, and who had been selected by the coöp members at that earlier meeting for the all-important job of running the fish freezer at the mouth of the George River. He was now the president of the coöperative, and a little behind him, walking slowly up the hill, was the stocky figure of that elder statesman, George Annanack, whose broad, seamed face with its long, mustached upper lip now reminded me of an aging lion. "They want to show you around," Mrs. Pruden said. I asked Mark if I could hire him as my interpreter until Pruden returned. He scratched his head and spoke to the others in Eskimo. There was an *"Aa-ah"* from the men, Willi and Stanley nodded,

George said something in his deep voice, and Mark replied to me, "Holy Smoke! I never done it before! O.K., I try."

The first thing I asked to see was the coöperative store. Willi told me it was being repainted and repaired, but said we could have a look. Walking toward it, I noticed tall poles that held modern, rectangular street lights at their tops. Power lines stretching from pole to pole made a pattern in the air above the dirt paths in four or five graduated parallel tiers from the water up the large slope on which the community rested. Willi pointed out the power house, a small shed close by the store, and said everyone had electric lights now. Two twenty-five kilowatt diesel motors provided the community's electricity. I noticed that among the neat new houses there were log and canvas tents and an occasional shack made from scraps of lumber, metal, and insulating material. The shacks, along with empty oil drums, which are to be found in rusty heaps wherever there are people from one end of the Arctic to the other, scarred the landscape here as they had at every northern settlement I had ever been in. I was surprised to see a few Eskimo dogs running loose. I well remembered the long discussion at the earlier meeting, in which it had been agreed that, to avoid contamination of the water supply, among other things, something must be done about the dogs, and the building of a compound had been considered preferable to tying the animals up. I also remembered how Pruden's son, Brian, had been mauled and badly injured by them shortly before the Frobisher Conference.

Before I could ask about the dogs, Willi was unlocking the heavy door of the warehouse. It was a large, windowless chamber, almost empty, with a few bright-red gasoline cans hanging from the rafters and a small pile of flour bags against the wall; in a corner, I made out boxes of soap, cereals, dried milk, and sugar, along with cans of soup, pork and beans, margarine, and coffee. A roll of sealskins waiting to be sent out for tanning rested on a platform. "When the boat comes in, this place will be full," Willi said, showing with his hands how high the supplies would be stacked against the wall. He listened closely while Mark translated this into English, and suddenly Willi said, halting before each word but speaking in English, *"This will make electric,"* and turned on the light. I exclaimed in surprise. I didn't know Willi could speak any English, and I could not get accustomed to electric lights at George River. Willi opened a door at the end of the storeroom and I found myself looking into the new store, the former community hall. Attached to the rafters from which we had hung a kerosene lantern at night among dirty fox and rabbit pelts and green fish nets, there were now shining electric fixtures. Ceiling, rafters, and walls had been whitewashed. A store counter and the trim for the shelves were an attractive salmon pink, and the floor was a soft gray. Through the window, where once the view was unobstructed landscape, I now glimpsed the nearby school, a neat single-story gabled structure with a wall of windows on the side that faced the store. When we left the store, it was beginning to get dark. The setting sun made a path of soft gray and green light across the low surrounding hills. The street lights—triggered, I was told, by a photoelectric cell—went on, and it was time for me to go back to the Prudens' for dinner.

The Pruden home, where I was staying, was much larger than the surrounding Eskimo houses, having a living room, a dinette, a modern kitchen, three bedrooms, a bath, and a storeroom. The Prudens' six-year-old daughter, Debra, and a twenty-year-old Eskimo girl who was minding their baby, David, joined us at dinner. We had scarcely finished eating when the door opened and Mark Annanack, accompanied by another young Eskimo whom I knew only as Sandy, entered.

"Aii, Davi-alook!" Mark called softly to the baby, who was lying on the sofa. Mark had come to say that he could not finish taking me around the community that evening, because one of the two diesel motors that ran the coöperative's fish freezer had broken down. He and Sandy, who were the coöperative's freezer maintenance men, would have to go immediately the twelve miles to the mouth of the river to keep an eye on the one good motor that remained, until Pruden

returned. The two boys were living for the summer at the freezer site. They could maintain the complicated machinery but they weren't trained to repair it, they said. Pruden himself had spent five weeks taking a course in diesel refrigeration in Halifax during the winter so that he could cope with minor mechanical failures. More than twelve thousand pounds of Arctic char, which was still the coöperative's main source of income, were stored in the freezer awaiting pickup by the boat which would take it to Montreal. After the freezer was emptied, the George River fishermen planned to set their nets for more fish and fill it a second time. Although one motor was sufficient to hold the temperature of the freezer steady, it would take two motors to freeze the new catch of fish, so no time could be lost.

While we were washing the supper dishes, there was a shout in the vestibule and the sound of boots being tugged off. Pruden appeared, smiling broadly, his body filling the doorway of the kitchen, with Brian behind him. "I was between here and Burwell when your pilot found me," he said as he greeted me. He immediately rolled up his sleeves, threw some onions, potatoes and a big steak into a frying pan, and continued talking while he cooked his and Brian's supper. Brian, I was happy to see, was a sturdy youngster, and, his mother had assured me, was totally recovered from his hair-raising encounter with the dogs.

"I was doing some experimental fishing for shrimp and oysters," Pruden said. "I wanted to boil them up, freeze them, and see how they would be next year. Until now, everything has centered around the char fishery, but there are less and less char every year, and it is harder and harder to catch our quota. Unlike salmon, char is a very slow breeder, a very odd fish. I think the char are being fished out in this area, even though the scientists say not."

While Pruden was eating dinner, his wife told him about the breakdown at the freezer. He paused, fork in air, scowling. "Damn!" he said, "I hope the motor isn't burned out. That would mean the end of fishing. The settlement's in pretty rough shape," he said to me. "Our tractor's broken down, and we can't keep the place properly cleaned up without a tractor. We need a resident mechanic. We're simply short of able-bodied men. Out of a population of a hundred and forty-six, only twenty-three are able-bodied men, and they're what you need when you are starting a new settlement like this. Before we get much further we are going to have to get more men. There are some from Chimo who want to come. We've several programs for the fall. We plan to make fifteen- and sixteen-foot net-tending boats and some larger Peterhead boats. We hope to build furniture for sale locally, and there's going to be a smokehouse for salmon. This past year, for the first time, we've done some stone carving, and we've just sent three thousand dollars' worth of it south. Our newest venture has been to hunt seal along the Labrador coast—a seven-hundred-and-fifty-mile round trip. Early last spring I took two men and two Skidoos and we went ahead to Labrador, then fourteen other men followed, with seven dog teams, three women, and nine children. We set up a hunting camp and hunted right up the coast all March, and came back in the middle of April with sealskins worth over five thousand dollars. This year we should do even better."

He got up from the table and carried his coffee cup over to an easy chair, sat down with a sigh, and stretched out his legs. "The biggest amount of my work is done after hours, when the Eskimos come in and talk things over," he said. "It takes a lot of talking to get things across. I never studied the Eskimo language, but I get along in it fine with most of these people. And now Gwen is teaching English to the young ones, and even some of the older people. Occasionally I have my closest friends for dinner—Willi, or Josepie, or Johnny George. George Annanack is a good buddy, too, but Josepie—well, he and I travel a lot together, and he's a great man on the trails. He's now up on the Ungava coast with the Long Liner boat."

I remarked that all the Eskimos looked pale to me. "What time were you here before? In March?" Pruden inquired. "They had their spring tan then, the reflection of the snow. I like spring, when the country comes alive. I get the color of that chair, myself," he added, pointing to a brown chair. "I have Indian blood. My folks were the first settlers on the prairies." He went to the kitchen for a second cup of coffee, came back, and continued, "When these hunting people moved into community life, in the early stages, men who formerly made their own decisions expected to be told what to do. They would even ask me if they could go hunting, and I would say, 'If you wish to go, go!' There's been one big change here lately: the people have been showing a willingness to take over, and I've been trying to make them make more of their own decisions. The materials are here to build a church and nursing station, and they are all waiting for me to tell them to start. Yet they handle the freezer, except for bookkeeping and major mechanical trouble, and the store and sawmill operate without my help. Government construction crews put up our departmental buildings during the summer, but the people build their own houses themselves from local timber. They only need me to handle something new and strange. If they could read and write, I am quite confident they could manage alone. Willi went ahead and remodelled the whole store. Even selected his own colors. It's all slow and long-range now," he said, rising to go to bed. "You've got to wait so long for anything to happen."

III

I GOT UP at a little after seven the next morning to the steady, throbbing sound of the sawmill, which was already at work. Mrs. Pruden asked if I wanted an egg for breakfast, and without thinking, I said, "Yes." When she had already cracked it in the pan, I remembered that eggs had to be brought all the way from Montreal and ranked as carefully rationed luxuries, along with liquor, beef, and green vegetables. At eight-thirty, Pruden went to his office to talk over the radio, and, repeating everything twice through the heavy static, asked a mechanic from Chimo, who was currently in Port Burwell repairing a boat, to come and fix the freezer motor and the tractor. "If we ever get that tractor started, we'll leave it going night and day," he said to me when he had signed off. "Let's get going to the freezer. It's about an hour from here by outboard canoe."

We started down the hill toward the river, but at the entrance to the nearest Eskimo tent, we met Willi Imudluk, who explained that the tent was his summer home. It consisted of spruce logs cut off and set upright into the ground for walls, a small door, and a slanting canvas roof through which a single, black stovepipe emerged. It was situated directly in front of a new Eskimo house, which also belonged to Willi. He invited us first into the tent, and we bent down and entered through the little red door. His old mother was sitting on the same iron bed that I had seen her sitting on three years before at the Hudson's Bay outpost, smoking, as she had been then, and looking just as bright-eyed. In addition to Selima, Willi's pretty young wife, and his daughter by his dead first wife, there were two new little girls, one of them a baby, who was playing on the floor with a blue plastic toy telephone. Children's drawings on manila paper were nailed to the log walls, and a Hohner accordion, a camera in a leather case, and a mirror hung from hooks. Besides the iron bed, there were two wooden bunk beds, a trunk, two wooden chairs, and a small iron stove. Pruden told Selima that I still had the sealskin boots she had made me. She smiled, and reaching under a bed, brought out a beautiful sealskin parka on which she was working, that Pruden was buying for himself. When we had admired it sufficiently, Willi said he would like us to see his new winter home. We left the tent and walked up the hill the few yards to the new house. It had a large rectangular living room, and, behind a partition, a small bedroom. Like Pruden's house, it was equipped with a chemical toilet and an oil heater, and Willi had purchased his own cookstove and a semi-automatic washing machine. A half-finished stone sculpture of a caribou that Willi had been carving stood on a shelf. I asked how long it took to make such a piece. Willi thought for a moment and replied to Pruden, who translated, "If I start early in the morning and work all day, late into the night, two days."

It was after ten and the tide was running out, so we hurried down the hill to the river, where we now had to walk for perhaps a mile through mud flats, slurping and sliding, to reach Pruden's large canoe. We were plagued by black flies, and I asked where they came from. Pruden said, "As the permafrost softens in summer, it makes little potholes that are ideal insect breeding grounds." We went on farther, picking our way around large stones on the river bottom. The tides in the Ungava area, officially measured at thirty-four feet, are among the highest in the world, and Pruden said that at nearby

Leaf Bay he had seen them reach more than sixty feet. The tide at George River had been so high at eight in the morning that it had covered the dock, but by the time we set off for the canoe the dock was so high above the river's exposed bottom that it looked like an engineering mistake.

When we finally reached the canoe, we found a young Eskimo boy sitting in the bow waiting for us. There were two outboard motors hooked to the stern, and Pruden started one and then the other. With this double power, we sped down the river. It was a gorgeous day, crisp and clear, and the hills had changed from mauve to slate color. The water was royal blue, and the sky a softer shade of the same color, with only a few white clouds that seemed permanently fixed in their positions. Pruden and the boy were wearing red knitted hats with long tassels, which, like the pointed hoods on the parkas made here and at Chimo, were distinctive to the Ungava area. Pruden zipped up his parka, and I pulled up the hood on mine as we swept along, making our own chilly breeze. Half-turning, I shouted at Pruden that I wondered how fast we were going, and he shouted back, "Thirty-nine miles an hour! This is a twenty-two foot canoe, and can hold six thousand pounds!"

After three quarters of an hour, the river broadened considerably and we passed an Eskimo fishing camp, consisting of two tents at the foot of some high, bare rocks. Ungava Bay lay directly ahead, and Pruden made a sharp left turn into a small cove. The thought swept through my mind that at last I was to see the George River fish freezer, something I had heard so much about at the first meeting that the words had a special ring for me—the freezer, keystone of a daring experiment, a modern appliance of the most delicate nature, constructed on this rocky, barren, uninhabited coast with colossal effort and somehow, miraculously, a success. I saw a small silver-gray metal building, a tired rectangle at the far end of a narrow beach, a curiously brave structure, all the more poignant for its weather-beaten shabbiness.

Pruden shut off the outboard motors and tied the boat around a large stone. Several Eskimo dogs came down and stared at us and went away as we waded through a foot of water to the beach, where sandpipers and snipe were seeking food among the pebbles. At the entrance to the freezer, my boot caught on a slatted platform and I fell flat on my face. Ashamed of my clumsiness, I hastily got up and looked around. The boy from our canoe had stayed near it to fish. Some Eskimo children and a woman in a tent several hundred yards away were staring at me, but they quickly vanished when I turned toward them. Pruden had disappeared, and I followed the sound of a noisy motor into a wooden shed on one side of the freezer building. I found Pruden on his knees examining a silent motor, while Mark and Sandy, in greasy overalls, looked on. Now Pruden smiled and said, "Not so bad as I thought. It just got dirty. I'm going to try to start it up for a while, but I'll have the mechanic strip it down and clean it when he comes."

I went outside to wait. I looked at the blue emptiness of Ungava Bay, but it was so big and motionless that it made me feel restless. I went around the side of the freezer to look at the wooden tables where the fish were weighed and dressed before they were frozen. I tried to imagine the furious activity that took place here when the fishing boats came in, but the place was too peaceful and too calm for me to imagine that. I heard the faulty motor start, and Pruden came out of the motor room and unlocked the heavy door of the freezer to show me the inside, where metal shelves were crammed with frozen char. "I'm going to move this freezer upriver to the community," Pruden said, slamming the door shut and locking it. "And I'm going to get rid of those diesel motors and convert to electricity."

We had been at the freezer site an hour. The tide had come in and the canoe was in deep water. We walked over the rocks along the side of the cove to the boat, where the boy was waiting, got in, and he paddled us out of the cove. Pruden started the motors and set our course up the George River. I had expressed a desire to see an Eskimo fishing camp, so Pruden stopped a short distance up the river at the Eskimo tents we had seen earlier, where we found Thomas Annanack, a brother of Stanley and Mark, with his family. The Annanacks' tent was small, and living had been reduced to its simplest form. The bed was a large quilt laid over a broad area of rocks and skins. The only other furnishings were a trunk, several rude wooden crates, and a small kerosene stove on which a teapot rested. Pruden asked if the sod underneath our feet was wet, and Thomas replied he had moved the tent yesterday and that the ground here was dry. When Pruden jokingly asked, "Why aren't you hunting caribou?" Thomas laughed and said, "Too many mosquitoes." Several large char, silver-green above, pinkish below, were drying on the ground. Thomas said he had caught them that morning in a net and that, although he had seen ducks lately, for the last week the family had eaten nothing but fish and bannock. His wife Elizabeth, he told us, had just returned from two years in a southern hospital where she had been treated for tuberculosis. Against her knee leaned her small son. Her husband patted the boy and said roughly, "We are glad to have her back, and she is through with all that sickness now." On my way out, I noticed a child's plaid schoolbag lying on the bare ground just inside the tent, partially covering a doll with pink cheeks and golden curls that was dressed in a Scotch tartan and white lace blouse. I guessed that it must belong to a small girl who had stopped to stare at us when we arrived and then had run off. Lying beside it was the sharp, pointed head of a harpoon. Pruden picked up the deadly looking piece of iron and showed me how it turns over when it is plunged into a seal so that it cannot slip out. Otherwise, he explained, the seal would sink or escape before it could be shot.

We embarked again, heading back to the settlement, hugging the shore while Pruden looked for a place to stop and have lunch. I could see reddish streaks of iron deposit in the black stones we were passing, and in a short while, Pruden brought the canoe in to another landing place, and we scrambled up some rocks to a spot where he began preparing lunch for the three of us on a small stove from provisions he had brought along. As we sat there high above the river, with nothing stirring and the only sounds our own, it seemed to me that no meal had ever tasted better. Over dessert, tea and bannock with jam on it, we talked about the settlement. Pruden half-crouched on his heels, Eskimo fashion. "I have one aim at George River," he said, stirring sugar into his tea. "I want to get every Eskimo there into a house. I won't leave for a year, anyway, and before I go, I intend to get rid of those shacks you saw at the settlement and finish the ten houses that are still to be done. I owe this to the people here, and I owe it to Don Snowden. When Snowden first came in, he had a dream about the settlement—the houses, the projects, logging, boatbuilding, things along that line. He told the Eskimos that the government wanted to help them to make their lives better and they believed him. Their name for Snowden is *Sielapalik*—which can be translated 'the man with the parka with the flat hood'—because the hood of the parka he was wearing the first time the Eskimos met him was rounded rather than pointed, like theirs. They quite often talk about when *Sielapalik* first came, in 1958. They think a lot of Snowden, these people do. Snowden told me that if, with our help in the beginning, these people at George River could make their own way and hold out against the growing tendency in the North toward a welfare society, their example might swing things in the other direction and the Arctic might serve as a proving ground for the treatment of other underdeveloped areas. I want to clean things up, so the settlement looks like a settlement *should* look, levelled off and landscaped. We'll ultimately have a boatbuilding shop and a church, and everything will be painted up, with fences, maybe even little white ones, around the houses and pathways. It looks rough now, but when the tents, shacks, and other temporary buildings are gone, it will be different. We organized an Eskimo council here two years ago, and I am encouraging it to pass a rule that a building be approved before it can go up so the kind of shacks that make Chimo and other places look like hell can't be put up at George River."

Pruden shook the last drops of tea from his cup and put it back into the box where he carried food and utensils. Descending the rocks to the canoe, I said that riding in an Eskimo canoe was one of the best means of travel I had ever experienced. Pruden laughed. "Don't fool yourself," he said. "In bad weather, with the wind blowing and the bow chopping up and down through the water, and water coming into the boat, there is nothing more miserable, cold and wet than an Eskimo canoe."

I NEVER had a chance to test the truth of this statement, for the weather remained glorious for the remainder of my visit. That same evening, after we had returned to the settlement, I went out with some Eskimos while they picked up the day's catch of salmon and char from nets that they had laid in the river. I was late in leaving the Prudens' house to meet them, and I ran headlong down the incline to the riverbank. As I settled myself in the canoe I heaved a great sigh and promptly swallowed a large black fly. I clapped my hand to my mouth, and everyone laughed, including myself. The owner of the canoe, Johnny George, started the outboard motor, and we chugged slowly off. Besides Johnny George, a small, solemn man, there was his chubby son in a red parka, an older boy, and in the bow, a man whose thin face was wrapped, as if he had a toothache, in a flowered blue kerchief that went under his chin and tied above his visored red cap. The only ripples on the calm water, glistening in the yellow-gold rays of the sun, were made by our canoe. The man in the bow was peering into the water, and when he held up his hand, we stopped, and he reached down into the river and lifted a length of black, wide-meshed net far enough above the surface for us to see that it was empty.

Johnny George turned the canoe toward the shore and brought it up on a beach, where I could see another net at the water's edge, supported by a string of bobbing cork floats. There were no fish here either, and at this point the motor stalled. After trying repeatedly to get it started again, Johnny said something to the others, and we all got out of the canoe. I hadn't the faintest idea what was happening, but assumed that since the motor didn't seem to work, we were disembarking to wait until someone came along and gave us a tow. This impression was strengthened by the fact that Johnny and the two boys started climbing the rather high hill in front of us, while the other man sat down by the canoe. Johnny looked at me, and when I started rather hesitantly after him, he nodded and began climbing more rapidly. On a lofty ridge he stopped and sat on a rock, and I sank down not far away, breathless. The older boy had disappeared over the top of the hill, and the younger one began picking blueberries, which were all around us on the gray tundra, their green leaves growing smooth and fresh through the spongy undergrowth. The boy interspersed his berrypicking with some kind of wonderful imaginary game, shouting and running joyfully from patch to patch, oblivious of his father and me. Johnny pointed at the river, and I looked where he directed but could not see any boat coming to our rescue, and puzzled, I turned again to him. He was gazing at the scene spread at our feet with rapt concentration. The cove where the settlement lay was on our right, and we were gazing straight down the George River. The sun cast a reddish light on the blue water, and all the colors of this Arctic world—the soft greens and yellows, the lavenders, browns, and muted blacks—were splashed lavishly across the gently rounded hills. The heavens were washed in gold and the river flowed to infinity. I thought, if there is a secret to the pull that the North has for some people, I had found it here, in the wild and peaceful beauty of this place.

We stayed on the ridge for perhaps half an hour. Then, at some signal from Johnny, the older boy reappeared and the younger one stopped his game. We descended the hill and resumed our places in the canoe. After Johnny had had a formidable struggle with the motor, it began chugging again, and we slowly crossed into the cove, stopping occasionally to lift nets. Finally Johnny exclaimed "*Ilkalu!*" I recognized the Eskimo word for char and, looking over the side of the canoe, I beheld two large, silvery fish caught in the mesh. Johnny quickly disengaged them from the net and dropped them into the boat. They weighed about six pounds each, and a little further along we found a third. By then we were almost at the settlement and when we came in, a crowd of youngsters at the beach followed us up the hill, chattering. It was after seven and the street lights went on, but the sawmill was still beating out its rasping tune, and Willi was kneeling at the entrance of the coöperative store, planing off the edges of a wooden door. Pruden, who had started down to meet us, talked briefly with Johnny George, then called out a question to Willi whose reply made him laugh. "I asked Willi what he was doing," Pruden said, "and what do you think he answered? He said he was making the door low enough so that a tall white man would hit his head."

We continued walking, and Pruden said, "Willi is overhauling the whole store himself. He gets paid seventy-five dollars a month while things are getting started, but later he'll make twenty-six hundred dollars a year. Two Eskimo government employees, the powerhouse operator and the school janitor, earn four thousand apiece annually, but Willi is the richest man in material things. He has a house, two canoes, two outboard motors, an Autoboggan, the three buildings he bought from the Hudson's Bay Company, a good team of dogs, and this winter he's buying a Skidoo. His father, by the way, was a white man. He worked for the Hudson's Bay Company, and left Willi's mother before she knew she was pregnant. She never married or had other children, and at seventy-three, is probably the oldest Eskimo in Ungava Bay."

Pruden asked how I liked the fishing expedition. "Very well," I replied, "but I was mystified by a stop we made to climb a hill."

"Oh, that was just to show you the view," Pruden said. "Johnny George was afraid that you would be disappointed because there were no fish in his nets."

For our evening meal we had caribou steak, which tasted like delicious beefsteak with a slightly gamy tang, and homemade lemon pie. Afterward, when we had settled again with our coffee cups in the living room, Mrs. Pruden told me that Johnny George had lost his wife the previous winter in childbirth. "Johnny and his wife were very close," Gwen said. "Every woman in the settlement has had trouble bearing children. When anyone is ill, we consult by radio with the health station at Chimo, and Don administers necessary drugs. I do it when he is away. If a person is too sick to be treated here, an aircraft is sent for the ill person. Both of us were Outside at official conferences when Johnny's wife, a big woman who already had five children, began to have trouble. Willi Imudluk radioed for a plane, but the people at Chimo have had experience with Eskimos' exaggerating and asking for aircraft when nothing is wrong, so no plane was sent. The other day I was explaining to Johnny about putting people to sleep with needles, because we have an emotionally disturbed child here who might need this so we can treat an injured eye from which he is suffering, and Johnny said, 'I would like to have a needle to put me to sleep, because my heart is hurting so much!' "

"By and large, though, this is a happy and productive community," Gwen continued, "and I doubt if any of the children will want to leave here." In fact, she added, there was a lot of inbreeding at George River. Johnny had been married to his first cousin, and among the dozen or so families many other cousins had married close cousins. "Sometimes an illegitimate child is adopted without the real father being named, and there is a good chance this child may marry a half brother or sister later," she said. "The people are only now beginning to realize how serious this is. Quite a few of my students are slow learners. So far the only new blood is Willi's wife, Selima, who comes from Chimo, but fathers shopping for husbands for their daughters now want to go to Burwell to look."

Pruden had shut his eyes, and I thought he had fallen asleep, but now he suddenly interrupted. "I love it here," he said. "I'm lucky. It's seldom you get a job you are really happy with. Pretty soon, though, I'd like to get another new settlement. I like having a hand in drastic change, especially change from the bloody life these people used to live. In 1959, the average income in this area was three hundred and twenty-five dollars, and everyone was on relief. Last year it was seventeen hundred and fifty dollars, only two people were on relief, and when the average income hits two thousand they'll be pretty well off. These Eskimos don't seem to care about money, but regard it as a means to an end. A man with a good hunting outfit—boats, motors, rifles, dog team, and Skidoo, can live off this country without much money, but all of this equipment tends to create a vicious circle, because once you have a motor, for instance, you have to have gasoline, and so on. You need cash, and inevitably, the old patterns of Eskimo life are being upset. Because of school, the young hunters can no longer accompany their fathers and the women their husbands, except in summer. Also, men who are working for cash wages don't have as much time to hunt, so their families sometimes don't really eat as well on store food as those of hunters, who bring in seal, char, and caribou."

He got up and walked around the room, stopping to peer out the window at the quiet community below. "There is no crime here, just a bit of petty theft, mostly of gas and tools," he went on. "I know who's doing it—two young men in one family—and I've warned them. Two years ago, I organized an Eskimo council, but so far the meetings have been confusing, always ending up with a discussion of coöperative business. There's no real leader yet, but old George Annanack still sits in the prominent spot at meetings and does a lot of talking. He's quite wise, you know. We have all our meetings in the schoolroom, and for recreation everyone who can walk or crawl goes there for movies. Some of the movies sent here are no good, though. The people don't like to watch jets being loaded on aircraft carriers, for instance, but they sit up and make lots of comments about movies on coöperative development, logging, or fishing."

I remembered to compliment Mrs. Pruden on our dinner, and this set her husband to talking rather worriedly of the shortage of game in the area. "A medical party surveying the Ungava Bay people last spring reported that George River was the only place on the bay where malnutrition existed among the children, and I feel this is directly due to a vitamin deficiency from lack of fresh, natural food. That's why I'm starting organized hunts and trapping expeditions to areas outside the usual range. In five or six years, I wouldn't be surprised if the coöps of this bay buy their own aircraft, hire a white pilot, and use planes in hunting and hauling game. Meanwhile, we want to can a good supply of dog food during summer months, and lay in canned seal and whale meat for humans, to be sold in the coöp store during slack hunting periods. You ask for trouble when Eskimos from remote inland areas come into a settlement like this and suffer from malnutrition, exposed as they are to new germs."

I inquired about the community's facilities for water and sewage. Water was provided in winter, he explained, by ice hauled by sled from the nearby lake and melted in large heated tanks, while in summer water from a spring was distributed around the community by means of plastic, above-ground pipes. The permanently frozen ground made the laying of conventional water and sewer pipes impossible, and sewage was collected in large tins and left on the tidal flats to rust away in the highly saline surrounding waters. I was also curious about what measures were taken to control the dogs. Pruden explained that compounds for them had proved impractical, because drifting snow in winter made it easy for the animals to clamber over the fences. In summer, he said, the Eskimos took most of their dogs to remote fishing camps. "To tell you the truth, the problem of controlling dogs hasn't been solved anywhere in the Arctic," he concluded. "The Eskimos don't like to tie them or pen them. We have to rely on persuasion and education of the Eskimos."

IV

WHEN I ROSE the next morning, the day of my departure, Mrs. Pruden suggested that I visit the summer-school classes she was conducting. "When David was born, I was going to stop teaching," she said to me, "but there was no one to take my place, and I couldn't let these children down. When we came three years ago, we lived in a tent, and I started teaching school right away, in a tent. Before fall, we're hoping, the full-time school principal will arrive. Then we're supposed to get a second classroom, and I'll probably go on teaching in that."

Gwen Pruden, dressed to teach school, was quite a different person. At home, less than five minutes from her classroom, she wore slacks or an old skirt and sweater, and had a shy, gentle manner. When she faced her pupils in a tailored skirt and blouse, with a pearl necklace and earrings, high-heeled shoes and silk stockings, she was pleasant but authoritative.

The interior of the schoolhouse contained a coatroom, a well-equipped book and supply room, two bathrooms, a modern kitchen, a hot-air oil furnace, a massive ice-melting tank, and the classroom itself, light and modern, with movable desks, maps, and two green slate boards. Mrs. Pruden explained that there would be only two small classes this morning: a group of girls and one boy, fourteen to seventeen years old; and some of the six men who were taking an adult education course she was trying out for the first time. Most of the children were away with their parents at the fishing camps now. It was a little before class time, so we sat down at two desks to talk. She opened a small book she held in her hand. "I want you to see this," she said. "It's the regular school attendance book. For instance, in December, the attendance record was ninety-eight per cent, ninety-eight, ninety-four—that's the lowest. It's inspiring for a teacher to see the Eskimos come out of the dark, with so much working against them, and no prior knowledge of what the rest of the world is like. The only time healthy children ever miss school in winter is when they are needed at home to help with other children or to get water and wood, if the father is away and the mother is unable to do so."

She closed the book. "The principal subjects I'm teaching are English and arithmetic, and, as you'll see, it's working out quite well even though I don't speak Eskimo. The Eskimos are very reluctant to use English at first, but they grasp new ideas very quickly. We have three grades in all now, pretty well grouped according to age, with students from fourteen to seventeen in Grade Three. I find the children fairly similar to those I used to teach in the South. In each grade I have a bright group and a low group. Some children are neat, some are untidy, and some are full of mischief, but I have hardly any real behavior problems —very little of that business of seeing how far you can go with the teacher, the way southern children do. On Parents' Day I mentioned that some of the children had been fighting, and that if they continued I would keep them in after school. All the parents backed me up, and they even suggested that it would be all right if I *spanked* the children. I was amazed. You always hear that Eskimos don't discipline their children and you don't *ever* see them spanking a child. I think things may be changing because they are living so close together. They have had to adopt a lot more rules and 'don'ts,' like ours."

She got up, walked over to the bookcases below the windows, and began to select books for the day's lessons. Through the window I could see children playing on the swings in the schoolyard, and a group of girls in summer dresses were standing by the door. "I have one deaf boy in my regular classes," Gwen said. "He had had a year at a special school in Montreal, where he was taught to lip-read, but his parents didn't want him to go back. At first, I wouldn't take him, because I didn't think I could cope with him. I had my hands full with seven new six-year-olds, who were immature for their age, as the very young often are here, and were really not ready for school. Finally I did let the deaf boy come to school, and I was surprised at how well he fitted in. He was very quick about visual things like arithmetic. I remembered reading somewhere that if you put a deaf child's hand on your throat it might help him learn to speak. He hadn't made a sound before, but as soon as I did that he started making sounds, very softly. I think his parents will send him back to Montreal next year. They talked to me on Parents' Day and said if he went south, he probably would stay there and would know only English. This is quite true. I told them, 'It's a decision you will have to make.'"

We were both silent for a moment.

"About the adults who will be coming this morning," she continued. "The adults here have never had an opportunity for schooling, and some of them, like Willi in the store, or Johnny George, who is school janitor, have a lot of responsibility. I asked those two if they would be interested in learning English, and when they said yes, I went down to the sawmill and announced that I was starting an English course for adults and anyone who liked could come. Don interpreted for me, and told the Eskimos that they shouldn't be afraid they were too old to learn English and shouldn't be ashamed if it was difficult, because it had taken him lots of time to learn Eskimo, too. Six men, including Willi and Johnny George, came the first day, a month ago, for an hour and a half. They don't all show up every day, because of their jobs. I had no training for adult teaching and no idea what to do. The radio was out and I couldn't talk over my problems by radio with any other teachers, which is what I often do, so I started right out in English, with things around the room that they had been using every day, and with a paperback book, *English Through Pictures*. One of my difficulties is that I have no special teaching books for Eskimos. I use southern books, the 'Dick and Jane' books of the Curriculum Foundation Series, about farms and automobiles and buses, apartment living in a city, the milkman, and the mailman who comes to the houses. It may be good for them to learn all this, but at the beginning it's very confusing. Sally is helping Mother set the table and Dick is working with Father in the garden, when it should be something about catching seals or caribou hunting, or other things with which they are familiar."

She looked at her watch, picked up a large bell and rang it at the door of the schoolhouse. Four girls in pretty cotton dresses and a teen-age boy came in and sat down at the desks by the windows, and I moved to a seat in the rear. A minute or two later, three men came in and took places at the center desks. They were Johnny George; Jobie, a cheerful-looking youth who, Mrs. Pruden had told me, was suffering from a mysterious muscular disease, and who for this reason was limping badly and holding his useless left arm in his right hand; and an older man whom I didn't recognize.

Mrs. Pruden wasted no time in getting started. First she wrote the day and date on the board and said very slowly in English, "Good morning! What is the day today?" One of the Eskimo girls answered, and then Gwen said, "What is the weather like today?" Another girl replied, with a little help from Mrs. Pruden. "It . . . is . . . good." Mrs. Pruden held up a cardboard clock face and, as she moved the hands around, asked each Eskimo what time the clock said. Next she asked everyone to count with her to one hundred by fives. After she had given the younger group assignments in some simple arithmetic workbooks, she called the three men to the front of the room, seating them in three chairs in front of her. She produced a set of colored picture cards with English words on them, and held up the first one, depicting a white woman in a pink dress, holding flowers, and asked Jobie to read the caption. "Mo-th-er," he said, so softly that you could hardly hear him. He had trouble with the "th" sound, so she tried again with a second card, a picture of a white man holding a baseball bat. "Fa-th-er," he read, more easily this time. Next she handed each of the men a "Look and See" book, in which were more pictures of "Mother" and "Father," and asked Johnny to tell her the color of Mother's dress. "Blue," he said. Now Mrs. Pruden asked him to read. In a voice scarcely above a whisper, Johnny read—slowly, painfully, with much prompting, "Look . . . at . . . Sally . . . and . . . Jane. They . . . are . . . standing . . . on . . . their . . . heads." Everyone laughed. "What is Spot doing?" Mrs. Pruden asked the third man, pointing to a picture of a dog. "Spot . . . is . . . sitting . . . up," he read, pausing for a long time between each word. After the pupils had worked their way painstakingly through several more pages in the book, Mrs. Pruden told them to take out their workbooks, and with these they settled down to the tasks of matching pictures of a needle and a thimble, a hammer and some nails, a can of paint and a brush, and so on.

While the adults were thus busying themselves, Mrs. Pruden called the young girls and the boy to the front, went over their workbooks, and then, seating them in a semicircle before her, carried on a brief and rather laborious English discussion of their summer fishing activities. A short session in arithmetic followed; then, pointing to cutouts of the alphabet above the slate boards, she called on all the students individually to pronounce the letters, and then just the vowels, going faster and faster. Finally, she wrote a large G on the board and asked, "Can anyone tell me a name that begins with G?" Nobody answered, and Mrs. Pruden smiled and said, "Oh, come on. Somebody say it." Jobie raised his good hand. "George," he said. Gwen said, "Let's put down the name of our settlement," and she wrote GEORGE RIVER in block letters. Writing a small g beneath this, she asked for a word that began with g, and one of the girls said "go." Gwen asked for a color and Jobie instantly said "green."

Finally, it was noon, and class was over. "Put . . . your . . . books . . . in . . . your . . . desks. Put . . . your . . . books . . . in . . . your . . . desks," Mrs. Pruden said, slowly and carefully.

The eight students complied, and then vanished instantly. We walked quickly back to the Prudens' house, but at the door Gwen paused. "You know, my children do not have the relationship with the Eskimo children that I hoped for," she said. "I think mine consider themselves a little bit better and are quite bossy, both with children and adults. Brian and Debra ask the Eskimo children for their toys or tell them to get off a swing if they want it, and the Eskimo children won't fight back. Our children were used to doing this in the South with other children who fought back and didn't give in, so this has really been worse for them than for the Eskimos. I have told the Eskimo parents that their children are to fight back when necessary, but still they won't be firm enough. The girls who work for us also give the children anything they want. I suppose the Eskimos are this way because in the past whenever they had contact with white people they were always treated as inferiors. Even Willi has a little of this attitude. If I go to the coöp store, he ignores all of his other customers, and if I say I'll wait, it upsets him very much."

After lunch of fresh salmon that one of the Eskimos had brought over as a treat for me, we chatted a while, and then it was time for me to leave George River. I said goodbye to Mrs. Pruden and the children, and when I walked down the steps of their house with Pruden, George Annanack appeared, and shook my hand. *"Aukchunie,"* he said, and then in English, slowly, "Goodbye." Pruden and I started down the path to the river. The sawmill, a giant pulse that never seemed to stop beating, was at work, and as we passed the coöperative store Willi Imudluk was bent over hammering on a new set of steps. His old mother was sitting on an upturned box not far away, smoking, wrapped in a green plaid shawl with a blue kerchief over her head. The air had a slight chill, even though it had been a dazzling, sunny day, and all the men were wearing jackets.

Willi stopped working when he saw us, and we sat down beside him on the new step. With Pruden acting as interpreter, I said to Willi that I knew that in the summer of 1958, when the government men first came to Ungava Bay and made an economic survey of the area, they had met with him and several other George River men who had come to Fort Chimo to find work; when the Eskimos were considering a move away from the George River area to avoid starvation, the government men had talked with them about the possible ways in which the people could make a living and still remain on their own land. This, I reminded him, had been the very beginning of George River, and I wondered what he, Willi, thought had been accomplished in those five years, and how he felt about George River now.

There was a silence for several minutes. Willi sat with his elbows on his knees, turning an unlighted cigarette around and around between his fingers, his head bent, staring at the ground. Suddenly he began talking rapidly, stopping only to nod brusquely at Pruden as a signal to translate what he had said to me, and quickly picking up the thread of conversation again as soon as Pruden stopped. Willi said, "At the first contact we ever had, at Fort Chimo, Don Snowden outlined the plans for the George River settlement and said everything. It didn't turn out quite the same, but when I look back before he came, we had many hard times when we were very hungry, and used to have to go to Chimo to get government relief. Now the plans are working out every year, and getting better and better as they go along."

Willi paused, and lit his cigarette. Then he continued, "At the very first meeting, I got such a good idea of what was planned that I became a supporter of the coöp idea. Don Snowden asked me to come back and tell the people in George River what the new ideas were, and get people ready to understand. Some of the Eskimos didn't really think anyone would come and help them. The white men had made promises before, and things like this never happened. But everything that has happened so far is good—the store, the sawmill, the freezer, the houses, the school. We aren't making much money, but that's going to get better, and the handicrafts aren't very good yet, but they will get better, too, as time goes on. Everything

Don said has not happened yet." He touched each of his eyes in turn. "But I can see now that it's all coming."

Willi stopped as abruptly as he had started. *"Aukchunie,"* he said to me, holding out his hand, with a warm smile.

"Goodbye," I said.

"Aukchunie means, literally, 'You are going,'" Pruden said.

He picked up my sleeping bag and knapsack, and then handed me a blue bag of Her Majesty's mail, which he had been carrying, that I was to give to the pilot when I boarded the plane. We started for the river. The tide was out, so we walked a considerable distance before we came to Pruden's canoe. Two Eskimo men were already sitting in it, and we rode out to the center of the river. Pruden turned off the motors, and we waited for the aircraft that was to take me away.

It was the beginning of a beautiful evening, bright and clear —blue sky and blue water, on which the sun had not yet begun to set. I heard the hum of a motor, and then I saw my plane, a small black and red line in the sky before it circled around and began to descend. It landed on the river and taxied toward our canoe. The pilot brought it alongside us, stepped out on the pontoon, and transferred an Eskimo woman and child he had brought to Pruden's canoe. My sleeping bag and knapsack, and the mailbag, were handed over to him, and I stood up in the canoe and prepared to leave.

"Aukchunie, Oneekatualeeotae," one of the Eskimos said softly, as he shook my hand.

"Oneekatualeeotae. That's a very long name," Pruden said. "It's the name the Eskimos have given you."

I winced.

"Don't make a face. It's a very nice name," Pruden said. "It means, 'The Woman Who Tells the Story.'"

EPILOGUE

THE GEORGE RIVER Eskimos were the first Inuit I ever met, and in the short time we were together I came to love their spirit. I later found that they arouse this same profound affection and admiration in all who know them, and time has proved how well they have earned it.

George River—Port-Nouveau-Québec—is now a settlement of three hundred, more than twice the number of inhabitants that were there in 1964. It has remained an Inuit community, sixty-six families whose main diet is still caribou, seal meat, wild fowl and the delicious Arctic char. In summer the Eskimos still set out their nets and pick them up in their canoes, sometimes with a twelve-pound salmon to reward them for their effort, or they go walking along the shoreline or move with tents to the coast. In winter there is a lot of hunting and trapping on motorized vehicles, especially for the white and colored foxes that are in some demand again. The Eskimos fish as they did before, through ice at the Kuurujuaq River (which I remember as the Korok) or on Long Lake, where our plane took off for Burwell, but the community freezer that is now at the settlement is no longer the center of economic activity. Every now and then the coöperative still gets a quota of fish to send south, but the Eskimos are not netting with the same interest they once had. The freezer is just as likely as not to contain ptarmigan or some other country food they may be storing or trading with other settlements along the coast, rather than the fish they used to ship south. Not even a plank remains of the once vital sawmill, constant throbbing sound in the background during my last visit, but there are now forty-seven houses, mostly prefabricated, some with three and four bedrooms. The new buildings fan up, out and behind the hillside and right down to the bottom along the bank, where once there was only the dock—which is still standing, still ridiculously poised in space when the tide is out. The scattered shacks are gone, but George River has a distinct business district at the top of the bank. It was marked off even when I was there by the presence of the old community hall that had become part of the coöp store. Nearby were the schoolhouse and four government structures, one of which had housed the Prudens. Now there are two major schoolhouses, a church, a nursing station, a number of government buildings—offices, warehouses, residences and garages—a long rectangular metal community hall that doubles as a movie theatre, and a large modern retail coöperative store. The coöp has several buildings. The old log community hall still stands, but it is a coöp warehouse now with numerous additions: a transformation that seems to me to be a suitable manifestation that what was meant to be has happened.

One of the most important changes is the addition of an airstrip. When it was completed four years ago, freeze-up and break-up lost their significance as isolating agents. A plane can now actually land at ten o'clock at night, as it did two years ago at Christmas when it brought home Willi Imudluk's daughter Maggie, who was taking her high school course in Ottawa. There are now two weekly scheduled air flights into George River from Fort Chimo at a cost of a hundred and six dollars round trip on Air Inuit. This is an Eskimo airline and was one of the first investments the Inuit made through their development corporation with funds received under the James Bay agreement. George River people like to make shopping sorties into Fort Chimo, and have also continued the practice of purchasing from the numerous mail-order catalogues they receive. Small items arrive by air parcel post the year round, but large orders still must wait for the summer resupply by sea, the sea lift. A dramatic alteration in life style has occurred with the introduction of telephones into almost every house. Before, the only way to communicate with one's neighbors and friends was to go visiting, sit down comfortably with a cup of tea and have a long talk, but now business can be concluded briefly by phone. Not just in George River but wherever settlements have diesel generators for electricity, there are freezers, washing machines and, to a lesser extent, refrigerators. Most Inuit households now possess tape recorders, radios, power tools and store furniture.

There are a few dog teams in George River, but they are bred chiefly for the benefit of winter tourists, notably a group of wealthy Italian alpinists—mountain climbers and skiers—who come regularly to Ungava Bay and pay handsomely for the privilege of travelling by *komatik* and dog team and sleeping in igloos. Before the Italians arrive at whichever place has been selected for them to start their overland journey—Fort Chimo, Payne Bay, Leaf Bay—snowmobiles are sent ahead to build igloos along the trails, and the dog teams, drivers and *komatiks* are flown in to meet the arriving Italians coming from Rome or Milan. Then all set off together, pausing en route in the freshly made igloos.

At various points in the Canadian Arctic, especially where outpost camps are being established by Inuit who want to return to the traditional way of life away from settlements for part of the year, dog teams are making a comeback. The Skidoo and other snowmobiles first appeared in the North in the early nineteen-sixties, when I was there, and then dogs seemed very slow to the Inuit. But snowmobiles and their maintenance are expensive, and they cannot take a lost hunter home. The Inuit are beginning to breed dogs again, especially for spring and fall hunting when the seals are plentiful and the ice is thin. Dogs, with their small feet, and *komatiks*, with their long runners, can travel over thin ice where a snow machine cannot.

Snowmobiles are still popular enough, however, to provide an unusual competitive situation in a business community as small as George River: the Bombardier Skidoo is sold at the coöperative store; Willi Imudluk has the dealership for a second variety, the Arctic Cat; and still a third Eskimo has begun selling Skidoos privately. The George River Coöperative's retail store is the main source of supply for almost everything else and has been enjoying a sharp increase in sales. It deals in a full line of groceries, hardware, clothing, hunting and fishing equipment, snow machines, boats, motors, toys, freezers, washing machines, radios and stereo and record equipment, and its current profitable condition is indicative of the general good health of the coöperative as a whole. Virtually everyone in the community is a coöp member, with almost two hundred thousand dollars invested in share capital and retained earnings to support future growth. This makes it one of the few coöperatives in the North that approaches the desired norm of having forty per cent of the assets owned by the members.

The George River Coöperative has never received any direct grants or other direct subsidies from either the provincial or federal governments since it was founded. In its first year it did twelve thousand eight hundred eleven dollars and seventy cents worth of business; by 1977 it was paying out one hundred thousand dollars to Inuit in the community in wages, in dividends, and in purchases of arts, crafts, fish, and furs. It has received a total of a quarter of a million dollars in loans from both governments, but steadily continues payments that are up-to-date on an outstanding debt of sixty-six thousand dollars. Eskimo Loan Fund interest rates in 1979 have gone as high as fifteen per cent—a long way from the five per cent simple interest rate with which Snowden and Paul Godt introduced the Eskimo Loan Fund concept and money borrowing charges to the George River men for the first time, by flickering lamplight, on that April evening in 1961.

Sales in the retail store have almost doubled in the past three years to over half a million dollars, enabling the coöp to pay out ninety thousand dollars in returns to its members over the same period. Besides running the retail store, the coöp ships stone and bone carvings, handicrafts, furs and fish to Montreal. Although George River has never been considered an art center like Cape Dorset, Holman Island or Baker Lake, it has developed some excellent carvers, among them some of my friends—my old friends as I think of them, for they have lived so long in my mind—Willi Imudluk, Josepie Annanack, Johnny George. The settlement has produced one extraordinary print maker, Tivi Etok, brother of Lucas Etok, whom I knew. Tivi, or David Etok, who is in his fifties, did a little carving in the early days of the coöp. In 1972 the community chose him to attend a print making course in Povungnituk that started him experimenting on his own. George River is still a settlement where in the spring more than half the inhabitants are out hunting, but it is said of Tivi Etok that he spends all day and all night at his work, putting on paper the vivid images and stories that in his own words are "whispering in my ears and mingling with my dreams." He had the distinction in 1975 of being the first Inuk in Canada to bring out a one-man catalogued print show.

The George River Coöperative has had its ups and downs. It hasn't always shown a profit, but it has fulfilled its original purpose: proving that a highly diversified multipurpose Inuit cooperative is viable in the North, and without white management. Willi Imudluk was its first manager, and there has never been a white one. In fact, since 1967 there have been no white managers in any northern Quebec coöps.

Stanley Annanack remains a major influence in the George River Coöperative today; Stanley of the green eyes and wild humor. The records show that Stanley made the very first Inuit coöp business transaction in Canada when he sold two fish. The date was August 23, 1959, and in retrospect the accident of Stanley in this historic role seems exactly right.

There are two separate Annanack families in George River, and Stanley is the nephew of "old" George Annanack, who served as a sort of elder statesman when I was there. George seemed old to me then, but he was actually in his late fifties, and he died at the age of sixty-five. Because of a heart condition, he had been warned not to continue hunting, but was determined to go one last time. While he was out with his dogs he suddenly fell off the *komatik*, victim of a heart attack from which he died instantly. Recently, his widow, Minnie, by now elderly and so crippled with arthritis that she couldn't walk, went to Montreal for an operation that gave her new artificial joints in plastic sockets and a steel femur. It was so successful that she has been reported to have been seen dancing at a community gathering in Fort Chimo.

Stanley Annanack and Willi Imudluk are each in their own way still the pillars of the George River community, but Stanley has the more tangible authority whereas Willi has continued to remain slightly detached. Stanley is the same outspoken confident individualist, and when he isn't holding one of a variety of official positions that he has had over the years he continues to wield power from behind the scenes. Lately he has been a teacher of native culture, helping the young to learn syllabics and taking the boys out to train them in skills connected with life on the land. His daughter Maggie manages the sewing shop which produces many of the excellent handicrafts for which George River women are well known. Maggie is married to a non-related Annanack, Sandy, one of the two young boys who accompanied Don Pruden and me at the disabled freezer at the mouth of the George River almost twenty years ago. Sandy is now the manager of the coöperative, and Jobie, the bright youth suffering from a muscular disease whom I met in Gwen Pruden's classroom when he was just beginning to learn English, has been holding down the important job of minding the store. He has taken a succession of courses on stocking, pricing and every other skill needed to manage a retail establishment, and he is said to be married to the store, since he has remained a bachelor. Although he must still hang on to his hand to prevent involuntary spasms, his condition has not deteriorated, and he hunts and fishes with a snowmobile. In the old nomadic life, Jobie might not have managed, but he has flourished with the responsibilities demanded of him in coöperative management.

Willi Imudluk still maintains his curious stance: one foot in the coöperative system—he is on the coöp's board of directors—the other in private enterprise, where until this year he owned and operated Ilkalu Lodge, a summer tourist camp twelve miles from the settlement, and a fall caribou hunting operation for southern sportsmen. There are a number of tourist camps owned and operated by Inuit coöps or individuals, but his was the first. He also has the Shell Oil concession and runs a little retail store at George River where he tries to offer goods the coöp store doesn't stock, such as wind pants and other special gear, in addition to the different brand of snowmobile. Recently, Willi decided to concentrate on the oil and snowmobile distributorships and the store, and to divest himself of the lodge and caribou hunting camps. He is said to be inspired not so much by a desire to slow down as by his concern that younger Inuit in George River be given the opportunity to have their own businesses. Negotiations are under way to sell the lodge and hunting camps separately, but in all probability the new owners will be former associates who were trained by Willi in the business.

In 1978, Willi was honored by having Canada's Governor General as his guest. His camp has been a kind of flagship, having provided the rationale for setting up private Inuit tourist facilities. Willi had been managing the coöperative store at George River two years when the Hudson's Bay Company offered to sell him, for two hundred and fifty dollars, the two old green-and-white outpost buildings where we had stopped on that first trip by *komatik* along the George River. He had once worked in a white man's fishing camp, so he began to think about starting his own lodge. He had a second motive as well: to broaden the economic base of the community. Everyone had such confidence in Willi that he received substantial government help, both financial and in the excellent advice and practical assistance given him by Don Pruden, who was still government administrator at George River at the time. He helped Willi obtain backing through the Eskimo Loan Fund, and then they took apart the frame buildings Willi had just bought, moved them to a new location on Qikiqtaaluk Island in the middle of the George River, and transformed them into a kitchen and dining room for his lodge, facing them with logs. Ilkalu Lodge opened in 1967 and has been in operation ever since. It accommodates from twelve to fifteen guests a week all summer and employs from twelve to fifteen George River men and women, the older men as guides. Willi always hired as many young boys from the community as he could to accompany the fishing canoes, with a double purpose: to provide communication between the guides and guests, who usually have a language barrier, and to give the boys knowledge of the river, teaching them the old skills of canoeing, fishing, and navigation. In the fall he also ran the caribou-hunting operation for three weeks, in two camps of six guests each, whom he took to the foothills of the Torngat Mountains in Labrador. The average cost to guests at almost all tourist camps in the North ranges around a thousand dollars a week, plus air fare, and the majority come from the United States. Many of them are in their late seventies, and Willi used to ensure that very few left without getting a caribou, or if they were fishermen, without a large char. It was indicative of Willi's concern for the resource that he gave fishermen only one night to fish at his outpost on the Kuurujuaq River, where the fish are largest. In an interview in the federal government's Eskimo language magazine, *Inuttituut*, he explained, "If I were to allow them, they would spend the whole week there, and Arctic char grow so very slowly and the big ones take so many years to replace."

Willi is in his mid-fifties now, has gray hair and wears glasses. Although he is on the community council and extremely active in the settlement's life, working on his own is easier for him than the togetherness of coöperative life but he has managed both. Some tourists—a few—who came to his lodge were "impossible to please," he said. "I try to prevent them from seeing my annoyance." With all these activities, Willi has always managed to turn out the occasional immaculate bear, walrus or caribou carving when he feels so inclined. He uses a special hard green soapstone that he has shipped in.

Willi's second wife, Selima, who made the sealskin boots I wore at the George River (which have stiffened up in two decades and repose high in a closet), has been his main business support. The summer operation confined the whole family for three months but financed the life Willi loves, since it left him free from binding hours of wage employment the rest of the year to hunt and fish. Selima supervised and cooked for the lodge, and her bread was reputed to be magnificent. She also became a first-rate seamstress, specializing in crocheted woollen toques, smoked caribou skin mitts, and parkas, which she sells to tourists once her large family's needs have been satisfied. The eldest daughter, Emily, the round-faced four-year-old who was playing on the floor of the Hudson's Bay Company outpost that first morning of my arrival, is married to a French Canadian, and they have had two children.

The Prudens stayed at George River six years, and by that time the lodge was a going concern. When Pruden was transferred to Ottawa to become Arctic District Tourist Officer, John MacDonald, a former Hudson's Bay Company man, came in to help Willi under government contract. Willi likes to do everything he does well, which is why although he can speak some English he prefers not to; and he likes someone else to keep his books and conduct his English correspondence. John MacDonald remained as Willi's interpreter and general factotum for eight years, and when MacDonald went to Ottawa for the winter to complete a university degree in social anthropology he acted as booking agent for the lodge. MacDonald married the school-teacher at George River, Carolyn Tincombe, whose Montreal family had many Eskimo friends (one of whom grew up with Carolyn and was one of the first Inuk graduates of McGill University). Willi not only acted as the MacDonalds' matchmaker but also made their wedding ring from a tooth of the huge jaw of one of the few sperm whales anyone remembers washing up on the shores of Ungava Bay. Later, when MacDonald returned to Ottawa to work in northern affairs for the government, Willi's son-in-law took on his duties. I have just discovered that Emily, who I thought was Willi's real daughter by his first marriage, was adopted according to Eskimo custom from Elijah Sam Annanack, the expert driver on my first dog-sled journey, while one of Willi's and Selima's own daughters was adopted out to Selima's brother's family. Recently the Imudluks adopted one of their daughter Emily's small boys, Noah. Willi's mother, Lucy, who seemed very old when I met her at the outpost and again on my return to George River, now *is* very old, in her late eighties. She lived for three years in a home for elderly people in Quebec City, but is now back at George River.

In Ottawa I recently met Willi's attractive sixteen-year-old daughter, Maggie, who has long black hair and looks like Willi. She was living with John MacDonald's family while she was attending high school there, but has been called home since to take care of her grandmother. Most George River girls leave school at thirteen or fourteen, but Maggie intends eventually to complete school in Ottawa, become a registered nurse, and return to George River to work. At home in the settlement, she enjoys going to dances, at which boys who normally wear blue jeans dress up in white shirts, ties, dress pants and boots. George River has the usual problems, endemic in the North, with drinking and drugs. Maggie thought her father and mother "the most strict parents at George River," and said, "If I started to drink my parents wouldn't let me come down to Ottawa." When she was studying in Ottawa she was one of approximately fifty Inuit high school students boarding in the Canadian capital while they pursued their education. They have their own meeting place, Inuit House, and a monthly newspaper, *Igalaaq*, that is published for the triple audience of students, vocational trainees who come south, and families back home.

Some people one never forgets, and although we communicated only in nods and smiles, I shall always remember the kindness of Elijah Annanack, who so quietly and courteously rescued me from the terrors of falling to the bottom of a steep hill on that first Arctic trip. I found later that he was specially selected to drive the *komatik* on which I rode because of his skill and competence at everything he does, since there never was a greener Arctic traveller than I; even at the time I was aware—from occasional hints dropped by George Koneak—of polite concern for my welfare mixed with amused tolerance of my inexperience. For quite a while, Elijah was assistant to the diesel mechanic who came into George River to repair machinery, and then he worked for Willi, doing the variety of jobs that Willi's extensive operations required, from building to guiding. He has always saved time to hunt and trap on his own, very successfully. Currently he is mechanic in Willi's Shell Oil business.

Josepie Annanack, George River's representative at the historic Frobisher Bay Conference who was, if possible, even quieter than his brother Elijah, has continued to be an excellent hunter and trapper. A close friend of Willi's, he has been one of his most trusted guides for many years. Josepie is highly respected in the community, and his advice is sought in a wide assortment of matters. He carves to supplement his income, but remains predominantly on the land, keeping to himself, as does Stanley Annanack's younger brother, Thomas, whose tent I visited at the mouth of the George River when I went with Don Pruden to examine the broken motor at the freezer. Thomas, a pleasant, affable man, recently suffered a stroke, but he continues to carve, hunt and fish as he always has done, leaving community affairs to his ebullient older brother.

Johnny George, the grieving widower who took me fishing on my return trip and then to see the view up the breathtaking expanse of the George River on that sunny, never to be forgotten afternoon, has remarried. For years he was head guide at a northern Quebec tourist camp run by a white man; later he served as president of the George River Coöperative. He is a prolific carver and manages now to supply all his needs hunting and carving. I recently discovered to my astonishment that Johnny George had an additional, last name, Annanack, and is the son of old George.

All the Snowballs moved from George River to Port Burwell shortly after our visit, where Daniel Snowball, whose tent I visited with Max Budgell on my first trip, died in 1966. Max wrote me once or twice a year, wonderful news-filled letters about the North. I received one of these dated December 30, 1966, that said:

> Bad news from Burwell. Daniel Snowball was accidentally shot in the back some time in October and died shortly after. Daniel and one of the young men were hunting duck in a small boat, the young man's shotgun accidentally discharged and the charge hit Daniel in the kidney region. The ship *Montcalm* was in the Straits at the time and brought a doctor, but all the doctor could do was to give him a sedative. He joined some other very good men on the hillside above the harbour.

THE INUIT population of Canada has almost doubled in the past twenty years, from twelve thousand to twenty thousand, with another two thousand or so more in Labrador. Inuit have one of the highest birth rates in the world, while the death rate has been cut in half by improved health care. Inuit health is still worse than the national average in Canada, but tuberculosis, the primary killer while the Eskimos lived in igloos, has been practically eliminated. (Igloos look romantic but above freezing they start to melt). Thus, all the settlements I visited are substantially larger, with one exception: Port Burwell, which has disappeared.

Various reasons are given for the demise of Burwell as a settlement. Located on Killinek Island, the hauntingly beautiful Outermost Place, Burwell seemed to have as promising a future as that of any place in the Arctic, with such an abundance of natural resources swimming past the front door. As both Snowden and Henry Annatuk, the gentle keeper of the coöperative store, had predicted, it could and did support many more people than the thirty-six inhabitants there when we went, shortly after the community had formed the Canadian Arctic's second coöperative. By 1967, one hundred and seventy-five people were living at Port Burwell, and a fish plant had been built to process cod. Burwell seems to have more or less faded away from then on until there were only twenty-eight persons in two big families still living on that rocky isle, huddled together a little more than a stone's throw across the narrow strait from the northern tip of Labrador.

Some say that the Inuit, who originally settled there from other places along the coast, left because of their close cultural relationship with northern Quebec and Labrador—that they were just going back home. Others point to a territorial government policy of discouraging settlements of less than two hundred inhabitants as too expensive to maintain. When we were there, Burwell's most direct contact with the outside world was through George River and Fort Chimo by land and sea. Shortly thereafter, Quebec established its presence more firmly in its northern regions, and Killinek Island, despite its proximity to Labrador, is in the Northwest Territories. Port Burwell therefore had to be administered from Frobisher Bay at a much greater distance solely by air, and it had no landing strip. Services diminished and then the nursing station closed. Finally, one day in February 1978 the territorial government sent aircraft to evacuate anyone wanting to leave. Everyone departed, but it was a bitter leave-taking. Specific clauses in the James Bay and Northern Quebec Agreement signed on November 11, 1975, protected Burwell's integrity, and the Northern Quebec Inuit Association immediately took up the matter of possible violation of the agreement.

The James Bay and Northern Quebec Agreement is the single most significant event in the past twenty years of northern history and will directly affect the lives of all Quebec Inuit, which includes those who live in George River and in the other thirteen communities on the Arctic coast. Faced with the inevitability of northern industrial development—the immediate threat in Quebec was a huge hydroelectric project—Canada's Inuit associations have been and are now engaged in the painfully slow and complex process of settling land claims. The James Bay Agreement, where Quebec Inuit negotiated side by side with Cree and Naskapi Indians, was the first claim to be settled and legislated. (The Inuit of the western Arctic have reached a comparable agreement-in-principle, but with less emphasis on political self-determination and more on land ownership; at least another year of negotiation is anticipated before final agreement.)

In return for relinquishing all claims to lands constituting the major part of James Bay and northern Quebec—land the Inuit have used and occupied for thousands of years—an Inuit development body, the Makivik Corporation, will receive a cash and royalty settlement amounting to some ninety million dollars; outright ownership, to the surface rights only, of three thousand, two hundred and fifty square miles of land; exclusive hunting, trapping and fishing rights over a large part of northern Quebec; and political rights that give them considerable self-government. (A rough translation of the Eskimo word *makivik* is "the place where you rise up.") The majority of Inuit accepted the agreement as a fait accompli, but several Inuit communities, led by Povungnituk, oppose the terms, maintaining they had not given their negotiators the mandate to relinquish title to the land.

Political rights already being implemented include the formation of the Kativik Regional Government administering its own educational system (*kativik* means "a place where people gather"). Its schools give priority to Inuktitut, the language of the Inuit, for the first three years; English and French are added after that, as second languages. Stanley Annanack's younger brother, Mark, a past manager of George River's coöperative and former president of the community council who also at one time had the Shell Oil agency, is a director of the Kativik School Board. Teaching materials based on the needs of Inuit school children, with relevance to their lives, is a priority, to replace the hand-me-down southern curricula to which they were subjected previously.

No account of the affairs of northern Quebec would be complete without mentioning Charlie Watt, who was in Fort Chimo when that settlement's coöperative was founded and who worked in its initial summer fishery. Watt is still a young man, in his mid-thirties, and has a remarkable facility in both his native Inuktitut and English. He, more than anyone else, was responsible for the Northern Quebec Inuit Association, NQIA, coming into existence. He has been its president since it was formed in 1972, and has also been a chief negotiator of native claims. He is now president of the Makivik Corporation, which seems likely to become the dominant organization in that area. The Makivik Corporation in effect has taken over most of the functions formerly performed by the NQIA, which will continue on paper as a signatory of the James Bay Agreement.

George Koneak, our inspired interpreter on that first trip and again at the Frobisher Bay Conference, is first vice-president of the Northern Quebec Inuit Association and was one of the signers of the James Bay Agreement. As an officer of the association, he helped to guide the negotiations, making decisions far more complex even than his brilliant work of communications accomplished for all of us. Interpreting is now in the hands of younger people said to be more fluent; I doubt if any are more imaginative.

Shortly after the Frobisher Bay Conference in 1962, Max wrote telling me that George had received a medal from the Royal Humane Society for rescuing a snowmobile load of children from drowning in a lake:

> The snowmobile broke through the ice and the driver fled. George got the kids out, got them ashore, built a fire and later a snowhouse and finally got them into Chimo. Nothing to George, all in a day's work . . .

In middle age George is still a good hunter when he has the time, as is his wife Johanna. The Koneaks moved from Fort Chimo not long after we last saw one another at Frobisher Bay, and George changed jobs, from interpreting to settlement administration. From Burwell they moved to Koartuk, on the west coast of Ungava, and now they are back in Chimo, where they have a married daughter; probably the little girl who leaned against her mother's knee at the meeting at Fort Chimo we attended the night that settlement's coöperative got its start.

Among former residents of Port Burwell, Henry Annatuk, the first president of its coöperative, lives at Koartuk and has a pacemaker to help out his ailing heart. I still see him in my mind's eye bent over with scholarly concentration working out coöperative financial business on an old-fashioned counting board. Both Senach Anglatweena and Thomas Thomas, who moved from Whale River to Port Burwell just before we came, are living now at George River; Senach Anglatweena worked as a guide for Willi, and Thomas Thomas has just recently arrived, having been in the last group to leave Killinek Island. Penina Assavak, with her beautiful smile and her family, moved from Burwell some time ago to George River, where her husband, Matthew, passed away after a long bout with ulcers. The little boy with round pink cheeks who hid behind her skirts is a widower with three small children, his wife having died last year in childbirth.

One of Max Budgell's favorite people on the Ungava coast was Noah Annatuk, whom he respected as the best guide for the uncharted waters of that treacherous area. Noah amused and intrigued Max, and he sent me a running account of his adventures, two of which bear repetition. On March 2, 1964, Max wrote me:

I spent from September 20th to December 28th at Port Burwell last year. That bad actor, Noah, who has two wives, is still at least when I left there, hale and hearty, and I hear his naughty wife Lizzie presented him with a son in January. I know this pleased him as an Eskimo without a son is an object of pity. They had a son, you know, when you were there, but he suddenly died last spring, and from what Noah told me I gather it was from T.B. meningitis. I felt very sorry knowing what it meant to them both; as Lizzie explained to me "when it die, I not happy." I sincerely hope this one lives.

The following year, on November 16, 1965, Max reported:

> Noah Annatuk has just been flown by RCAF to hospital in Halifax. He had fallen on board our vessel and dislocated his hip. Noah's accident is peculiar in that it happened while he was wearing rubber sea boots made not to skid on a wet deck. Noah's story is that "Had I been wearing my own sealskin boots this would not have happened." (Sealskin boots on a painted wet deck are something like skates on ice).

Noah lives now in George River with his pretty second wife, Lizzie; his first one, Emily, sensibly departed some time ago for Koartuk.

THAT FIRST Conference of Arctic Coöperatives at Frobisher Bay in 1962 seems to me now even more remarkable than it did at the time. Logically, such a conference was the next move in the development of an Eskimo coöperative system across the one third of Canada that lies in the North; but to have the right event at the right time! A minor miracle. It was the springboard for so many later developments: the proliferation of coöperatives, the coöp federations and the native organizations. The total effectiveness of that conference can never be calculated, for it was the first place Inuit met Inuit from west to east and were able to exchange experiences and ideas.

Shortly after the Frobisher conference, Snowden obtained federal government classification of Eskimo art products as works of art for customs purposes. This achievement was enormously helpful when, as a direct result of the conference, a marketing agency was formed through which Inuit coöperatives were able to sell their products not only in southern Canada but also in the United States and Europe. The agency, Canadian Arctic Producers, or CAP as it is known everywhere, is located in Ottawa. Until 1975 the whites on the board of directors outnumbered the Inuit. That year, the Eskimo coöperatives acquired more than half CAP'S share capital, and the balance shifted. In 1978 for the first time CAP had an Inuk chairman, thirty-five-year-old William Noah from Baker Lake, who is the son of Jessie Oonark, one of the earliest and most eminent of the print makers. Noah, besides being president of the Baker Lake coöperative and chairman of its hamlet council, has been drawing and carving since 1963 and an active print maker since 1969. Recently he has begun experimenting with oil and plywood. He is so busy when he is at home in Baker Lake that his only holidays are promotion trips on behalf of CAP as far away as Houston, Texas.

When it was formed, CAP was designed to be the marketing agency for all Inuit coöperatives, most of whom had white, government-appointed managers. CAP has become a financial success with the help of such dedicated people as Alma Houston and her assistant Mary Craig. The former spent ten years at Cape Dorset when she was married to James Houston, and was with CAP from the very beginning. From time to time friction has developed between the coöperatives and CAP about prices paid for carvings, about directives to make smaller carvings for a softening market, and the practice of sending back to the coöps the carvings that did not sell within a certain time, especially the large ones. Cape Dorset, the richest member of the system, recently began marketing its prints separately—though not its carvings or handicrafts—through its own small Toronto outlet. CAP has been slow to respond to the wishes of its Inuit members to convert to a coöperative, as was originally planned by its founders, but at the February 1979 meeting of CAP's board of directors, the decision was made unanimously to proceed with the conversion forthwith.

In 1967, the northern Quebec coöperatives, including George River, withdrew from CAP and formed a separate, all-inclusive organization, *La Fédération des Coöperatives du Nouveau Québec* (referred to as FCNQ) which not only markets products of the coöperatives but also conducts education and training programs; provides resupply and merchandising assistance to the coöp stores; and assists the coöps to develop the sports fishing and hunting tourist operations that number at least half a dozen now. In 1972 the coöperatives in the Northwest Territories followed suit, forming a federation of their own. The Canadian Arctic Coöperative Federation Limited, CACFL as it is known, coördinates all NWT coöp activities except southern marketing of arts and crafts, which is still done separately through CAP. The coöperatives continue to send the bulk of their production to CAP, but

CACFL operates a chain of retail stores, called Northern Images: two in the Northwest Territories, at Inuvik and Yellowknife; one each in the Yukon at Whitehorse and in Churchill, Manitoba. Lately CACFL has been discussing marketing below the sixtieth parallel. A joint committee of CAP and CACFL that includes both presidents and general managers has been set up to look into all aspects of a merger.

Peter Murdoch, who has had long experience in the North, first working for the Hudson's Bay Company and then as a federal administrator, has been general manager of the Quebec federation since it was organized in 1967, shortly after the province of Quebec took a firmer hold on its northern areas. Murdoch, although he is not an Inuk and still has a gentle Newfoundland accent, is said to be more Eskimo than white. He was on holiday before taking on a new assignment with the federal government's Industrial Division and was travelling around the North with the writer Farley Mowat when he was asked by the people of Povungnituk if he would set up a federation for the northern Quebec coöperatives. Murdoch speaks Inuktitut like an Inuk, and on that trip he was convinced, from what the Eskimos said to him once he assured them their views would not be translated into English, that the government was definitely doing things for them "the wrong way." He still believes that the Inuit would have been better off if some system of helping them had been devised other than bringing them into settlements. He is a tall, spare, brusque man in his early fifties, and when I visited him not long ago at the federation's main office in Montreal, he discussed with great feeling the situation of Inuit in settlements as he perceives it.

"A primitive culture cannot co-exist with a civilized race, which will devour it," he said. "The government has not been interested in the Eskimos as people. Education to me is the process by which somebody becomes an adult and succeeds in his own environment. Until now, the environment has been one thing, the education another, so that we have had a whole generation of misfits, shaped in one way by their environment and in another by their education, whom we are still destroying by our good intentions. In fact, the utter destruction is just beginning; we never gave them the tools to destroy themselves before, but now we have done it with ninety million dollars and the land settlements.''

Murdoch believes in the coöperative system with religious fervor. He sees it as a political as well as an economic movement ''based on the idea of the resources being controlled and operated by the people.'' He therefore agreed to set up a federation for the northern Quebec coöperatives on the condition that Inuit take on all the jobs and responsibilities in the coöps. ''When we started, the people didn't understand anything about an economic system even in George River,'' he said. ''When we asked the Eskimos, 'Do you want to be boss and control your coöp?' they naturally said, 'We want to be boss!'

''How then do you manage this?'' Murdoch continued. ''No other way than to force them to be boss, so we took the whites away and said, 'If you need help ask for help from outside the community and you have to pay for it or you are not boss. If you decide to go with the federation you can expect to lose the support and help of the government.' This took a lot of discussion, because Eskimos are conservative and they knew what they had with the government, but even so they chose to go on their own. From my previous experience, I felt that they always work better in a crisis, and when action is made imperative they always succeed; otherwise they sit back and let the white man do it. When I get out, I would hope that they will not have another white man as federation manager, but just hire white people when they need help for accounting or tourist development, marketing, and so on. After all, I wouldn't be belittling the white race if I hired an Eskimo to get me from Pond Inlet to another place if that was the most efficient way!

''Getting back to the beginning of the federation, after the federal government withdrew their white development officers who had in effect been running the coöperatives, then you had the Eskimo people and no management whatsoever. We had designed a very simple accounting system which had been translated into the Eskimo language and we put this in immediately. Then we met with our board of directors, all native, and asked the government for one hundred thousand dollars to run the federation: for a southern arts and crafts wholesaling operation, education and training programs and the stores. We thought eventually we could pay for all this ourselves but in the beginning we needed subsidies."

The federation began with five coöps and six more were added later, including the James Bay Cree coöp, Paint Hills. "The Quebec government transferred a grant to us of between sixty and seventy thousand dollars, but once we got rid of all the white people, the federal government felt there was no possibility we could succeed," Murdoch went on. "We had asked for a hundred thousand—it now costs over a million to run the federation—and finally after two years the federal government said they would give us the thirty-seven thousand dollars that it had cost them to do economic development in the communities. Meanwhile we lived from hand to mouth, just surviving. Most of us took practically no salary, used our own cars and gas, went into hock to keep alive. Until three years ago we built all our stores without a professional staff. The Eskimos and I did the planning, ordering, building, electricity, plumbing and heating, and we learned as we went. It's only when we started to succeed, only in the last three or four years, that Quebec and the federal government have really said that what has happened was worth happening and came in with us."

"I don't know where it goes from here," he said. "It could be, in two to three years, that the coöperative movement no longer will exist in northern Quebec. All it takes is fifteen million dollars badly spent and our own people will destroy it. At our last meeting Eskimos were saying, how come things were cheaper at the Hudson's Bay Company, which doesn't have to pay for the training of managers, doesn't have to borrow money at twelve-and-a-half per cent the way we do to finance the sea lift, and basically derives vast financial strength from its land grants. All that has to happen is that millions of free dollars from the land claims be spread around for cheaper merchandise, flashier ideas, and hiding operating costs, and we can't compete. What took twenty years to get going can be destroyed, and then there will be nothing left but a little reservation, like in the South. What will prevent it? An Eskimo is no more honest or dishonest than anyone else. Is it ethical for a coöp president to use his position to build a five thousand dollar debt? No. But what prevents it? Nothing, except that at a certain point a business ethic evolves, and that doesn't exist yet. The safeguard in the coöps is that they are controlled by a group, through which, given time, a system of ethics *will* evolve.''

It is doubtful that most Inuit thoroughly understand the economic intricacies of the coöperative system, which at its best is a highly sophisticated way for human beings to work together. One of the Eskimos who grasped the whole concept is Pauloosie Napartuk of Great Whale River. At that first conference at Frobisher Bay it was Napartuk, making careful notes to take back to report to his people, who demanded,so eloquently of Snowden that someone be sent to help their fledgling coöperative, whose only activity then was carving. He was the founding president of La Fédération des Coopératives du Nouveau Québec in 1967 and was reëlected annually until he stepped down in 1974, but he is still a director. His memory for the important things said at FCNQ board meetings is fantastic, especially for promises made by government people. The annual FCNQ board meetings last for three weeks, during which time all management personnel at the federation—manager, assistant manager, department heads and so on—appear before it and are quizzed in tremendous detail about the previous year's performance, upcoming plans and the budget. All the board's proceedings are in Inuktitut, with interpreters present for French and English-speaking employees, and there is no doubt in anyone's mind that the Inuit run their own federation and provide its direction, which was the way Murdoch wanted it to be from the very beginning. In 1978, the federations in the Northwest Territories (CACFL) and northern Quebec (FCNQ) established a bond with the election of the president of the Quebec federation to CACFL's board. The Quebec federation, for its part, now provides CACFL with office space in its Montreal headquarters.

A couple of years ago when the Quebec coöperatives were having financial difficulties—finding funds for the annual sea lift is usually the last straw—the Quebec federation's board of directors met with government officials who gave them an ultimatum: if they wanted government help, they must accept a government administrator, which meant getting rid of Peter Murdoch and his assistant, Bruce Myers. The officials requested that both Murdoch and Myers leave the room while the subject was discussed. The board of directors promptly demanded that the meeting be taped if their employees were absent, and then flatly refused to go along with the demand for a change of administration. They won their point; they were financed without government control.

Quebec coöperatives collectively guarantee the federation debt to their suppliers, so that if one coöp goes under, the others will support it until it gets back on its feet, lending it funds through the federation without interest. All Inuit coöperatives suffer from a lack of working capital, and most are expanding at a faster rate than their profits can support—difficulties due, paradoxically, to their success. The coöperatives still are regarded by many of their advocates as a learning opportunity, and the Inuit see certain enterprises—sewing centers and tourist camps, for example—as performing needed work in the community even though they are slow to make money. The gravest crises inevitably occur over the sea lifts, because even though suppliers may extend credit to the Inuit coöperatives over the whole year of the sea lift, the goods must be paid for before the next year's purchases can be made, and that cost is over two million dollars annually in northern Quebec and more than double that amount in the Northwest Territories.

ULTIMATE responsibility for the Inuit in Canada rests with the federal government, which has consistently taken an enlightened approach of supporting with capital funds the slow learning and adjustment process through which the Inuit have been passing. Administration of this policy rests in the capable and sympathetic hands of Gunther Abrahamson, chief of the Social and Cultural Division of the Department of Indian Affairs and Northern Development. Abrahamson, a discreet and knowledgeable administrator, first went to the North in 1953, and operated the government's reindeer herd in the Mackenzie Delta until in 1962 Don Snowden persuaded him to undertake area economic surveys. He has been in Ottawa ever since, and now has the position with the government that is the nearest equivalent to what Snowden had when he hired him. Perhaps because Abrahamson lost most of his family in Nazi Germany and has been on his own since he was twelve, he has managed to retain a resilient approach to Inuit problems with the same fresh air of enthusiasm I so admired among the government people I met in the North in the early nineteen-sixties.

Like everyone else directly involved with the Inuit coöperatives, Gunther has regarded them as an enormous success in social development and as a major economic tool; but in 1974 the chronic problem of their economic well-being came to a head when requests for funds made to the department by the coöps in both the Territories and northern Quebec exceeded ten million dollars, for periods up to five years.

Gunther's first move was to have a detailed examination done of the whole Eskimo coöperative system by the federal government's Bureau of Management Consulting. In 1977, as a result of this study, a fifteen million dollar five-year self-development program was put into effect to provide the coöperatives through the two federations with grants, loans and bank loan guarantees "to develop native management skills, implement a system of financial planning, inventory control and accounting procedures and provide sufficient working capital." Abrahamson, who has long respected Peter Murdoch's commitment to coöperatives, then hired Bruce Myers, who had been with the Quebec federation as assistant manager for the past ten years, to coördinate the program.

When Gunther Abrahamson talks about the progress that has been made in the Inuit's thinking about their new way of life, he likes to tell about the time in 1975 when a management contract was proposed by the government under which CAP would provide marketing services to its Indian equivalent, the government-operated Central Indian Marketing Services, which had been in existence since 1932 but, unlike CAP, had never turned a profit: "The government went to CAP and said, 'Help us, and we will give you a management contract, plus a fifty-thousand-dollar fee and expenses, and a share of the profits.' In return CAP, which was then an obvious success, would send one of its key men to the Indians and get their marketing service on the rails," Abrahamson related. "The contract was drawn, and brought to the CAP board for approval in April. The whites all said it was a great idea, would increase CAP's profits, and would benefit the Eskimos. But the Eskimos said they had to think about it and take it back to their communities and discuss it with the people they represent. Mark Evaluarjuk from Igloolik, who understands English but refuses to speak it, said through an interpreter after a three-hour discussion, 'How long has CAP been talking to Indian Affairs about this?' and our people said, 'Since before Christmas.'

"Mark then asked, 'Why are you only telling us now?' This was not the kind of question that would have been asked before; it would have been, 'The white man knows what he's doing, that's good enough for us!' " Gunther continued, "Mark then stated that the Indian people needed the fifty thousand dollars more than the Eskimos did. When he said that, a light dawned in our heads and we sent for an Indian on our staff to explain the situation. He said to the Eskimos, 'Look, we really want you to help us, and the government is paying the fifty thousand dollars, not us.' Mark said, 'If this helps you, no problem,' and all the other Eskimos fell in with it, and I realized how far we had come. What bothered Mark and all the Eskimos was taking fifty thousand dollars from the Indians who needed it!"

The Northwest Territories federation, CACFL, is slowly adopting the independent Inuit attitude pioneered by its Quebec counterpart. The BMC report, as the federal study of coöperatives is referred to, strongly recommended the sale of the DC-4 aircraft which had been purchased with high hopes by the federation after it had been sitting idle at Pelley Bay for two years in the open, unprotected from the elements. CACFL has a twenty-eight-year-old Inuk president, Louis Tapardjuk, from Igloolik, and a white manager. The CACFL board of directors told their manager that if the aircraft were sold, he could go with it; or as Tapardjuk wrote in his President's Report, quoting another Inuk delegate, if the federation sold the aircraft, "they would also sell the manager, real cheap." At this point Abrahamson tactfully suggested leasing the plane instead to a Winnipeg airline, with the coöperatives having first call on it, and painting the aircraft with the federation's colors.

Tapardjuk, who is bilingual and a communications specialist, is having the Northwest Territories coöp bylaws, a small dictionary of financial terms, and the John Deere Snowmachine Owners Manual translated from English into Inuktitut, and typed out in Eskimo syllabics. Sam Metcalfe, an Inuk from Labrador who works for Abrahamson's department in the federal government, is chairman of an all-Inuit committee of translators and interpreters from the various regions that has been established to guide the standardization of Inuktitut technical words and phrases being introduced into the language through contact with the South as the society becomes more complex: legal, medical, and resource development terms, and so on. The use of Inuktitut in the Inuit's rapidly changing world received a further boost from a syllabic typewriter element that has been designed to conform to the revised Inuktitut syllabic writing system, a ball that can be used on a standard IBM typewriter. One thing leads to another: Abrahamson's department now offers a touch-typing course and training manual for Inuit typists.

GOVERNMENTAL policy in the North is never to unload its experimental industries on a coöperative unless they show a profit on the books. The whale-meat canning program in the Keewatin that looked so promising when we were there in 1964 came to an abrupt end when the whales and seals were found to have a dangerously high mercury content. However, experimental canning of other products continued, and the cannery that originally had started in a tent in Whale Cove was moved to Rankin Inlet, which is now the administrative center of the Keewatin. Certain kinds of fish were processed there, chiefly lake trout and Arctic char. The cannery was subsequently sold to a Winnipeg firm that then canned northern smoked fish, salmon and trout and marketed them as delicacies in southern stores until the plant closed down in 1976. Erich Hoffman continued in Alaska his frenetic and inspired canning activities among the Inuit.

I always wondered what was happening to Celestino Magpa, whom I had last seen at Whale Cove when we were making the rounds of the Keewatin on the survey of Eskimo canned goods. He had mastered the capitalist system enough even then to have his own pleasure boat and a pet German shepherd dog. I found out that he was one of the first directors of CAP. He also borrowed enough money from the Eskimo Loan Fund to buy a long liner, and is in the transportation business today at Whale Cove.

When I inquired about Magpa, I also asked what had happened to two other Inuuk whom I scarcely knew but never forgot. Pauloosie Seuak of Povungnituk had asked a key question at the first Frobisher Bay Conference of the eminent carver, Oshaweetuk: "Who is the boss at Cape Dorset, the white man or the Eskimo?" Oshaweetuk, I learned, is still carving as beautifully as ever and still active in coöperative affairs in Cape Dorset; Seuak, who is himself a fantastic carver and print maker, spent a number of years setting up new coöperatives for the Quebec federation. He has also continued to be involved in coöp and community matters in Povungnituk. Lately, he has added to his several careers; he is writing Inuktitut history books and curricula for the schools, preparing courses for the youth on living the Inuit way, surviving off the land.

THE INUIT continue to smoke as heavily as they ever did—their reasoning being that it doesn't seem to harm them, since they see so much less tuberculosis—but the attitude toward alcohol is changing. Alcoholism has been a severe problem, especially in large communities, and the Inuit have decided to do something about it themselves. About a dozen communities in the Northwest Territories have voted a complete ban on alcohol— which means a ban on possession, purchase, sale, transportation or manufacture of alcohol. Others, including Igloolik and Frobisher Bay, have instituted forms of local control: in Frobisher, the local store has been closed, although liquor can still be shipped in from Outside or bought at licensed premises. Even so, there has been a tremendous decline in the crime rate in Frobisher Bay. The ban on alcohol has been handled variously around tourist camps, which are entirely dependent on trade from the South. At Snowdrift, on Great Slave Lake in the western Arctic's Mackenzie District, a total ban extends twenty-five kilometres from the center of the community with the exception of a nearby fishing lodge owned by a white man; its guests are permitted to have alcohol although Snowdrift residents working at the lodge are not. At the opposite end of the country, at Pangnirtung on Cumberland Sound—a gorgeous spot—the white owner of Clearwater tourist camp has had to adjust his business to a total local prohibition against liquor.

Art skills have flourished at many coöperatives since I was there. From the beginning, Povungnituk had the benefit of the energetic presence of an Oblate priest, Father Steinman, who was an early initiator of coöps and is now in Montreal as a translator with the Kativik school board. Cape Dorset has had for many years a white manager, Terry Ryan, who is still there and encouraging experimentation in new media. At Holman Island, Father Tardy long remained a guiding gentle force as the coöperative developed its own art and handicraft styles that were totally Inuit but very distinctive. Father Tardy has stepped back from coöperative. affairs and become a dignified figure in retirement among the Inuit he loves so much. Holman Island also runs a tourist program that includes a hotel, a restaurant and a coffee shop.

The Fort Chimo coöperative, shortly after we were there, achieved international fame when Jeannie Snowball invented a little furry big-eyed animal which she called an *ookpik*, the Eskimo word for owl although Jeannie Snowball's invention had no wings. Not only did the *ookpik* bring financial profit to the coöp but also it became the occasion for the first copyright of an Eskimo product. It was so popular, following its introduction at a southern trade fair, that manufacturers, cartoonists, film and advertising people were clamoring to use it, and in order to bring a halt to its exploitation, Snowden obtained a copyright for it. From then on the little *ookpik* was protected in the name of the Queen, setting an important precedent for Inuit art and handicrafts. In the intervening years, Fort Chimo has changed considerably. It has a modern air terminal, paved roads, about eight hundred inhabitants, and plans for a fifteen to twenty-bed hospital.

When we stopped at Baker Lake on our journey through the Keewatin, our concern was with Eskimo food, not art, but the pioneering work originally by Bill Larmour of the Industrial Division to develop the latent artistic genius of those inland Eskimos has produced a generation of superb artists. Their magnificent carvings, often in heavy black stone, have a distinctive spiritual quality. Baker Lake is much bigger now, with over a thousand people and many more buildings. Its coöperative has been one of the largest shareholders of CAP after Cape Dorset, but had bad luck when its print and craft shop was razed in a fierce fire just before Christmas in 1977. Everything was destroyed: all the prints, papers, inks and stone blocks. Baker Lake prints are just beginning to be produced again, with construction of new and larger facilities. This disruption did not disturb the production of carvings, however, since they are mostly done at home.

ONE OF the best things about the North is that once you have been there, not only the memories but also the friends you meet there stay with you forever. It is like joining a special club as a lifetime member, and you never quite get over a longing to go back. Max Budgell expressed it in a letter he wrote to me after he heard that I had attended the Frobisher Bay Conference. In 1962 he wrote: "I think you are on the road to becoming a Northerner. I seem to recognize the symptoms. First the bug bites you, then you find a reason for going back, and this time you leave the door open so you can return again; after that you are captured, and you can go back and forth without any special reason."

When someone from that special northern club dies, a rend is made in the closely woven fabric of those relationships, and the death of Max Budgell several years ago was such a loss. He had always been a heavy smoker, and died from lung cancer when he was barely sixty. He had worked in the North for some years, but later on turned his attention to freshwater fisheries and was the department's adviser in the development of fishing resources in Indian communities. Shortly after we were in the North together,

Paul Godt became progressively crippled by multiple sclerosis. He remained the same cheery helpful person and continued working as long as he could, but now lives in Ottawa on a disability pension. Bill Larmour, who helped so many of the early settlements to develop unsuspected artistic talents, has retired, as have Sam Dodds, the senior northern service officer at Fort Chimo when I was there, Alex Laidlaw of the Coöperative Union of Canada, who sat next to me at the Frobisher Bay Conference, and Alex Sprudz, the government coöperative development officer, both of whom gave a lifetime to the coöperative movement. Dr. Frank Vallee has continued his career as a distinguished sociologist, as a professor at Carlton University in Ottawa. Simonie Michael, the first chairman of that first Inuit conference, became the first Inuk elected to the Northwest Territories Council and was subsequently president of the Baffin Region Inuit Association, an Inuit Tapirisat affiliate.

Jon Evans, who succeeded Don Snowden as head of the Industrial Division, is now director of social and economic development in the federal government's Indian program in his native province, British Columbia. He is helping the Indians get a solid base either in coöperatives or business in the same way he did in the North, and with the same fervor.

Keith Crowe, whose house I stayed in that first night in the Arctic, at Fort Chimo, has continued working for the Inuit, making full use of his administrative and scholarly talents. He left Fort Chimo to become the first government administrator of Pangnirtung, in 1962, remaining there for two years. Two years more were spent completing his master's degree at the University of British Columbia; he worked the intervening summer in Igloolik doing government research that became part of his thesis, on the cultural geography of Foxe Basin. Back with the federal government in Ottawa in its northern community development and adult education program, in 1968 he organized a course in northern Quebec that took one married couple from each northern community on a tour of southern Canada. Representations made by the Inuit delegates on this trip to the then Minister of Northern Affairs, Jean Chretien, were first steps toward regional political organization. Keith and Edna Crowe's knowledge of Inuktitut and Japanese subsequently took them to Japan as advisors and interpreters for the Inuit artists at the World's Fair at Osaka, and shortly thereafter, Keith transferred to the Northern Science Research Division, where he produced a book already considered to be a classic on the subject, *The History of the Original Peoples of Northern Canada*, published in 1974. His career since has been interspersed with leaves of absence to assist the Inuit with native claims negotiations in the James Bay Agreement, and he is now working for the federal government as assistant claims negotiator for Labrador, the eastern Arctic and the Mackenzie Valley. On the side, he manages from time to time to write articles for magazines about the North, and he wrote the first course on coöperatives both in English and Inuktitut. Adult education is both a vocation and avocation with Keith, and he once wrote in two days an elementary book on learning Inuktitut for the Superintendent of Education for Northern Quebec, who wanted to study on the bus going to work.

When the Prudens left George River, they first went to Ottawa, where as a tourist officer Don organized the first tourist trip to the North Pole for a group of wealthy Americans from Boston. He and Gwen were transferred then to Yellowknife, where they have remained ever since, except for four years in Africa. Don set up a development corporation in the South African kingdom of Lesotho, under the direction of CIDA, the Canadian International Development Agency. In that tiny landlocked country he was able to use his rich variety of skills to set up craft organizations, small manufacturing businesses, a rock crushing operation, and a hotel business, among others, all run locally. During his stay there, he brought a number of his colleagues to Africa from the North to assist him, among whom were Barry Gunn, whom I had known at Baker Lake, and Jack Veitch, now retired, who shared a table with me and Alex Laidlaw at the Frobisher Bay Conference.

The Prudens are again back in Yellowknife, where Don heads the territorial park system, which includes camp grounds, and he has recently been asked to be on the board of directors of the new NWT Métis Development Corporation, an investment vehicle similar to the Makivik Corporation. Gwen never went back to teaching; she is now assistant administrator of lands for the government department that has responsibility for the disposition of federal lands in the Territories. She writes that she finds "land claims, moratoriums, and environmental concerns very interesting, but it will take years to learn the work thoroughly, so I am happy in this work." While the Prudens were still at George River, on a visit to Gwen's family in British Columbia their baby son David was stricken with spinal meningitis and died very suddenly. The other two children, Brian and Debra, are of course grown now, and Brian has recently married.

As for Don Snowden, he has had a distinguished career since he left the federal government in 1964. He went directly to St. John's, Newfoundland, where he produced a full study of the coöperatives there for both Ottawa and the government of the province (whose official name is Newfoundland and Labrador). He liked St. John's so well that he has made it his residence ever since. He became head of the Extension Service of Newfoundland's Memorial University, and under this umbrella helped change for the better the lives of the rural people of that province. He began by helping to organize a fishing coöperative that now sells more of the traditional Newfoundland product, salt codfish, than any other fish business in the province. At the same time he aided in establishing local development associations for the rural population that cut across economic and social lines to include not only fishermen but also doctors, teachers, woodsmen, housewives and sometimes even the clergy. Meanwhile, together with members of Canada's National Film Board he began experimenting with the use of film and later half-inch videotape in a new form of communication where oral and visual consensus can be obtained between people without actual meeting, a method that is being used in other parts of the world: in South America, Tanzania, the South Pacific Islands including Fiji, in Guyana, Latin America and the Caribbean, in India (where the National Dairy Institute wants to teach illiterate farmers better farming methods) and periodically in Alaska. Because the experiment was started on the offshore Fogo Islands of Newfoundland, where the population was successfully resisting a government plan for resettlement on the mainland, it is known as the Fogo Method. Using first film, and later videotape that has equipment so light that it can be carried from community to community easily, a staff organized by Snowden interviewed the local people of Fogo Island and elsewhere in the province on their attitudes—in their own homes and local meetings, where they were able to speak freely in a way that these unassuming people could never have done before an official body. These interviews were then played before government bodies, and the replies carried back, on film and videotape, to the communities. Two-way communication ensued that could never have occurred otherwise and that finally reached even the cabinet ministers in Ottawa, who could then see the devastating effects of some of their policies on people who were otherwise distantly removed.

Possibly as a result of this work, Snowden was appointed to a six-year term on the board of governers of the National Film Board, and was also on the executive of the Canadian Council on Rural Development, a citizens' advisory group to the federal government. From 1972 through 1974, he was chairman of the Royal Commission on Labrador, which completed a six-volume study on the problems in that underdeveloped area, with comprehensive recommendations of which an unusually high proportion are already being adopted provincially and federally. Snowden likes to work with his old friends whenever he can, and managed to borrow Max Budgell, a native of Labrador, to serve as executive director of the Royal Commission.

Snowden, a person of seemingly unlimited energy, also works for the United Nations from time to time as an advisor on rural development and rural education. At the present time he has come full circle: he is a member of the Canadian Eskimo Arts Council, which advises coöps on standards, and he is counselling the Labrador Inuit Association on setting up a fishing coöperative along the whole north coast of Labrador, whose waters contain salmon, char and a huge potential shrimp fishery. Up until now, the local people have had no control of resource development.

I OFTEN think about how it was when I first considered going to the Canadian Arctic. I didn't even know where Ungava Bay was when I first heard about it, and had no idea how to spell it. The editor of *The New Yorker* magazine, William Shawn—who has extraordinary intuitions and perceptions—accepted on faith my sketchy explanation of what the story was likely to be about: a vague description of an Eskimo meeting somewhere in the North of Canada.

The other day I was reading through my old files and I came across Don Snowden's first letter, written when I was trying to decide whether I would or would not ask *The New Yorker* to send me to the second meeting of the first coöperative at George River; whether it was really worth writing about. His letter was dated October 28, 1960, and it was a long one, in which he first discussed the problems involved; especially the isolation of the area in a completely undeveloped region with no docks, warehouses, regular communication or transportation networks.

He then went on to write:

> Canada has only a short history of involvement with Eskimo people. Our programme is based on preparing them for abrupt changes they will face with an industrial society in their land and on the assumption that some—perhaps many—will choose to remain as people of the land. When the time comes to make a decision on how they wish to live, they must be fully aware of the choices before them. In the long run this may be the most significant factor of the programme.
>
> To be more precise, we believe coöps will provide operational techniques for living with the white man and opportunity for getting not just economic but political power, and we hope eventually to extend the idea in the whole Arctic. We have made a beginning with a group of Eskimos who met with us last winter in a tent on the Korok River not far from the place selected for a settlement. . . .

I picked up the telephone and called Newfoundland, and asked Snowden if he could remember what had happened at that first meeting, the meeting that occurred before I had met him.

Snowden replied, "There were a hundred and ten people in that tent, twenty-one of them eligible to vote, because women couldn't vote in coöperative affairs in Quebec. Twenty ballots were cast in favor of a coöperative, and no negative, but Willi Imudluk didn't vote. He said, 'I work for the Hudson's Bay Company and as their employee I can't vote for a coöp because I know we'll have a store some day.' As you know, when the coöp voted to have its own retail store, Willi closed his Hudson's Bay Company outpost and became the coöp store's first manager.

"It was Willi who turned the tide at that first meeting," Snowden continued. "We demanded from the start that the George River coöp pay its own way, and old George Annanack was reluctant to borrow money, because he didn't know any Eskimos who had done that. They were talking all night, and finally Willi said, 'Without the coöp, we will all go into Chimo on relief,' and that settled it.

"George and Stanley and Josepie and Willi, the outsider with no relatives at George River, got the coöp started, and that wise old man, George Annanack, persuaded the others to go along. The climate in the South was hostile to coöperatives and to the idea that Eskimos could run them. Without government support, they would not have had the resources, so if George River had said no, maybe we would never have had the chance again."

How glad I am that the George River said yes—and that I had the chance to see it all happen.